H. Rider Haggard
A Bibliography

H. Rider Haggard

A Bibliography

D.E. Whatmore

MECKLER PUBLISHING CORPORATION

First published 1987 in the United States of America and Canada
by Meckler Publishing Corporation, 11 Ferry Lane West, Westport,
Connecticut 06880, U.S.A.

First published 1987 in Great Britain by Mansell Publishing Limited,
6 All Saints Street, London N1 9RL, England

Library of Congress Catologing-in-Publication Data

Whatmore, D.E. (Denys Edwin)
  H. Rider Haggard.

  Includes indexes.
  1. Haggard, H. Rider (Henry Rider), 1856–1925——
Bibliography. I. Title.
Z8377.5.W47 1987   [PR4732]   016.823′8   86–33272
ISBN 0–88736–102–1

Set by Colset Private Limited, Singapore
Printed and bound in Great Britain

FOR MY WIFE

Contents

Preface

Bibliographies are not ends in themselves. They are a beginning, for book collectors, bibliophiles, librarians, book sellers and, not least, researchers. They provide a starting point for further work on authors of interest. In my own case, I hope this Rider Haggard bibliography will facilitate further research into Haggard's works of fiction and non-fiction which, reflecting as they do the values and perceptions of a Victorian country gentleman of undoubted imagination and wide knowledge of events both at home and abroad, reveal insights into the man and his times worthy of an attempt at understanding. I sincerely hope, too, that Rider Haggard collectors both experienced in and new to this happy pastime, will find interesting material in the following pages.

DENYS WHATMORE
October 1985

Introduction

'. . . You're looking for adventure,' I cried; 'well, you've found it here. The devils are after me, and the police are after them. It's a race I mean to win.'
'By God!' he whispered, drawing his breath in sharply, 'it is all pure Rider Haggard and Conan Doyle.'

The Thirty Nine Steps
JOHN BUCHAN

Sir Henry Rider Haggard was born on 22 June 1856 and he died on 14 May 1925. His history is well recorded in several excellent biographies (see section 9). Additionally, Haggard's autobiography, ending in September 1912, is an original source of information about his life as an official and farmer in South Africa, a junior lawyer and budding author in England, a traveller and successful writer, to, ultimately, a respected agriculturalist and establishment figure. Haggard is best known to the general public for his works of romantic fiction: these, as well as his other, more down-to-earth writings, increasingly attract collectors of books and researchers interested in the late nineteenth and early twentieth centuries.

The early editions of Rider Haggard's books are now much sought after in the United Kingdom and in the United States of America. The First Editions are becoming rare and expensive, adding the incentive of the chase to the collector's interest in the man, his works, his times and his message about many subjects.

After a slow start, Haggard's literary career suddenly blossomed with the publication of *King Solomon's Mines* in 1885 and *She* in 1887. Thereafter, he wrote steadily and successfully until his death. True, his later works lacked the originality and style of the earlier stories: one at least — *Mary of Marion Isle* — was, frankly, puerile. Public interest in Haggard works declined. In recent years, however, that interest has been regenerated, and editions of the more popular stories continue in print and are read by young and old alike.

Haggard's romantic imagination was, I believe, unique and his tales have a quality about them unequalled since his death. Perhaps the essence of his continuing appeal is held in the period of history during which his books were written. For these were the times of Empire, when the British, from all walks of life, went adventuring into unexplored lands, to pit their wits against wild terrain and strange peoples often of savage aspect, to win a fortune or lose their lives in the attempt. There was little or no soul searching about the rights and wrongs of such enterprise. Those who shouldered 'the white man's burden' — civilizing, Christianizing, bringing government, education and medicine to an undeveloped world — rubbed those same shoulders with farmers, traders, adventurers, outcasts and criminals pursuing their private ends in territories where it was every man for himself and the law was unenforceable and often unestablished.

All this was the very stuff of adventure. Bold spirits, unexplored lands, hostile native tribes, hazardous obstacles and killing climates were all to be found in Africa. There was no communications infrastructure and travel was slow. The African interior was uncharted. Mystery therefore knew no bounds; the imagination could conceive fantastical events untrammelled by the fear of contradiction based on experience or even common sense. Today, the science fiction *genre* exploits the same limitless opportunities.

This is the appeal of Rider Haggard's African adventures: the places, events and characters he invented and the themes he developed strike still at the spirit of adventure latent in all his readers, young and old. Whether we are reading *She* or *Allan Quatermain*, or other, less well known stories, the indefinable appeal of enterprise and freedom to act, of Empire and the Victorians, of life, love and death under the stars, add an unique quality to what otherwise could be rip-roaring adventure for its own sake.

Rider Haggard's works include many other stories of pure imagination set elsewhere than in nineteenth century Africa. Scenes of action range from Scandinavia to Mexico, from ancient Egypt to an imaginary island. Haggard visited many parts of the world to collect material for these romances, adding to the authenticity of the settings against which his characters act out their roles. He also wrote several novels of a more conventional nature. Though not regarded as great works of literature, they nevertheless remain perfectly readable today. The first two, *Dawn* (1884) and *The Witch's Head* (1885), are now the most rare, in their original three volume form.

Nor should it be forgotten that complete lists of Haggard's books include works not only under the headings 'Romances' and 'Novels', but also under 'Parliamentary Blue Books', 'Political History', 'Agriculture and Country Life' and 'Travel'. Rider Haggard was involved with several Royal Commissions and was immensely interested in the agricultural problems of his day. All the major works on these matters are included in this bibliography.

Numerous articles and letters of literary and historical interest were written by Haggard for publication in magazines, periodicals and newspapers. Many of these have not been republished in book form, though I have found no work of fiction in this category. He wrote introductions to several works by other authors and some anthologies include contributions by him. He made many speeches, some of which were thereafter published as pamphlets. Parodies have been made of his characters and plots. All these are of interest to collectors and researchers and reference is made to them in the following pages.

It is obvious from the above that Rider Haggard collectors have a very wide field from which to choose if they wish to specialize. Most collectors are interested, however, in the whole range of the works and aim for a complete set of the First Editions. Perhaps someone may care to consider a narrower line of approach, and set out to collect a copy of *every* edition of just one or two of the works. *King Solomon's Mines* and *She*, for example, have long and involved publishing histories right up to the present day, and there are certainly dozens if not hundreds of editions of these two works alone.

Guide to the Bibliography

In laying out the following pages, I have tried to avoid the strict textbook severity often associated with bibliographical works. I want readers to enjoy the book as much as I have enjoyed compiling it. My aim throughout has been simple. It has been to provide a readable yet comprehensive guide to the First and other notable editions of H. Rider Haggard's works: and to list items about Haggard and his work for future reference. Thus, collectors at all levels of experience, when searching for Haggard's published works, will be able to identify them and, when they have acquired a volume, will be able to check its authenticity and completeness. Researchers will have easy reference to the plethora of items written about Haggard.

For collectors, the recognition of Haggard First Editions is sometimes difficult. Some include no date of publication. Later editions and First Editions are often superficially the same. Various issues are known. These factors are identified in the following pages, so far as my research makes possible. Reference is also made to the first publication of works in magazines and periodicals when this precedes the first book version.

The pages of the bibliography are laid out in a logical, standardized form, to make reference to them easy. In Sections 1 and 2, readers should note the progressive approach to the information required when searching a bookshop's shelves. The colour and size of a volume, coupled with the publisher's name, are obvious starting points. Technical details come last, for although they are necessary for the final authentication of a volume, they are not vital to its initial identification. This layout differs from other bibliographies and I hope it will be of assistance to the reader, especially new collectors.

Sections 3 to 11 are less standardized in layout but provide clear chronological guides to Haggard's writings other than his principal works; to dramatizations of his works; and to writings by others about him and his works.

My research towards compiling the material for this book has indicated that details of every facet of every Haggard work may now be unobtainable. The records seem no longer to exist. Some of the details which I should have hoped to include in the following pages are, therefore, missing. Nevertheless, this volume does include all the information I have been able to find and it is not inconsiderable. I have excluded the many foreign language editions of the works, though they are represented in most European languages and others in the Far East.

Arrangement of the Material

Each section is arranged chronologically in order of date of publication. Items are numbered sequentially separately within each section, each with its own prefix, for example, F (fiction); NF (non-fiction); L (letters); etc.

SECTIONS 1 AND 2: PRINCIPAL WORKS OF FICTION AND NON-FICTION
Each volume is described under the following headings:

1 PUBLISHER

2 IDENTIFICATION FEATURES
a. Binding	Colour of material and size of covers.
b. Spine	Detail of printing.
c. Front Cover	Detail of printing.
d. End Papers	Description and colour.
e. Preliminaries	Half title, title page, frontispiece and any other leaves before the text.
f. Text	Number of pages.
g. Supplements	All the leaves following the end of the text, including catalogues of advertisements.
h. Illustrations	Number of illustrations and astists' names. All illustrations are in black and white unless otherwise stated.
i. Errors	Included because sometimes they help to identify First Editions from others.
j. Dust Jackets	Described only when seen or proved by research to have existed. It is very difficult to find copies of Haggard First Editions with dust jackets still in place.

3 TECHNICAL
a. Format	Most of the works described are Crown Octavo (approximately 127 × 191 mm). Some are Demy Octavo (approximately 143 × 222 mm). One or two are Crown Quarto (approximately 190 × 254 mm) or other sizes.
b. Edges	The state of the edges is an aid to identification.
c. Collation	1. I use this term in its narrowest sense, to account for the number of leaves in a volume. This includes preliminaries, text, supplements and illustrations, but excludes end papers. I have related illustrations to gatherings as well as to page numbers. 2. Collation is by gatherings (identified by signatures). Note that signatures can be letters (a, b, c, etc to z, or A, B, C etc to Z, followed

if necessary by AA, BB, CC etc to ZZ; it was a printer's convention to omit the letters J, V and W); or figures (1, 2, 3 etc onwards as required).

3. An example of an entry under 'Collation' is:

6; B to I × 8; K to T × 8; U × 4; catalogue 8. Illustrations — Frontispiece; H (facing p. 102);
P (facing p. 210); T (facing p. 288). Total 166 leaves.

This means:

a. There are 6 preliminary leaves (excluding end papers and Frontispiece) with no signature.

b. The gatherings with signatures B, C, D, E, F, G, H and I each have 8 leaves (Signature 'A' is seldom used).

c. The gatherings with signatures K, L, M, N, O, P, Q, R, S and T each have 8 leaves. (Signature 'J' has been omitted).

d. The gathering with signature U has only 4 leaves.

e. The catalogue of advertisements at the end of the volume has 8 leaves.

f. The illustrations are inserted into the gatherings as shown, that is Frontispiece in the preliminaries and others in gatherings H, P and T.

g. The total number of leaves to be found in a complete volume is 166.

4 NUMBER OF COPIES IN FIRST EDITION AND DATE

I take *First Edition* to mean the first appearance of a work between its own covers. The copies printed and bound ready for the launch of the work comprise the *first issue*. Any copies thus printed but left over for binding up at a later date, and any later print runs from the same type setting, comprise the *second (third*, etc), *issue(s)*. When the original type setting is substantially amended, or is completely reset, *Second (Third*, etc) *Editions* result. The date in this paragraph is the date of first publication of the first issue, in the number of copies stated.

5 EARLIER PUBLICATION IN MAGAZINE

Haggard's stories were written in the heyday of the popular weekly and monthly literary and illustrated magazines. It was commonplace (and a measure of an author's popularity) for works both of fiction and non-fiction to appear in serialised form in these magazines before publication in book form.

6 OTHER EDITIONS OF NOTE

These are selected for their bibliographical, historical and general interest. They include English editions, the Tauchnitz copyright editions and American First Editions. The details, even in the case of American editions, are the result of research in England. It is clear that American editions published before the US Copyright Act of 1891 are numerous and in many cases compete for the accolade 'First'. In this work, therefore, 'American First Edition' before 1892 means only the edition which, so far as I can discover, appears to be the earliest. Some popular and uniform editions, both English and American, are also listed at Appendix 1.

7 NOTES

These have been compiled from points that have interested me during research.

8 SOME HAGGARD NOTES

Rider Haggard himself provides some interesting comments on his works, chiefly in his autobiography. I have quoted such items as help to reveal some of the background to the writing of the works.

SECTION 3: PAMPHLETS AND REPORTS

This section describes the several pamphlets which were written by Rider Haggard for various purposes, or which reproduce his speeches on a number of topics. Also included are the Reports of the Royal Commissions in which Haggard was involved and other official documents in which Haggard contributions have been traced.

SECTION 4: THE AFRICAN REVIEW

Haggard's association with this weekly journal and the items he contributed to it seem to me to deserve a separate section, to emphasize his real depth of knowledge about and continuing interest in the African problems of his day.

SECTION 5: MISCELLANEOUS WRITINGS

The items in this section comprise a list of Haggard contributions to magazines and periodicals other than the serialized versions of his principal works, which are mentioned in Sections 1 and 2. Most of the items in Section 5 have not been collected for publication in book form.

SECTIONS 6 TO 11

These sections are self-explanatory, chronological guides to Haggard's letters in the press, to reports of his speeches, to dramatizations of his works, and to items written about Haggard and his works.

Abbreviations and Symbols

p/pp	page/pages. Two pp equals one leaf.
vol/vols	volume/volumes
para	paragraph
Cr 8vo	Crown Octavo
Dmy 8vo	Demy Octavo
Cr 4to	Crown Quarto
no/nos	number/numbers
[ ]	square brackets enclose information, e.g. page numbers, inferred from the text of a work, but not printed therein.
/	oblique line appearing between words and phrases indicates a new line of printing in the work.

Sources and Acknowledgements

Sources

1. The collection of Rider Haggard manuscripts, ephemera, letters and books held in the Norfolk Record Office, Norwich. This is a fascinating collection, particularly as to Haggard's manuscripts in his own handwriting, revealing the labour of writing undertaken to produce his early works. A list of the items of bibliographical interest can be found in Appendix 2.
2. The British Library copies of First Editions and reference books, as well as their copies, in the original state or on microfilm, of magazines, periodicals and newspapers, at the British Library Newspaper Library, Colindale, London.
3. The collection of First Editions held in the Norwich Reference Library.
4. Notes made from examining my own collection of First and other editions and magazines, and from other items seen in passing.
5. The archives of the Longmans Group, Harlow, Essex, including Longmans Quarterly Analysis of Works.
6. The archives of the Routledge and Kegan Paul, London.
7. The archives of the Hutchinson Publishing Company, London, including the Hurst and Blackett ledgers.
8. The Macmillan Publishing Company, New York, regarding the publishing records of Messrs Cassell and Co. Ltd.
9. The Library of the Royal Commonwealth Society, London.
10. The Public Record Office, Kew, London.
11. The Dr. Williams Library, Gordon Square, London.
12. The Library at Lambeth Palace, London.
13. The Library of the British Film Institute, London.
14. The Library of the BBC, London.
15. The printing records of Messrs Richard Clay, PLC, Bungay, Suffolk.
16. The Head Office of the National Society for the Prevention of Cruelty to Children, London.

17. The Head Office of Dr Barnardo's Homes, Ilford, Essex.
18. The International Headquarters of the Salvation Army, London.
19. The Head Office of the *Surrey Herald*, Chertsey, Surrey.
20. The source book *A Bibliography of the Works of Sir Henry Rider Haggard 1856–1925*, by J.E. Scott (Elkin Mathews Ltd, 1947), to which occasional reference is made in the following pages.
21. Several American libraries, by correspondence.

I also had confirmation that collections of Rider Haggard material are held by the Rare Book and Manuscript Library, Columbia University, New York, and the Department of Manuscripts, Henry E. Huntington Library, San Marino, California.

The interpretation of the information gathered during research at the places listed above is, of course, my own. The responsibility for any errors in that interpretation is mine. Comment would be welcome from readers finding errors in the bibliography or who are in a position to remedy omissions.

Acknowledgements

My thanks are due to all the members of staff in record offices, libraries, publishing houses and charities who, with unfailing good humour, assisted in answering my enquiries and in furthering research. Of all the organizations I approached only one turned me away. I should particularly like to thank the following for their assistance and goodwill.

Dr J.A. Edwards of the University of Reading Library, in regard to the Longmans Archives and other matters; Mr D.H. Simpson, Librarian of the Royal Commonwealth Society Library, London; Mr Charles G. Birchall of Messrs Richard Clay, PLC, Bungay, Suffolk, for sight of the Richard Clay printing records; the Longman Group Limited, Harlow, Essex, for permission to reproduce extracts from the Longman Quarterly Analysis of Works; Mrs L.K. Coverdale of Tiptree Book Services Limited, Tiptree, Essex, for her help with the Hutchinson and Hurst and Blackett records; and the staff of the Library at University College London, in regard to the Routledge and Kegan Paul Ltd archives.

1 Principal Works: Fiction (F)

F1 Dawn 1884

1 PUBLISHER Hurst and Blackett, London.

2 IDENTIFICATION FEATURES

a. Binding   Three volumes, all light green cloth. Each 125 × 195 mm.

b. Spine   DAWN / By / H. Rider / Haggard / [three red lines] / Vol. I. [or II., or III.] / [three red lines] / London / Hurst & Blackett. [All between green decoration and red line at top, and red line and green decoration at bottom. Lettering all in gold].

c. Front Cover   [Red and green decoration top left, red bird top right] / DAWN / By / H. Rider Haggard [this lettering within a rough outline of a scroll, all in red] / [red and green decoration to lower fore edge and bottom right hand corner.]

d. End Papers   Plain grey.

e. Preliminaries

Vol I   Half title — DAWN. / Vol. I; verso, list of 5 New and Popular Novels. Title page — DAWN / By / H. Rider Haggard / 'Our natures languish incomplete; / Something obtuse in this our star / Shackles the spirit's winged feet; / But a glory moves us from afar, / And we know that we are strong and fleet.' / In Three Volumes / Vol. I. / London: / Hurst and Blackett, Publishers, 13, Great Marlborough Street. / 1884 / All rights reserved. Verso — 19 lines of verse.

Vols II and III   As for Vol I, but Vol numbers are II and III, and verso to title and half title pp are blank.

f. Text

Vol I   pp [1] to 325, with imprint at foot of p 325 — London: Printed by Duncan Macdonald, Blenheim House.

Vol II   pp [1] to 334, with same imprint at foot of p 334.

Vol III   pp [1] to 332, with same imprint at foot of p 332.

g. Supplements   Vols I and II, none. Vol III, four unnumbered pages, followed by pp 1 to 16, all comprising Messrs. Hurst and Blackett's List of New Works.

h. Illustrations   None.

i. Errors

Vol I

p 53, line 22. 'lable' should read 'label'.

p 63, line 4. 'Caresfort' should read 'Caresfoot'.

p 287, line 26. 'i' in 'him' has been printed upside down.

Vol II

p 220, line 4. 'then' should read 'than'.

p 286, line 25. 'lord' should read 'Lord'.

p 315, line 2. 'is' has been omitted at the end of the line.

Vol III

p 99, line 14. 'knowlege' should read 'knowledge'.

p 300, line 1. The first word should read 'and'.

3 TECHNICAL

a. Format   Cr 8vo

b. Edges   Top and fore edges uncut, bottom edge cut.

c. Collation

Vol I   2; B to I × 8; K to U × 8; X × 8; Y × 3. Total 165 leaves.

Vol II   2; B to I × 8; K to U × 8; X × 8; Y × 7. Total 169 leaves.

Vol III   2; B to I × 8; K to U × 8; X × 8; Y × 8; catalogue 8. Total 178 leaves.

4 NUMBER OF COPIES IN FIRST EDITION AND DATE
500; 10 Apr 84.

5 EARLIER PUBLICATION IN MAGAZINE
None.

6 OTHER EDITIONS OF NOTE
a. First one-volume edition by Messrs. J. and R. Maxwell, Feb 1887. This had a black and white frontispiece by H. French.
b. Another early one-volume edition, with a coloured frontispiece by E. Hume, was produced by Spencer Blackett (successor to J. and R. Maxwell) in about 1888, pp 371.
c. Another illustrated edition, with 16 illustrations by Laslett J. Pott, was produced, also by Spencer Blackett, in 1890. This included an Author's Note.
d. Messrs. Longmans, Green and Co. produced a further illustrated edition in 1894, at 3*s.* 6*d.*, as well as a Silver Library edition in the same year at the same price. These had 16 illustrations by D. Murray Smith and included for the first time a dedication — 'After many years, I dedicate this my first story to that unknown lady, once seen, but unforgotten, the mould and model of Angela, the magic of whose face turned my mind to the making of books. 1894.' pp 371.
e. Tauchnitz of Leipzig copyright edition 1892, (Nos 2825—6).
f. Early (First?) American Edition by J.W. Lovell, New York, 1887.

7 SOME HAGGARD NOTES
a. '. . . the first draft of it (Dawn), I think I wrote at Norwood. Towards Christmas of 1882 my wife and I made up our minds to return to this house at Ditchingham, which was standing empty and furnished, while I pursued my studies at the bar . . .'
b. '. . . Whilst we were at Norwood a little incident occurred which resulted in my becoming a writer of fiction. At the church which my wife and I attended we saw sitting near us one Sunday a singularly beautiful and pure-faced young lady. Afterwards we

agreed that this semi-devine creature — on whom to the best of my knowledge I have never set eyes again from that day to this — ought to become the heroine of a novel. So then and there we took paper, and each of us began to write the said novel. I think that after she had completed two or three folio sheets my wife ceased from her fictional labours. But, growing interested, I continued mine, which resulted in the story called "Dawn".'

c. '. . . There appear to be three drafts of this work, the first of which (incomplete) is named "Angela", after the heroine; the second, five hundred and fifty-four closely written foolscap sheets long (!), . . . called "There Remaineth a Rest"; and the third . . . unnamed.

d. '. . . Mr. Trübner, with whom I had become personally acquainted since the publication of "Cetewayo and his White Neighbours" . . . was good enough to take some interest in the story, and to suggest that it should be sent to the late Mr. Cordy Jeaffreson for his opinion. . . . he found time on behalf of an individual totally unknown to him . . . to write a masterly criticism . . . I took his advice . . . I began to rewrite "Dawn", or "Angela", as it was then called, on May 15th, 1883, and finished . . . on September 5th of the same year.'

e. '. . . My criticism on "Dawn" considered as a whole — that is, so far as I recollect it, for I have not reread the book for many years — is that it ought to have been cut up into several stories. However, it has pleased, and apparently still continues to please, a vast number of persons.'

f. '. . . Messrs. Hurst and Blackett wrote to me, and well do I remember the jubilation with which I read the letter: . . .' (The firm offered to publish the work at their own expense and risk and to pay Haggard £40 on the sale of 400 copies and £30 on the sale of every 100 copies thereafter. They mentioned that 'Angela' had already been used as a title.) . . . 'Needless to say I accepted the offer with gratitude and promised to find another title. . . . In their . . . letter they informed me that they only proposed to print five hundred copies in the three-volume form, leaving me at liberty to make any arrangements I liked for a cheap edition . . .'

The Days of My Life
Vol I, pp 209–15

g. 'I worked so hard at re-writing this MS. that I went nearly blind and had to finish it in a darkened room. For weeks afterwards I was not allowed to read anything and might only amuse myself by throwing a ball against a wall, like a child, and catching it again.'

A note in Haggard's handwriting
on the MS to *Dawn* held in
Norfolk Record Office

F2   The Witch's Head   1885

1 PUBLISHER   Hurst and Blackett, London.

2 IDENTIFICATION FEATURES

a. *Binding*   Dark greeny-grey cloth. 127 × 195 mm.

b. *Spine*   [Two lines] / [Two lines] / THE / WITCH'S / HEAD / [two lines] / Vol. I [or II or III] / [two lines] H. Rider / Haggard / [two lines] / [one line] / Hurst & Blackett / [one line]. [All in silver.]

c. *Front Cover*   THE WITCH'S HEAD / BY / H. Rider Haggard. [All in silver,

	printed diagonally between two lines in blind at top and two at bottom.] (The lines in blind also appear on the back cover.)
d. End Papers	Plain dark brown.
e. Preliminaries	
Vol I	Half title — THE WITCH'S HEAD / Vol. I.; verso, list of 5 New and Popular Novels. Title page — THE WITCH'S HEAD / By / H. Rider Haggard, / Author of 'Dawn'. / In Three Volumes. / Vol. I. / London: / Hurst and Blackett, Publishers, / 13, Great Marlborough Street. / 1885. / All rights reserved; verso, 12 lines of verse by A.M. Barber. Contents page; verso blank.
Vol II	Half title — THE WITCH'S HEAD / Vol. II.; verso, blank. Title page — (as Vol I, but Vol. II., not Vol. I.); verso, imprint — Clay and Taylor, Printers, Bungay, Suffolk. Contents page; verso blank.
Vol III	Half title — THE WITCH'S HEAD / Vol. III.; verso blank. Title page — (as Vol I, but Vol. III., not Vol. I.); verso, printer's imprint. Contents page; verso blank.
f. Text	
Vol I	pp [1] to 295, with verso to p 295 blank except for printer's imprint at foot.
Vol II	pp [1] to 303, with printer's imprint at foot of p 303, verso blank.
Vol III	pp [1] to 334, with printer's imprint at foot of p 334.
g. Supplements	Vols I and II, none. Vol III, pp 1 to 8, list of New Works.
h. Illustrations	None.
i. Errors	
Vol I	p 97, line 6. 'his' should read 'her'.
Vol III	p 90, line 16. 'Dartwell' should read 'Dartnell'.
	p 99, line 19. 'Inslhazatze's' should read 'Inhlazatye's'.
	p 154, line 9. 'rakisk' should read 'rakish'.
	p 155, line 11. A hyphen is missing between 'rig' and 'out'.
	p 245, line 14. 'must' should read 'most'.

3 TECHNICAL

a. Format	Cr 8vo
b. Edges	Top edge uncut, fore edge rough cut, bottom edge cut.
c. Collation	
Vol I	3; B to I × 8; K to T × 8; U × 4. Total 151 leaves.
Vol II	3; B to I × 8; K to U × 8. Total 155 leaves.
Vol III	3; B to I × 8; K to U × 8; X × 8; Y × 7; catalogue 4. Total 174 leaves.

4 NUMBER OF COPIES IN FIRST EDITION AND DATE
500; 22 Dec 84.

5 EARLIER PUBLICATIONS IN MAGAZINE
None.

6 OTHER EDITIONS OF NOTE
a. The first one-volume edition was produced by Messrs J. and R. Maxwell in May 1887. This included a black and white frontispiece.

b. As in the case of *Dawn*, Messrs. Spencer Blackett and Hallam (successors to J. and R. Maxwell) produced another single volume edition of *The Witch's Head* in 1887, with a coloured frontispiece by E. Hume. An 1889 issue of this edition includes at the end a supplement of 32 pp — 'A Catalogue of Books' — dated London, September 1889, the same as is found in *Allan's Wife*, 1889 (Fll).

c. In 1893, Spencer Blackett and Hallam issued another edition with 16 illustrations by Charles Kerr.

d. Early American Edition by D. Appleton and Co., New York, 1885.

e. Tauchnitz of Leipzig copright edition 1887, (Nos 2482–3).

7 SOME HAGGARD NOTES

a. '. . . The new novel upon which I embarked ultimatley appeared under the title of "The Witch's Head". Failing to find any magazine that would undertake it serially, in the end I published it with Messrs. Hurst and Blackett on practically the same terms as they had offered me for "Dawn".'

b. '. . . The notices of "The Witch's Head" naturally delighted me; indeed, after a lapse of more than a quarter of a century they still make pleasant reading. Also they caused the book to go quickly out of print and to be pirated in America. But this success would not tempt my publishers to reissue it in a cheaper form.'

c. '. . . Ultimately, after various "business complications", in the course of which I lost some money that was due for royalties, . . . "Dawn" and "The Witch's Head" passed into the hands of Messrs. Longmans.'

The Days of My Life
Vol I, pp 218, 219, 267, 268

F3   King Solomon's Mines   1885

1 PUBLISHER   Cassell & Co., Ltd., London.

2 IDENTIFICATION FEATURES

a. Binding   Red cloth. 125 × 192 mm.

b. Spine   KING / SOLOMON'S / MINES / H. Rider / Haggard / [ornament of mountainous landscape]. [Title in gold, remainder in black.]

c. Front Cover   KING SOLOMON'S / MINES / by / H. Rider Haggard [author's name underlined] / [device of shield over spear, knobkerry, tusk and leaves]. [All in black.]
(Back cover has a design of a flowering plant, in black.)

d. End Papers   Plain light yellow.

e. Preliminaries   Half title — KING SOLOMON'S MINES; verso blank. Folded facsimile of a map of the route to the mines. Title page — KING SOLOMON'S /MINES. / by / H. Rider Haggard / Author of "Dawn," "The Witch's Head." &c. / [line] / Cassell & Company, Limited: / London, Paris, New York & Melbourne. / [line] / 1885. / (All Rights Reserved.); verso blank. p[i] Dedication; verso blank. p[iii] Contents list, with printer's mark B2 at foot; verso blank. pp[v] and vi, Introduction.

f. Text   pp[7] to 320, with printer's imprint (Cassell) at foot of p 320.

g. Supplements   Catalogue of 8 leaves, dated 5G. 8. 85.

h. Illustrations   Apart from the map before the title page, there are no illustrations except another map in the text, p 27.

i. Errors p 10, line 14. 'Bamamgwato' should read 'Bamangwato'.

p 122, line 27. 'to let twins to live' should read 'to let twins live'.

p 307, line 29. 'wrod' should read 'word'.

3 TECHNICAL

a. Format Cr 8vo

b. Edges Top edge cut, other edges rough cut.

c. Collation 1; map; 1; B to U × 8, catalogue 8. (Signature J is unusually included.) Total 179 leaves including map.

4 NUMBER OF COPIES IN FIRST EDITION AND DATE

2,000; Sep 85. (Many of the Cassell's publishing records were destroyed in the Second World War. Messrs Cassell are unable, therefore, now to corroborate the information given by Scott, that the sheets for 1000 copies of the book (the First issue) were bound up in Sep 85 with a catalogue date 5G. 8. 85.: that a further 500 sets of the sheets were bound up in Oct 85 with a catalogue dated 5G. 10. 85 (the Second issue): and that the last 500 sets of sheets were sent to the Cassell's New York office and were bound up there in Nov 85 (to form the First American issue.)

5 EARLIER PUBLICATION IN MAGAZINE

None.

6 OTHER EDITIONS OF NOTE

a. The 'People's Library Edition' (Cassell & Co, 1920) states, in a Bibliographical Note:
'First published 1 Sep 85
Reprinted — Oct, Nov, 10 Dec and 27 Dec 85
          10 Jan, 25 Jan, Feb, Mar, Apr, May, Jul,
          Sep, Oct, Nov and Dec 86
          Feb, Apr, Jun and Nov 87
          Jan 88, Nov 89, May, Jul and Nov 90, Aug and Nov 91
          Jul 92, Jan 94, May 95, Feb 97, Jun 99,
          Jul 02, Jan 05.'
b. Tauchnitz of Leipzig copyright edition, 1886, (No 2386).
c. The first illustrated edition was the 53rd Thousand (1887), with 9 illustrations by W. Paget.
d. A revised edition, with 32 illustrations by Russell Flint (and therefore much sought after today) was published in Nov 1905 (pp xii, 306).
e. A further issue of 6d above (Sep 1907, pp xii, 306) states, in a Bibliographical Note:
  1. First Edition — Sep 85 (no date given.)
  2. Reprint dates as in para 6a above.
  3. Additional reprint dates, viz:
     New Illustrated Edition Nov 05, 07
     Abridged Edition May 03, 06
     Popular Edition Apr 1898. Reprinted Aug and Dec 98,
     1900, 01, 02, 03, 04, 05, 06, Jan and Sep 07.
     Pocket Edition Jul 07
     Peoples Library Oct 07
f. First American Edition — see para 4 above.
g. An Oxford University Press edition, published in Hong Kong in 1976 in the Oxford Progressive English Readers series (Grade 3). This is a simplified version of the text, published with unusual monochrome illustrations.

7 NOTES

a. The adventurers in the story, at the time of a full moon, seek to prove their (supposed) omnipotence by using an eclipse of the sun (forecast in a pocket almanac they carry) as a sign. Here, Haggard made a mistake; an eclipse of the sun is impossible when the moon is full. This was pointed out to him and in later editions of the book, an eclipse of the moon is substituted, requiring considerable re-writing of the chapter 'We Give a Sign'. Scott believed that the moon eclipse first appeared in the 37th Thousand (1887) edition and that all subsequent editions include the moon eclipse. (See Scott, p 35.) But the moon eclipse appears in the 31st Thousand (1886) edition, and the sun eclipse is not unknown to re-appear in later editions. The 31st Thousand may be the first appearance of the moon eclipse; it certainly does not feature in the 28th Thousand.

b. A further change became necessary when Haggard's hero, Allan Quatermain, became so popular that the reading public began to follow his career. *King Solomon's Mines* opens with '. . . my age — fifty-five last birthday — . . . .'. This did not fit in with the chronology of other stories written later, so it was changed (in a 1912 edition) to '. . . I shall never see sixty again . . .'. Subsequent editions use either of these opening sentences, apparently arbitrarily.

c. As shown in para 4 above, the dates of the catalogues bound in at the end of the early editions give interesting clues to publication dates. Eg. my copies show;

   1. 1885 edition. 'Eighth Thousand' on the title page. '20.1285' on p 320. Catalogue dated '5G.11.85' (p 3) and '5B.11.85.' (p 11).

   2. 1886 edition. No reference to any 'Thousands' on title page. '20.1285' on p 320. Catalogue dated '6G.9.85' (p 3) and '6B.9.85 (p 11).

   3. 1886 edition. 'Twenty-eighth Thousand' on the title page. '30.886' on p 320. Catalogue dated '5G.9.86' (p 5) and '5B.9.86' (p [13]).

8 SOME HAGGARD NOTES

a. '. . . I read in one of the weekly papers a notice of Stevenson's "Treasure Island" so laudatory that I procured and studied that work, and I was impelled by its perusal to try to write a book for boys.'

b. '. . . I think the task occupied me about six weeks. When the tale was finished, I hawked it round to sundry publishers . . . At length . . . the MS . . . reached the late W.E. Henley who . . . brought it to the notice of Mr Andrew Lang.'

c. '. . . Ultimately that book found its way to Messrs Cassells.'

d. '. . . "King Solomon's Mines", which was produced as a five-shilling book, proved an instant success. Published about the beginning of October, on December 9th Messrs Cassells wrote to me that they had already sold 5,000 copies more or less.'

The Days of My Life
Vol I, pp 220, 226, 231, 233

F4   She   1887

1 PUBLISHER   Longmans, Green, and Co., London.

2 IDENTIFICATION FEATURES

a. Binding   Dark blue cloth over bevelled edge boards. 122 × 195 mm.

b. Spine   SHE / [line] / H. Rider / Haggard / [scarab ornament] / Longmans & Co. [All in gold.]

c. Front Cover   [Scarabus] / SHE / by / H. Rider Haggard. [All in gold.]

d. End Papers	Patterned, brown on grey, of swans, sailing ships and 1726, all entwined with leafy twigs.
e. Preliminaries	Half title — SHE; verso, list of 4 works by the same author. One page blank; verso, coloured facsimile of the Sherd of Amenartas, numbered 1 at top of page. Opposite page, coloured facsimile of the reverse of the sherd, numbered 2 at top of page; verso blank. Title page — SHE / A HISTORY OF ADVENTURE / by / H. Rider Haggard / Author of 'King Solomon's Mines' 'Dawn' 'The Witch's Head' Etc / In earth and skie and sea / strange thynges ther be / Doggerel couplet from the Sherd of Amenartas / London / Longmans, Green and Co. / 1887 / All rights reserved; verso, Printed by / Spottiswoode and Co., New-Street Square / London. Dedication to Andrew Lang; verso, list of plates. Contents list; verso, Allan Quatermain advertisement.
f. Text	pp[1] to 317, with printer's imprint at foot of p 317, the verso of which is blank.
g. Supplements	One leaf of Longmans, Green & Co. advertisements, undated.
h. Illustrations	Apart from the sherd facsimiles (see above), there is one illustration in the text, on p 26. This represents an impression of the scarabus on the front cover.
i. Errors	p 88, line 4. 'mysogymist' should read 'misogynist'.
	p 126, line 26. 'had' should read 'have'.
	p 258, line 37. 'it' should read 'if'.
	p 269, line 38. 'Godness me' should read 'Goodness me'.

3 TECHNICAL

a. Format	Cr 8vo
b. Edges	Top edge uncut, fore edge rough cut, bottom edge cut.
c. Collation	6 (including two illustrations); B to I × 8; K to U × 8; X × 8. Total 166 leaves.

4 NUMBER OF COPIES IN FIRST EDITION AND DATE

10,000; 1 Jan 87. (10,003 were printed in Dec 86. There were three further print runs in Jan 87 of 5001, 5005 and 5006. Another 5001 were printed in Mar 87. The Jan and Mar print runs do not quite add up to the '25,000' mentioned by Longman — see para 8 below.)

5 EARLIER PUBLICATION IN MAGAZINE

Serial story in The Graphic, Oct 86 to Jan 87, Vols 34 and 35, Nos 879 to 893. Illustrated by E.K. Johnson.

6 OTHER EDITIONS OF NOTE

a. The Second Edition, also 1887, is exactly the same as the First except for 'Second Edition' on the title page, and all errors corrected except for p 126, line 26.

b. Tauchnitz of Leipzig copyright edition 1887, (Nos 2445−6).

c. The First Illustrated Edition was published by Longmans, Green, and Co. on 1 Nov 88. It included 19 full page illustrations and numerous illustrations in the text, specially drawn for this edition by Maurice Greiffenhagen and Charles Kerr. 10,000 of the Illustrated Edition were printed in Oct 88 and 5011 in Dec 89.

d. Early American Edition by Harper and Brothers, New York, 1886.

e. A Colonial Library and a Silver Library edition were published in 1892. 2,500 and 7502 copies were printed respectively.

f. An edition in Esperanto was published in Amsterdam by the 'Populara Esperanto Biblioteko' in 1934. Bound in rough cloth in shades of brown, with 'H. Rider Haggard / ŜI' printed in gold on the front cover. My copy has, pasted over the publisher's name on the title page, a slip reading 'The Esperanto Publishing Co. Ltd., / 142, High Holborn, London, W.C.I., Anglujo.' The volume is undated. pp 276.

7 NOTES

a. In the serial version in *The Graphic*, the horrible method of execution called 'hot-potting' was actually used on Mahomed. In the book version, Mahomed is shot dead in the struggle while resisting the attempt to kill him. This required several other textual amendments in later chapters.

b. The error recorded by Scott (see Scott, p 37), ie, the incorrect spelling of 'gentleman', is not, in my view, an error at all, but Haggard's deliberate attempt to express Job's colloquial style of speech.

c. Longmans Magazine, No LXV (Mar 88), Vol XI, pp 492 to 497, includes a 'Suggested Prologue to a Dramatised Version of "She" ', by Rider Haggard. He states in a note — 'This Prologue is designed to explain to the spectator, in as few words as possible, such of the antecedent circumstances as are necessary to the right understanding of the tragedy'.

d. '. . . a silly, sensational novel just published by J.S. Ogilvie & Co.' was reported in *The Literary World* (Boston, USA) in Apr 87. The title page was deliberately ambiguously worded to read 'Me. A Companion to She. A Story of Adventure' 'By H. Rider Haggard'. The actual writer is not shown. On 25 Sep 87, the *New York Times* published a letter from Rider Haggard, repudiating authorship.

8 SOME HAGGARD NOTES

a. 'So soon as "Jess" was finished, or rather about a month later, I began . . . "She". The exact date of commencement is uncertain, for it has been obliterated by a clip that fastened the MS together, and all that remains is "Feb/86". At the end, however, it is inscribed "Finished 18 March 1886".'

b. '. . . Having run through the *Graphic*, where it attracted a good deal of attention, "She" appeared as a six-shilling volume, . . . some time in December 1886. It was brought out by Messrs. Longmans and very well got up, the elaborate sherd compounded by my sister-in-law, then Miss Barber, and myself, being reproduced in two plates at the beginning of the volume.'

c. '. . . On March 15th [1887] Charles Longman wrote to me in Egypt: "I am glad to tell you that 'She' keeps on selling capitally. We have printed another 25,000 already and have ordered another 5000, and I do not think we shall have many left when the printers deliver them. . . . Last week we sold over 1000 copies".

The Days of My Life
Vol I, pp 245, 248, 251

F5   Jess   1887

1 PUBLISHER   Smith, Elder, & Co., London.

2 IDENTIFICATION FEATURES
a. Binding   Red cloth. 125 × 195 mm.
b. Spine   JESS / H. Rider / Haggard / Smith Elder & Co. [All between two
                  lines at top and two at bottom. All in gold.]

c. Front Cover	[Square decoration top right corner] / JESS / By / H. Rider Haggard / Author of King Solomon's Mines, Etc / [spiral decoration bottom left corner]. [All between a single horizontal line at top and at bottom. All in black.] (The back cover has the horizontal lines at top and bottom in blind.)
d. End Papers	Grey patterned, of leaves and flowers.
e. Preliminaries	p[i] Half title — JESS; verso, list of 5 works by the same author. p[iii] Title page — JESS / by / H. Rider Haggard / Author of / King Solomon's Mines' 'She, A History of Adventure' / Etc. / London / Smith, Elder, & Co., 15 Waterloo Place / 1887 / (All rights reserved); verso blank. p[v] Dedication — To My Wife; verso blank. pp[vii] and viii, Contents list.
f. Text	pp[1] to 336, with printer's imprint at foot of p 336.
g. Supplements	8 pages of advertisements, undated. The last page, however, mentions that Volume X of the *Dictionary of National Biography* 'will be issued on 26th of March'.
h. Illustrations	None.
i. Errors	On the title page, the inverted comma has been omitted, or appears only faintly, before 'King' in 'King Solomon's Mines'.

3 TECHNICAL

a. Format	Cr 8vo
b. Edges	Top and fore edges uncut, bottom edge cut.
c. Collation	4; B to I × 8; K to U × 8; X and Y × 8; Z (advertisements) 4. Total 176 leaves.

4 NUMBER OF COPIES IN FIRST EDITION AND DATE
2,000; Mar 87.

5 EARLIER PUBLICATION IN MAGAZINE
Serial story in *The Cornhill Magazine*, Vols VI, VII and VIII, May 1886 to April 1887, Nos 35 to 46.

6 OTHER EDITIONS OF NOTE
a. Tauchnitz of Leipzig copyright edition 1887, (Nos 2451−2).
b. A New Edition by Smith, Elder, & Co., 1888 (pp viii 335, and 8 pp of advertisements.)
c. The first illustrated edition, Oct 1896, with 12 illustrations by Maurice Greiffenhagen.
d. Early American Edition by Harper and Brothers, New York, 1887.

7 NOTES
a. As in the case of *She*, critics took the opportunity to level accusations of plagiarism against Haggard over *Jess*, in particular about the use of some verses Haggard had received from an acquaintance who, Haggard thought, had made them up and implied he could use them. In fact, they had been copied from elsewhere and, with some embarrassment, Haggard withdrew them from susequent editions.
b. Much of the background to the story of *Jess* was drawn from real events experienced by Haggard and some characters were real personalities thinly disguised.
c. The British Library copy of the First Edition is bound in green cloth but otherwise is as described above.

8 SOME HAGGARD NOTES
a. '. . . To put it mildly, the lawyers who frequented the Transvaal courts were not the

most eminent of their tribe. . . . Thus one . . . subsequently became notorious in connection with the treatment of the loyal prisoners at the siege of Potchefstroom. He was fond of music, and it is said that before two of these unfortunate men were executed, or rather murdered, he took them into a church and soothed their feelings by playing the "Dead March of Saul" over them. He, by the way, was the original of my character of Frank Muller in "Jess".'

b. '. . . On my return to town in late autumn (from a holiday in 1885) I began . . . "Jess". The MS . . . does not state the date of its commencement, but at the end appears the date of December 31, 1885, . . . This book I wrote for the most part in the chambers, at 1 Elm Court,. . . .'

c. '. . . In the winter of 1886, as I remember very much against my own will, I was worried into writing an article "About Fiction" for the *Contemporary Review* . . . to spring a dissertation of this kind upon the literary world over (my) own name was very little short of madness. Such views must make . . . enemies . . . these foes found a very able leader in the . . . editor of the *Pall Mall Gazette*.'

d. '. . . It is a gloomy story and painful to an Englishman, so gloomy and painful indeed that Lang could scarely read it, . . . except when I went through it some fifteen years ago to correct it for a new illustrated edition, I too have never reread it, and I think that I never mean to do so. The thing is a living record of our shame in South Africa.'

The Days of My Life
Vol I, pp 108, 109, 244, 264, 265

F6   Allan Quatermain   1887

1 PUBLISHER   Longmans, Green and Co., London.

2 IDENTIFICATION FEATURES

a. *Binding*	Dark blue cloth over bevelled edge boards. 136 × 194 mm.
b. *Spine*	ALLAN / QUATERMAIN / [Line] / H. Rider / Haggard / [vertical outline of a battleaxe] / Longmans & Co. [All in gold.]
c. *Front Cover*	ALLAN / QUATERMAIN [at top left]; H. Rider Haggard [at bottom right]. [All in gold.]
d. *End Papers*	Patterned, brown on grey, of swans, sailing ships and 1726, all entwined with leafy twigs.
e. *Preliminaries*	Half title — ALLAN QUATERMAIN; verso, Andrew Lang verse in Greek and English. One page blank; verso, frontispiece with tissue guard. Title page — ALLAN QUATERMAIN / Being an account of his / Further Adventures and Discoveries / in company with / Sir Henry Curtis, Bart., Commander John Good, R.N. / And One Umslopogaas / by / H. Rider Haggard / Author of 'She' 'King Solomon's Mines' Etc / Ex Africa semper aliquid novi / London / Longmans, Green and Co. / 1887 / All rights reserved; verso, printer's imprint. Dedication to Arthur John Rider Haggard, dated 1887; verso blank. Contents page; verso, list of plates.
f. *Text*	pp[1] to 278.
g. *Supplements*	One page of the Author's acknowledgement of certain 'Authorities'; verso, list of 6 works by the same author, with printer's imprint at foot.

h. Illustrations	There are 20 full page illustrations including the frontispiece, all engraved on wood by J. Cooper from drawings by C.H.M. Kerr. All have blank backs and are not included in the pagination. Additionally, 11 drawings and 2 charts appear in the text on pp 39, 51, 54, 71, 78 (chart), 134, 142, 143, 144 (2), 145, 146, 162 (chart).
i. Errors	p 17, third line from bottom. 'Dongo' should read 'Donyo'.

3 TECHNICAL

a. Format	Cr 8vo
b. Edges	Top edge uncut, fore edge rough cut, bottom edge cut.
c. Collation	4; B to I × 8; K to S × 8; T × 4. The 20 illustrations have been sewn into the gatherings as follows: Frontispiece; B (facing p 10); C (facing p 24); D (facing p 36); F (facing p 76); G (facing p 86); H(2) (facing pp 98 and 110); I(2) (facing pp 116 and 124); K (facing p 140); N(2) (facing pp 184 and 188); O (facing p 204); P (facing p 224); R(2) (facing pp 224 and 254); S(2) (facing pp 258 and 264); T (facing p 274). Total 164 leaves.

4 NUMBER OF COPIES IN FIRST EDITION AND DATE
20,000; 1 Jul 87. (20,000 copies were printed Jun 87).

5 EARLIER PUBLICATION IN MAGAZINE
Serial story in *Longmans Magazine*, Vols IX and X, Jan to Aug 87, Nos LI to LVIII. No illustrations. The serial and the book forms of the story differ in several places, but only to minor effect; for example see, Vol IX, p 343 — text and note; p 561 note; p 562 text: and Vol X, p 10 text; p 19 note.

6 OTHER EDITIONS OF NOTE
a. Longmans published a large paper issue (Cr 4to) on the same date as the Cr 8vo edition. Only 112 copies were printed. It was illustrated as for the smaller version but the plates were printed on India paper and mounted.
b. There were further printings of 500l (Aug 87) and 5002 (Oct 87) which may have reached the public as 2nd and 3rd issues of the First Edition. (Cr 8vo.)
c. A New and Cheaper edition was published on 1 Nov 88 at 3*s.* 6*d.* (10,000 printed Jul 88 and 10,000 Oct 88). This edition includes a footnote to the frontispiece, but otherwise the illustrations are the same as in the First Edition.
d. A further issue of the Cheap Edition was made in 1891 which included a portrait of Haggard's son Jock, to whom the work had been dedicated and who tragically died on 8 Feb 91. (5000 were printed Aug 91, including the photo-tint of the portrait.) This edition was reissued in 1893.
e. A sixpenny Edition was published by Longmans in 1904 (50,000 printed Apr 04).
f. The book was reprinted for Longmans Silver Library and Longmans Colonial Library many times. The first such printing was:

Silver Library	5000	Jan 93
Colonial Library	3000	Jan 93

f. Tauchnitz of Leipzig copyright edition, 1887, (Nos 2472–3).
g. Early American edition by George Munro, New York, Jun 1887.

7 NOTES
a. In *Longmans Magazine*, No LXI, Nov 87, Vol XI, pp 61 to 66, in an article titled 'On Going Back', Rider Haggard records his thoughts on returning to a village he had not

seen since early boyhood. During the visit, Haggard asked for William Quatermain who, with his wife, had been kind to Haggard. Here we can see the origin of Allan Quatermain's name.

b. The accusations of plagiarism levelled at Haggard over *She* and *Jess* have been mentioned. He was upset by this and was thereafter sensitive on the subject. The acknowledgement of his 'Authorities' inserted at the end of *Allan Quatermain* is one manifestation of this sensitivity.

c. A Longmans ledger includes this work under the title *Frowning City*, but this is crossed through and *Allan Quatermain* substituted.

8 SOME HAGGARD NOTES

a. '. . . While on my summer holiday in 1885 I wrote "Allan Quatermain" the sequel to "King Solomon's Mines", from the first word to the last, although it did not appear until a couple of years later, after it had run through *Longmans Magazine*. . . . I made a present [of the MS] to Charles Longman.'

b. '. . . "Allan Quatermain" came out about the end of June 1887. Charles Longman, in a letter dated June 20th, writes:

> You have broken the record — at least so I am told. We have subscribed over 10,000 copies of 'Quatermain' in London, which they say is more than has ever been subscribed of a six shilling novel before . . . We printed 20,000 of 'Quatermain' as you know and we are now ordering paper in readiness for another lot.

c. '. . . By one of the saddest of all coincidences, if such things are pure coincidence, 'Allan Quatermain' opens with a description of the death of Quatermain's only son. I dedicated it to *my* only son, and shortly afterwards that fate overtook him also!'

The Days of My Life
Vol 1, pp 243, 244, 274, 275

F7   Maiwa's Revenge   1888

1 PUBLISHER   Longmans, Green, and Co., London.

2 IDENTIFICATION FEATURES

a. Binding   Issued in two bindings: Black cloth. 125 × 196 mm
                    Pale green-grey boards. 121 × 187 mm.

b. Spine   MAIWA'S / REVENGE / By / H. Rider / Haggard / Longmans & Co. [All in brick red, both bindings.]

c. Front Cover   MAIWA'S / REVENGE / By / H. Rider Haggard. [All in brick red, both bindings.] (The rear cover of the boards version carries advertisements for *She* and *Allan Quatermain*, within a box, all in brick red.)

d. End Papers   Cloth binding — patterned, light green, of swans, sailing ships and 1726, all entwined with leafy twigs. Boards binding — plain white.

e. Preliminaries Both bindings: Half title — MAIWA'S REVENGE; verso, list of 7 works by the same author. Title page — MAIWA'S REVENGE; / or, / The War of the Little Hand. / by / H. Rider Haggard. / London: / Longmans, Green, and Co. / and New York: 15 East 16th Street. / 1888. / All rights reserved; verso, printer's imprint (Richard Clay). Preface; verso blank. Contents list; verso blank.

f. Text   Both bindings — pp[1] to 216.

g. Supplements   Cloth binding — pp[1] to 16, General List of Works dated June 1888 on p[1]. Boards binding — None.

h. Illustrations   Both bindings — None.

i. Errors   Both bindings — None.

3 TECHNICAL

a. Format   Cr 8vo

b. Edges   Cloth binding — top edge uncut, fore edge and bottom edge rough cut.

Boards binding — all edges cut.

c. Collation   4; B to I × 8; K to O × 8; P × 4. Total 112 leaves (plus 8 leaves in catalogue in cloth binding.)

4 NUMBER OF COPIES IN FIRST EDITION AND DATE

30,000; 3 Aug 88. (The records do not disclose how many were bound in cloth and in boards.)

5 EARLIER PUBLICATION IN MAGAZINE

Two-part story in *Harper's Monthly Magazine*, Vol XVI (European Edition), Vol LXXVII (American Edition), Jul and Aug 88, pp 181–209 and 345–63. With 10 illustrations by Thulstrup.

6 OTHER EDITIONS OF NOTE

a. The First Illustrated Edition was published by Longmans in 1891, (pp 115) with 8 illustrations by C.H.M. Kerr, in two bindings — red cloth and pictorial boards. 10,000 copies were printed, of which 5,000 appear to have been bound in cloth.

b. A further illustrated edition — Longmans 'New Edition with portraits etc . . .' came out in 1923 (pp vii, 152).

c. Early American edition by Harper & Brothers 1888.

d. Tauchnitz of Leipzig copyright edition, 1888, (No 2530).

7 NOTES

The simultaneous issue of the book in two bindings was aimed at high sales. The cloth version sold at 2*s*. 6*d*. and the boards version at 2*s*.

8 AN HAGGARD NOTE

'. . . We have sold 20,000 copies of "Maiwa" on the day of publication'. (Quote from a Charles Longman letter to Haggard dated 4 Aug 88.)

The Days of My Life
Vol I, p 280

F8   Mr Meeson's Will   1888

1 PUBLISHER   Spencer Blackett, London.

2 IDENTIFICATION FEATURES

a. Binding   Dark red cloth. 145 × 232 mm.

b. Spine   Mr. / MEESON'S / WILL / by / H. / Rider / Haggard / Illustrated / Spencer Blackett. [All in gold except 'Illustrated' which is in black.]

c. Front Cover   Mr. MEESON'S / WILL / [picture of the heroine at a dressing table,

	in a frame superimposed upon a seascape.] / H. Rider Haggard. [All lettering in black and gold. Picture all in black.]
d. End Papers	Plain black; or, more rarely, a light floral pattern.
e. Preliminaries	p[i] Half title — Mr. Meeson's Will; verso, list of 8 works by the same author, in a box. p[iii] blank; verso, Frontispiece. p[v] Title page — Mr. MEESON'S WILL / by H. RIDER HAGGARD / Author of / "King Solomon's Mines", "Dawn", "The Witch's Head", "She", / "Allan Quatermain," etc. / With Sixteen Illustrations / London / Spencer Blackett. / Successor to J. & R. Maxwell / Milton House, 35 St. Bride Street, E.C. / 1888 / [All Rights Reserved]; verso blank. pp[ix] to xiv — Preface; pp xv and xvi — Contents list. p[xvii] List of illustrations; verso blank.
f. Text	pp[19] to 286, with printers imprint at bottom of p 286.
g. Supplements	One leaf blank. pp[1] to [32] Catalogue of Books, dated at top of p[1] — London, October, 1888.
h. Illustrations	16 full-page engravings by A. Forestier and G. Montbard, as listed on p[xvii]. All with blank backs, both sides unnumbered but included in the pagination. Additionally, there are 26 decorated chapter headings, 24 decorated initial letters and 18 end-of-chapter decorated devices.
i. Errors	p 284, line 1. 'Johnson' should read 'Johnston'.

3 TECHNICAL

a. Format	Dmy 8vo
b. Edges	All uncut
c. Collation	[A?] × 8; B to I × 8; K and L × 8; [M] × 8; N to S × 8; 16 (catalogue). Total 160 leaves.

4 NUMBER OF COPIES IN FIRST EDITION AND DATE
Oct 1888

5 EARLIER PUBLICATION IN MAGAZINE
Illustrated London News, Summer Number, June 1888. Several minor changes were made in the book version of the story. Illustrated by A. Forestier and G. Montbard.

6 OTHER EDITIONS OF NOTE
a. Some copies of the First Edition can be found without the catalogue bound in at the end.
b. Griffith, Farran and Co., London and Sydney, published an edition in 1888, similar to the First Edition. In these copies, the frontispiece has a tissue guard.
c. Early American edition by Harper Brothers 1888.
d. Tauchnitz of Leipzig copyright edition 1888, (No 2556).

7 NOTES
a. Mr Meeson is a publisher. The treatment he gives the heroine, who is an aspiring authoress, is totally unsympathetic. By this story line, Rider Haggard works off some of his own annoyance with one of his own publishers, whose contractural terms, accepted for the re-publication in a cheap edition of *Dawn* and *The Witch's Head*, later cost the author some money. See the Preface to the First Edition and below.
b. The Preface also deals with accusations of plagiarism 'which are now so freely brought against authors', as Haggard knew to his cost in respect of *She* and *Jess*. See also my note under *Allan Quatermain* (qv).

8 SOME HAGGARD NOTES

a. '. . . some other publishers — who have long since ceased to publish . . . agreed to bring out [*Dawn* and the *Witch's Head*] in a two shilling edition, and nobly promised me one-third of the profits. But in that generous agreement was a little clause that afterwards nearly proved my ruin. It bound me to allow this firm to republish any other novel I might write during the following five years, in the same form and in the same terms. To such a document as this in my ignorance . . . I set my hand . . .'

b. '. . . The unfortunate agreement to which I have already alluded, entered into with the firm in which I believe Mr Maxwell . . . was a partner, had been abrogated without a lawsuit. . . . But this was done at a price, and that price was that I should write them two stories. . . . The tales that I wrote for them were called respectively "Mr. Meeson's Will" and "Allan's Wife".'

c. '. . . It is curious how often imagination is verified by fact . . . in Mr Meeson's Will, I set out very fully indeed the circumstances under which a new and splendid liner was lost at sea and the great majority of those on board of her were drowned owing to lack of boats to accommodate them. . . . During the present year this prophecy, and indeed the whole scene of the sinking of the Kangaroo, has been fearfully fulfilled in the instance of the great White Star liner Titanic.'

The Days of My Life
Vol I pp 219, 267; Vol II pp 95 to 97

F9   Colonel Quaritch V.C.   1889

1 PUBLISHER   Longmans, Green and Co., London.

2 IDENTIFICATION FEATURES

a. Binding   Three volumes, all red cloth. Each 126 × 197 mm.

b. Spine   COLONEL / QUARITCH V.C. / [line] / H. Rider Haggard / Vol I. [or II., or III.] / Longmans & Co. [All in black.]

c. Front Cover   COLONEL / QUARITCH V.C. [on all three volumes. All in black.]

d. End Papers   Plain white.

e. Preliminaries

Vols I, II and III   Half title — COLONEL QUARITCH V.C.; verso, list of 9 works by the same author. Title page — COLONEL QUARITCH, V.C. / A Tale of Country Life / by / H. Rider Haggard / In Three Volumes. / Vol. I. [or II., or III.] / London: / Longmans, / Green and Co. / 1888 / All rights reserved; verso, Printed by Kelly and Co., Gate Street, Lincoln's Inn Fields, W.C.; / and Middle Mill, Kingston-on-Thames. Dedication to Charles Longman; verso, blank. Contents list; verso blank.

f. Text

Vol. I   pp[1] to 247.

Vol II   pp[1] to 263.

Vol III   pp[1] to 261.

In each volume, the last page of the text has the printer's imprint on the verso, as on verso of title page.

g. Supplements   Vol III only has one blank leaf before the loose end paper.

h. Illustrations   None, though all the chapters except the last in each volume end with a decorated device.

i. Errors
Vol I   p 149, line 10. 'Tapestrie' should read 'tapestried'.
                p 149, line 23. 'reasure' should read 'treasure'.
                p 206, line 1. 'relatinoship' should read 'relationship'.

3 TECHNICAL
a. Format   Cr 8vo
b. Edges   Top edge uncut, fore edge and bottom edge rough cut (all three volumes).
c. Collation
Vol I   4; 1 to 15 × 8; 16 × 4. Total 128 leaves.
Vol II   4; 17 to 32 × 8; 33 × 4. Total 136 leaves.
Vol III   4; 34 to 49 × 8; 50 × 4. Total 136 leaves.

4 NUMBER OF COPIES IN FIRST EDITION AND DATE
3000; 3 Dec 88. (3000 in the three-volume edition printed Nov 88).

5 EARLIER PUBLICATION IN MAGAZINE
Serial story in the periodical *England* and in various newspapers in England (eg *Newcastle Chronicle*, *Yorkshire Post*, *Liverpool Daily Post*) and in the Dominions overseas.

6 OTHER EDITIONS OF NOTE
a. The first single volume edition was published by Longmans on 1 Mar 89, at six shillings, in blue cloth over bevelled edge boards, lettered in gold on spine and front cover. It has no half title, opening instead with the title page — COLONEL QUARITCH. V.C. / A / Tale of Country Life. / by / H. Rider Haggard. / In One Volume. / London: Longmans, Green, & Co. / and New York: 15 East 16th Street. / 1889. / All rights reserved.; verso, printer's imprint (Kelly). Dedication page; verso, Contents list. pp 341. Cr 8vo. Top edge rough cut, fore edge and bottom edge cut. Collation, 2; 1 to 21 × 8; 22 × 4. Total 174 leaves. No illustrations. The errors in the First Edition have been corrected. 5000 printed Nov 88 and 10,160 printed Feb 89.
b. Tauchnitz of Leipzig copyright edition, 1889, (Nos 2564−5).
c. The work appeared in Longmans Silver Library in 1890, with a frontispiece and tissue guard, and a vignette of the heroine Ida de la Molle, and '1890' on the title page. The illustrations were by C. Whymper. 5000 were printed Feb 90.
d. First American edition by John W. Lovell, New York, 1888.

7 NOTE
This, the last of the Rider Haggard works issued originally as a 'three-decker', is rare but is more frequently seen than either *Dawn* or *The Witch's Head*.

8 AN HAGGARD NOTE
'. . . I made money . . . for instance I sold . . . "Colonel Quaritch V.C.", a tale of English country life which Longman liked — it was dedicated to him — and Lang hated it so much that I think he called it the worst book that ever was written. Or perhaps it was someone else who favoured it with that description.'

The Days of My Life
Vol I, p 266

F10 Cleopatra 1889

1 PUBLISHER   Longmans, Green, and Co., London.

2 IDENTIFICATION FEATURES

a. Binding Blue cloth over bevelled edge boards. 123 × 195 mm.

b. Spine CLEOPATRA / [line] / [a cartouche of Egyptian hieroglyphics] / Longmans & Co. [All in gold.]

c. Front Cover CLEOPATRA / By / H. Rider Haggard. [All in gold.]

d. End Papers Patterned, light green, of swans, sailing ships and 1726, all entwined with leafy twigs.

e. Preliminaries p[i] Half title — CLEOPATRA; verso, list of 10 works by the same author. One page blank; verso, Frontispiece with tissue guard. p[iii] Title page — CLEOPATRA / Being / an Account of the Fall and Vengeance of / Harmachis, the Royal Egyptian, As / Set Forth by His Own Hand / by / H. Rider Haggard / Author of / 'King Solomon's Mines' 'She' 'Allan Quatermain / Etc / London / Longmans, Green, and Co. / 1889 / All rights reserved.; verso, printer's imprint (Spottiswoode). p[v] Dedication to Haggard's mother; verso blank. pp[vii] and viii, Author's Note. pp[ix] to xiii, Contents list. pp[xv] and xvi. List of illustrations. (A slip has been pasted into p[xv] to state 'The Illustrations by Caton Woodville are reproduced by permission of the Proprietors of the Illustrated London News'.)

f. Text pp[1] to 336, with printer's imprint at foot of p 336.

g. Supplements pp[1] to 16, General List of Works, dated January 1889 on p[1].

h. Illustrations There are 29 illustrations including the frontispiece. 18 are by Maurice Greiffenhagen and 11 by R. Caton Woodville. All have blank backs and are not included in the pagination. The wood engravings were executed by Edward Whymper, J.D. Cooper and B. Lloyd. In addition, the initial letter at the start of each chapter is elaborated into a design, signed EW (perhaps Edward Whymper?)

i. Errors An inverted comma has been omitted from the end of 'Quatermain' on the title page of some copies, possibly the result of poorly inked type.

3 TECHNICAL

a. Format Cr 8vo

b. Edges Top edge uncut, fore and bottom edges rough cut.

c. Collation 8; B to I × 8; K to U × 8; X and Y each 8; catalogue 8. The 29 full page illustrations have been bound into the gatherings as follows: Frontispiece; B (facing p 4); C(2) (facing pp 19 and 25); D(2) (facing pp 37 and 45); E(2) (facing pp 56 and 58); F (facing p 78); G (facing p 90); H(2) (facing pp 99 and 103); I(2) (facing pp 119 and 126); K (facing p 145); L(3) (facing pp 151, 152 and 155); M (facing p 167); N (facing p 188); O(2) (facing pp 196 and 208); P (facing p 222); R(2) (facing pp 244 and 250); T(2) (facing pp 280 and 284); U (facing p 296); Y (facing p 323). Total 213 leaves.

4 NUMBER OF COPIES IN FIRST EDITION AND DATE
25,000; 24 Jun 89. (25,043 copies printed Jun 1889.)

5 EARLIER PUBLICATION IN MAGAZINE

Serial story in the *Illustrated London News* Vol XCIV, Jan to Jun 89, Nos 2594 to 2619. Included were 29 illustrations by R. Caton Woodville and 33 initial letters by 'EW'. The *Illustrated London News*, No 2591, 15 Dec 88, on p 714, advertised the forthcoming serial story.

6 OTHER EDITIONS OF NOTE

a. A large paper issue (Cr 4to) was published by Longmans on the same date as the Cr 8vo edition, in an edition of 50 copies. 57 copies were printed Jun 89 on Dickinson's Fine Art paper, with the same illustrations as in the Cr 8vo edition but mounted. The binding is of brown pebble cloth with a brown leather spine. Lettering all in gold. Top edge gilt.

b. First American Edition by George Munro, New York, 1889.

c. Tauchnitz of Leipzig copyright edition 1889, (Nos 2592−3).

d. An edition was produced by Messrs. Bryce of Toronto, Canada, in 1890.

7 SOME HAGGARD NOTES

a. '. . . I started, in January 1887, on a journey to Egypt. From a boy, ancient Egypt had fascinated me, and I had read everything concerning it on which I could lay my hands. Now I was possessed with a desire to see it for myself, and to write a romance on the subject of Cleopatra.'

b. '. . . I revisited these tombs . . . and I remember also the millions of bats . . . afterwards I incarnated them all in the great bat that was a spirit which haunted the pyramid where Cleopatra and her lover, Harmachis, sought the treasure of the Pharaoah . . .'

c. '. . . I dedicated "Cleopatra" to my mother, because I thought it the best book I had written or was likely to write, although since then I have modified that opinion in favour of one or two that came out after it.'

The Days of My Life
Vol I, pp 254, 259, 271.

F11   Allan's Wife   1889

1 PUBLISHER   Spencer Blackett, London.

2 IDENTIFICATION FEATURES

a. Binding   Brown pebbled cloth, with spine, 30 mm of covers, fore edge corners and centre panel on front cover all in plain brown cloth edged with black lines. 133 × 197 mm.

b. Spine   ALLAN'S / WIFE / H. Rider Haggard / Illustrated / Spencer Blackett. [All in gold between two black lines at top and two at bottom.]

c. Front Cover   ALLAN'S WIFE / by / H. Rider Haggard. [All in gold in centre panel.]

d. End Papers   Plain purple.

e. Preliminaries   p[1] Half title — ALLAN'S WIFE; verso, list of 11 works by the same author. p[3] blank; verso, Frontispiece with tissue guard. p[5] Title page — ALLAN'S WIFE / And Other Tales / by / H. Rider Haggard / Author of / "Dawn," "The Witch's Head," "Mr. Meeson's Will," "King / Solomon's Mines." "She," Etc., Etc. / With Thirty-Four

Illustrations / By Maurice Greiffenhagen and Charles Kerr / London / Spencer Blackett / 35, St. Bride Street, Ludgate Circus, E.C. / 1889. / [line] / (All rights reserved.); verso, five line note about the publishing history of the present work. pp[7] and 8, Dedication to Arthur Cochrane. pp[9] and 10, Contents list. pp[11] and [12], List of Full-Page Illustrations.

f. Text   pp[13] to 331. Verso p 331 blank.

g. Supplements   p[333], Advertisement for 3 Haggard works; verso blank. p[335], Imprint — The Gresham Press, / Unwin Brothers, / Chilworth and London. —; verso blank. Followed by pp[1] to [32], Catalogue of Books dated September 1889 on p[1].

h. Illustrations   8 full page illustrations are included, 5 by Greiffenhagen and 3 by Kerr. They are unnumbered but are included in the pagination. Additionally, there are 12 illustrations in the text, plus 8 at chapter heads and 4 at chapter ends, as well as 12 decorated devices at chapter heads, 13 initial letters and 13 decorated devices at chapter ends.

i. Errors   None.

3 TECHNICAL

a. Format   Cr 8vo

b. Edges   Rough cut.

c. Collation   [1] × 8; 2 to 21 × 8; catalogue 16. Total 192 leaves.

4 NUMBER OF COPIES IN FIRST EDITION AND DATE

Dec 89.

5 EARLIER PUBLICATION IN MAGAZINE

a. Allan's Wife did not previously appear in a magazine. The 'Other Tales' were previously published as follows: 'Hunter Quatermain's Story' in *In A Good Cause*, 1885. This was a volume of stories, poems and illustrations, published for the benefit of the North Eastern Hospital for Children, in Hackney Road, London. It was Edited by Margaret S. Tyssen Amherst, published by Wells Gardner, Darton, & Co., and dedicated to Her Royal Highness The Princess of Wales. Haggard's story appears on pp[211] to 237, with 3 illustrations by S. Carter.

b. 'A Tale of Three Lions' was first published in *Atalanta Magazine*, Vol I, Nos 1 to 3, in three parts, viz; No 1, Oct 1887, pp 26–32; No 2, Nov 1887, pp 79–84; No 3, Dec 1887, pp 156–62. There are four full-page illustrations and one illustration at the head of a chapter (Ch II), all by Heywood Hardy. Haggard's signature in facsimile also appears twice. (*Atalanta Magazine* was published by Hatchards', Piccadilly, London, with the sub-title 'Every Girl's Magazine, New Series'.)

c. 'Long Odds' first appeared in *Macmillan's Magazine*, Vol LIII, No 316, Feb 1886, pp 289 to 297. There were no illustrations, and there are minor differences in the text when compared with the book version.

6 OTHER EDITIONS OF NOTE

a. A large paper issue (Cr 4to) was published by Spencer Blackett on the same date as the Cr 8vo edition. Only 100 copies were printed. The same illustrations as in the Cr 8vo edition are used. The binding is red cloth with leather spine. Lettering all in gold. Top edge gilt.

b. In 1891, Griffith, Farran, Okeden and Welsh, of London and Sydney, published an edition which, externally at first glance, could be mistaken for the first English Edition;

the volume is, however, 7 mm shorter and the lettering on spine and front cover is in silver not gold. This volume has pp 331 followed by a two leaf list of recent novels.

c. The British Library lists a 16 pp pamphlet produced by Alexander P. Watt in 1889, publishing short extracts from *Allan's Wife*. (Watt was Haggard's friend and agent for some time.)

d. Tauchnitz of Leipzig copyright edition 1890, (No. 2634).

e. First American Edition by Frank F. Lovell & Co., New York, 1889.

f. When the rights passed to Longmans, 5000 copies were printed in Feb 95 for a Silver Library edition.

7 NOTES

a. This was the second work written by Haggard as part of the price for extracting himself from his obligations to Messrs Maxwell; see the notes to *Mr. Meeson's Will* (F8).

b. The short story 'Long Odds' was republished in America by F. Tennyson Neely, in 1899, under the title 'The Spring of a Lion'.

c. Similarly, 'A Tale of Three Lions' was reproduced in America by Lothrop Publishing Co, Boston, in 1898, under the title 'Allan the Hunter: A Tale of Three Lions (and Prince, another Lion)': and by J.W. Lovell in the 'Lovell's Library' series, as 'Allan the Hunter' — see Appendix 1.

F12   Beatrice   1890

1 PUBLISHER   Longmans, Green, & Co., London.

2 IDENTIFICATION FEATURES

a. Binding   Blue cloth over bevelled edge boards. 123 × 195 mm.

b. Spine   BEATRICE / [line] / H. Rider / Haggard / Longmans & Co. [All in gold.]

c. Front Cover   BEATRICE / by / H. Rider Haggard. [All in gold.]

d. End Papers   Plain black.

e. Preliminaries Title page — BEATRICE / A Novel / by / H. Rider Haggard / Author of "She" "Allan Quatermain" / "Cleopatra" Etc. / London / Longmans, Green, and Co. / 1890 / All rights reserved; verso blank. Quotation of ten lines of verse; verso blank. Contents list; verso, list of 12 works by the same author. Dedication to Beatrice; verso blank.

f. Text   pp[1] to 312, with imprint — Printed by Kelly and Co. Kingston-on-Thames; and London — at foot of p 312.

g. Supplements   pp[1] to 16, General List of Works dated 30,000/3/90 at foot of p 16.

h. Illustrations None.

i. Errors   None.

3 TECHNICAL

a. Format   Cr 8vo

b. Edges   Top edge uncut, fore edge cut, bottom edge rough cut.

c. Collation   4; 1 to 19 × 8; 20 × 4; catalogue 8. Total 168 leaves.

4 NUMBER OF COPIES IN FIRST EDITION AND DATE
10,000; 12 May 90 (10,000 printed Apr 90.)

5 EARLIER PUBLICATION IN MAGAZINE

Serial story in newspapers, including *The Yorkshire Post*, *Ipswich Journal*, *Cardiff Times*, *Liverpool Daily Post* and *Nottingham Guardian*, on various dates.

6 OTHER EDITIONS OF NOTE

a. Longmans printed 1558 copies in Aug 90 for a 'Library' edition, the details of which I have not traced.

b. Longmans Fourth Edition, published in 1890, included a Frontispiece and a vignette on the title page, both by Maurice Greiffenhagen.

c. A New Edition appeared in Longmans Silver Library in 1894. 5000 printed May 94.

d. A revised edition came out in 1895, with a Preface and sundry amendments to the text. These resulted from public, especially feminine, reaction, to the work. See 7 below.

e. Tauchnitz of Leipzig copyright edition, 1890, (Nos 2656–7).

f. First American Edition by George Munro, New York, 1890.

g. Longmans made stereo plates for Messrs Bryce of Toronto, Canada, who sold 5000 copies of the book up to Jun 90.

7 SOME HAGGARD NOTES

a. (Extract from a letter written by Charles Longman, dated 2 August 1888) — '. . . I was very much interested in "Beatrice". It is of course a terrible tragedy — unrelieved in its gloom which increases from start to finish. Still there is no denying its power . . .'

b. 'Some years after "Beatrice" was published I was horrified to receive two anonymous or semi-anonymous letters from ladies who alleged that their husbands, or the husbands of someone connected with them — one of them a middle-aged clergyman — after reading "Beatrice", had made advances to young ladies of that name; or perhaps the young ladies had made advances to them which they more or less reciprocated — I forget the exact facts. Also I heard that a gentleman and a lady had practised the sleep-walking scene, with different results from those recorded in the book. These stories troubled me so much — since I had never dreamed of such an issue to a tale with a different moral — that I wished to suppress the book. . . . The end of the matter was that I went through the tale carefully, modified or removed certain passages that might be taken to suggest that holy matrimony is not always perfect in its working, etc., and wrote a short preface which may now be read in all copies printed since that date . . .'

The Days of My Life
Vol I, p 279; Vol II, pp 13, 14, 15.

F13   The World's Desire   1890

1 PUBLISHER   Longmans, Green, and Co., London.

2 IDENTIFICATION FEATURES

a. Binding	Dark green cloth over bevelled edge boards. 120 × 195 mm.
b. Spine	THE / WORLD'S / DESIRE / [line] / H. Rider Haggard / And / Andrew Lang / Longmans & Co. [All in gold.]
c. Front Cover	THE / WORLD'S DESIRE / By / H. Rider Haggard & Andrew Lang. [All in gold.]
d. End Papers	Plain black.
e. Preliminaries	p[i] Half title — THE WORLD'S DESIRE; verso blank. p[iii] title page — THE WORLD'S DESIRE / By / H. Rider Haggard / And /

Andrew Lang / London: Longmans, Green, and Co. / 1890. / (All Rights Reserved); verso, printer's imprint. p[v] Dedication to W.B. Richmond, A.R.A.; verso blank. pp[vii] and viii, Contents list. p[1] second half title — THE WORLD'S DESIRE, with signature B bottom right; verso, 32 lines of verse.

f. Text   pp[3] to 316.

g. Supplements   One page containing 15 lines of verse (Palinode); verso blank. One page blank except for printer's imprint; verso blank. pp[1] to 16, General Lists of Works, dated 10,000/10/90 on p 16.

h. Illustrations   None

i. Errors   None

3 TECHNICAL

a. Format   Cr 8vo

b. Edges   Top edge uncut, fore and bottom edges rough cut.

c. Collation   4; B to I × 8; K to U × 8; X × 8; catalogue 8. Total 172 leaves.

4 NUMBER OF COPIES IN FIRST EDITION AND DATE
10,000; 5 Nov 90. (10,123 copies printed Oct 90.)

5 EARLIER PUBLICATION IN MAGAZINE
Serial story in *The New Review*, Vols II and III, Apr to Dec 1890, Nos 11 to 19. (Vol II also includes an article by Rider Haggard, 'The Fate of Swaziland', pp 64–75.)

6 OTHER EDITIONS OF NOTE
a. Longmans brought out the first illustrated edition in 1894, with 27 illustrations by Maurice Greiffenhagen and a three page preface by the Authors.
b. A Longmans Silver Library edition was also published in 1894, for which 5050 copies were printed.
c. Tauchnitz of Leipzig copyright edition, 1891, (Nos 2694–5).
d. The work is believed to have had various publishers in America in 1890/91.

7 AN HAGGARD NOTE
'. . . let us return to "The World's Desire", "The Song of the Bow" as it was called at first. Roughly the history of this tale, which I like as well as any with which I have had to do, is that Lang and I discussed it. Then I wrote a part of it, which part he altered or rewrote. Next in his casual manner he lost the whole MS. for a year or so; then it was unexpectedly found, and encouraged thereby I went on and wrote the rest. The MS in its final form I have, bound up, and with it a very interesting preface or rather postscript by Lang which was never published, eight sheets long. . . .'

The Days of My Life
Vol I, p 280

F14   Eric Brighteyes   1891

1 PUBLISHER   Longmans, Green, and Co., London.

2 IDENTIFICATION FEATURES

a. Binding   Blue cloth over bevelled edge boards. 123 × 195 mm.

b. Spine   ERIC / BRIGHTEYES / [line] / H. Rider / Haggard / Longmans & Co. [All in gold.]

c. *Front Cover*	ERIC / BRIGHTEYES / by / H. Rider Haggard. [All in gold.]
d. *End Papers*	Plain black.
e. *Preliminaries*	One leaf blank. p[i] Half title — ERIC BRIGHTEYES; verso, list of 14 works by the same author. p[iii] Title page — ERIC BRIGHTEYES / by / H. Rider Haggard / Author of / 'King Solomon's Mines' 'Allan Quatermain' / Etc / With Numerous Illustrations / By Lancelot Speed / Longmans, Green, and Co. / 1891 / All rights reserved; verso, printer's imprint (Spottiswoode). pp[v] and vi, Dedication to H.I.M. Victoria, Empress Frederick of Germany. pp[vii] to x, Introduction. pp[xi] and xii, Contents list. pp[xiii] and xiv, List of illustrations.
f. *Text*	pp[1] to 319, with printer's imprint at foot of p 319, the verso of which is blank.
g. *Supplements*	pp[1] to 16, A General Selection of Works dated 75,000/12/90 at foot of p 16.
h. *Illustrations*	There are 17 full page illustrations though, oddly, a Frontispiece is not provided. 16 are not included in the pagination. All 17 have blank backs. Additionally, 34 woodcuts appear in the text, including 13 initial letters. All these are included in the list of illustrations (see para 2e above.)
i. *Errors*	None.

3 TECHNICAL

a. *Format*	Cr 8vo.
b. *Edges*	Top edge uncut, fore edge rough cut, bottom edge cut.
c. *Collation*	8; B to I × 8; K to U × 8; X and Y × 8; catalogue 8. The full page illustration facing p 106 is one of the 8 leaves of signature H, included in the pagination though unnumbered. Strange, as all the other full page plates are sewn into the gatherings as follows: B (facing p 2); E (facing p 50); F (facing p 68); G (facing p 88); K (facing p 130); M(2) (facing pp 162 and 172); N (facing p 190); P(2) (facing pp 216 and 222); Q (facing p 240); S (facing p 258); T(2) (facing pp 280 and 286); U (facing p 305); X (facing p 317). Total 192 leaves.

4 NUMBER OF COPIES IN FIRST EDITION AND DATE
10,000; 13 May 91. (10,003 copies printed Apr 91.)

5 EARLIER PUBLICATION IN MAGAZINE
Serial story in *The People*, 1891.

6 OTHER EDITIONS OF NOTE
a. There was a Second Edition in 1892 and a Third in 1893.
b. First American Edition by John W. Lovell, New York, 1891.
c. Messrs Bryce of Toronto, Canada, published an edition there in 1891.
d. Heinemann and Balestier English Library edition, Leipzig, Vols 25–26, 1891.

7 NOTES
In June 1888, Rider Haggard visted Iceland with a friend, to gather background material for a saga he intended to write. He travelled there in a trading vessel named *Copeland* and, although she was laden with Iceland ponies for the return journey, Haggard decided to make the run home in her. On 25 Jun, the *Copeland* foundered on rocks in a gale. The lifeboats failed (shades of *Mr Meeson's Will!*) and, at some peril, the passengers —

including Haggard — had to be rescued by another ship. Many of the ponies were drowned. Haggard later wrote of his experiences in 'The Wreck of the Copeland', in the *Illustrated London News*, Vol XC111, Aug 1888.

8 SOME HAGGARD NOTES

a. '. . . I conceived the idea of writing a saga, but determined that before I attempted this, I would visit Iceland and study the local colouring on the spot.'

b. '. . . I began to write "Eric Brighteyes", the saga which was the result of my visit to Iceland, on 29 Aug 88, as the MS shows, and I finished it on Christmas Day 1888.'

c. '. . . "Eric" came out in due course, and did well enough. Indeed, as a book it found, and still continues to find, a considerable body of readers.'

The Days of My Life
Vol I, p 278; Vol II, pp 1 and 7.

F15   Nada the Lily   1892

1 PUBLISHER   Longmans, Green, and Co., London.

2 IDENTIFICATION FEATURES

a. Binding   Blue cloth over bevelled edge boards. 123 × 195 mm.

b. Spine   NADA / THE / LILY / [line] / H. Rider / Haggard / Longmans & Co. [All in gold.]

c. Front Cover   NADA THE LILY / by / H. Rider Haggard. [All in gold.]

d. End Papers   Plain black.

e. Preliminaries   p[i] Half title — NADA THE LILY; verso, list of 15 works by the same author. One page blank; verso, Frontispiece with tissue guard. p[iii] Title page — NADA THE LILY / by / H. Rider Haggard / Author of / 'King Solomon's Mines' 'She' 'Allan Quatermain' Etc. / [vignette] / London / Longmans, Green, and Co. / And New York: 15 East 16th Street / 1892 / All rights reserved; verso, Printer's imprint (Spottiswoode). pp[v] to vii, Dedication to Sir Theophilus Shepstone, K.C.M.G., Natal.; p[viii] blank. pp[ix] to xiii, Preface; pp[xiv] and xv, Contents list. p[xvi] List of illustrations.

f. Text   pp[1] to 295, with printer's imprint at foot of p 295, the verso of which is blank.

g. Supplements   pp[1] to 24, A Catalogue of Works in General Literature dated 50,000−2/92 at foot of p 24.

h. Illustrations   There are 23 full page illustrations including the Frontispiece, all by Charles Kerr. All have blank backs and are not included in the pagination.

i. Errors   None.

3 TECHNICAL

a. Format   Cr 8vo.

b. Edges   Top edge uncut, fore and bottom edges rough cut.

c. Collation   8; B to I × 8; K to T × 8; U × 4; catalogue 12. The illustrations are sewn into the gatherings as follows: Frontispiece; B(2) (facing pp 4 and 8); C (facing p 24); D (facing p 44); E (facing p 62); F (facing p 72); G(2) (facing pp 82 and 92); H (facing p 112); I (facing p 126); K

(facing p 134); L (facing p 154); M(2) (facing pp 166 and 172); N
(facing p 192); P(2) (facing pp 210 and 216); Q (facing p 234); S
(facing p 266); T(2) (facing pp 282 and 288); U (facing p 292). Total
191 leaves.

4 NUMBER OF COPIES IN FIRST EDITION AND DATE
10,000; 9 May 92 (10,003 printed Apr 92.)

5 EARLIER PUBLICATION IN MAGAZINE
Serial story in the *Illustrated London News*, Vol C, 2 Jan 92 (Jubilee Number) to 7 May
92. Illustrated by R. Caton Woodville.

6 OTHER EDITIONS OF NOTE
a. An additional 10,000 copies were printed in Apr 92 for a Longmans Colonial Library
edition. 3,000 cloth covers were made but the record indicates that only 2,500 copies were
bound up (*2s.*). The remainder were sewed (*1s. 6d.*).
b. First American Edition by Longmans, Green, and Co., New York, 1892.
c. Heinemann and Balestier English Library edition, Leipzig, Vol 133, 1892.

7 NOTES
a. Sir Theophilus Shepstone was Haggard's revered chief and friend during Haggard's
early days in South Africa.
b. Few writers of Haggard's day, and few since, have attempted to write sympathetically
and in depth in a work of fiction about the life and loves of native African peoples. It is a
measure of Haggard's understanding of and respect for the natives, especially the Zulus,
that *Nada the Lily* was such a success.
c. In years of collecting Haggard, I have seen only one volume in a Colonial edition. This
is *Nada the Lily* in the Longmans Colonial Library edition, dated 1892, pp ix, 295, with a
catalogue of pp 24 dated 50,000−2/92.; in other words, it is the same as the First Edition,
including illustrations, and appears to be from the same type setting. The only differences
from the First are: (1). The exterior; the book is slightly smaller, bound in light grey
cloth, printed in gold on the spine and in brown on the front cover, with the Colonial
Library imprint boldly set at the top. (2). Inside, the pages carrying the signatures each
have the letter C added at bottom left.

8 SOME HAGGARD NOTES
a. '. . . from my friend Fynney (the Chief Interpreter of Natal colony) . . . I gathered
much information as to Zulu customs and history which in subsequent days I made use of
in "Nada the Lily" and other books.'
b. '. . . I think that the next book I wrote after "Eric", or at any rate the next that was
printed, was "Nada the Lily", which I began upon June 27, 1889, and finished on
January 15, 1890. It is a pure Zulu story, and, as I believe I have said, I consider it my
best or one of my best books.'

The Days of My Life
Vol I, p 56; Vol II, p 16.

F16   Montezuma's Daughter   1893

1 PUBLISHER   Longmans, Green, and Co., London.

2 IDENTIFICATION FEATURES

a. Binding   Blue cloth over bevelled edge boards. 123 × 195 mm.

b. Spine   MONTEZUMA'S / DAUGHTER / [line] / H. Rider / Haggard / Longmans & Co. [All in gold.]

c. Front Cover   MONTEZUMA'S / DAUGHTER / by / H. Rider Haggard. [All in gold.]

d. End Papers   Plain black.

e. Preliminaries   One page blank; verso, Frontispiece with tissue guard. p[i] Title page — MONTEZUMA'S DAUGHTER / by / H. Rider Haggard / Author of / 'She' 'Allan Quatermain' Etc. / [vignette] / Otomie, Princess of the Otomie / London / Longmans, Green, and Co. / And New York: 15 East 16th Street / 1893 / All rights reserved; verso, list of 16 works by the same author. p[iii] Dedication to J. Gladwyn Jebb, Esq. and Note; verso, Note on Aztec history. pp[v] and vi, Contents list. pp[vii] and viii, List of plates.

f. Text   pp[1] to 325, with printer's imprint at foot of p 325.

g. Supplements   One blank leaf. pp[1] to 24, Classified Catalogue of Works in General Literature dated 50,000/11/93 at foot of p 24.

h. Illustrations   There are 24 full page illustrations including the Frontispiece, all by Maurice Greiffenhagen. They have blank backs and are not included in the pagination.

i. Errors   None.

3 TECHNICAL

a. Format   Cr 8vo.

b. Edges   Top edge uncut, fore and bottom edges rough cut.

c. Collation   4; B to I × 8; K to U × 8; X × 8; Y × 4; catalogue 12. The illustrations are sewn into the gatherings as follows: Frontispiece; C(2) (facing pp 20 and 30); D (facing p 48); E (facing p 58); F (facing p 74); G(2)(facing pp 84 and 92); H (facing p 108); I (facing p 124); K (facing p 138); L(3) (facing pp 146, 148 and 152); M (facing p 174); O(2) (facing pp 194 and 198); Q (facing p 230); R(2) (facing pp 242 and 250); S (facing p 270); U(2) (facing pp 298 and 302); Y (facing p 324). Total 204 leaves.

4 NUMBER OF COPIES IN FIRST EDITION AND DATE
10,000; 13 Nov 93. (10,002 copies printed Jul 93.)

5 EARLIER PUBLICATION IN MAGAZINE
Serial story in *The Graphic*, Vol 48, Jul to Nov 93, Nos 1231 to 1250. Illustrated by Seymour Lucas and J.R. Weguelin.

6 OTHER EDITIONS OF NOTE
a. An additional 10,002 copies were printed Jul 93 for a Longmans Colonial Library edition. Of these, 2,500 were used for binding in cloth (2s.); the remainder were sewed (1s. 6d.).

b. The Second Edition was issued in 1894. 'Second Edition' and '1894' appear on the title page.

c. The Longmans Silver Library edition of 1895 and later editions omit the note on the immuring of nuns, to be found on pp 71 and 72 of the First Edition. Haggard explains this in a note: in summary, criticism from religious representatives led to the note's withdrawal.

d. A New Edition was published by Longmans in 1896 (pp xii, 325).

e. Tauchnitz of Leipzig copyright edition, 1893, (Nos 2953–4).

f. First American Edition by Longmans, Green, and Co., New York, 1894.

7 NOTES

a. J. Gladwyn Jebb was managing director of the Santa Fe Copper Mines in Mexico. Haggard met him in 1889 through city friend and later visited him in Mexico where they became firm friends. It was while staying with the Jebbs that Rider Haggard and his wife received the entirely unexpected and shocking news of the death of their son Jock — news which profoundly affected Haggard's health for several years.

8 SOME HAGGARD NOTES

a. '. . . During the year 1889 I made the acquaintance of my later friend J. Gladwyn Jebb, one of the most delightful persons whom I have ever known. . . . .I have described his character in my introduction to "The Life and Adventures of J.G. Jebb," by his widow. . . .'

b. '. . . Jebb urged me to come to Mexico and write a novel about Montezuma, both of which things I did in due course; also as a bait he told me a wonderful and, as I believe, perfectly true tale of a hidden treasure which we were to proceed to dig up together.'

c. '. . . It is strange, but when I went to Mexico I knew, almost without doubt, that in this world he [Jock] and I would never see each other more. Only I thought it was I who was doomed to die . . . I said nothing of this secret foreknowledge of mine . . . only I made every possible preparation for my death . . .'

d. '. . . My son died suddenly of a perforating ulcer after an attack of measles.'

e. '. . . On my return from Mexico I wrote a romance called "Montezuma's Daughter". In this tale the teller loses his children, and I put into his mouth what myself I felt.'

The Days of My Life
Vol II, pp 39, 40, 42, 44

F17   The People of the Mist   1894

1 PUBLISHER   Longmans, Green, and Co., London.

2 IDENTIFICATION FEATURES

a. Binding   Blue cloth over bevelled edge boards. 120 × 190 mm.

b. Spine   THE / PEOPLE / OF THE / MIST / [line] / H. Rider / Haggard / Longmans & Co. [All in gold.]

c. Front Cover   THE / PEOPLE OF THE MIST / by / H. Rider Haggard. [All in gold.]

d. End Papers   Plain black.

e. Preliminaries   Half title — THE PEOPLE OF THE MIST; verso, list of 17 works by the same author. One page blank; verso, Frontispiece with tissue guard. p[i] Title page — THE / PEOPLE OF THE MIST / by / H. Rider Haggard / Author of / 'Allan Quatermain' 'She' 'King Solomon's Mines' Etc. / London / Longmans, Green, and Co. / And

New York: 15 East 16th Street / 1894 / All rights reserved; verso
blank. p[iii] Dedication to 'my godsons' dated 1894; verso blank. pp[v]
and vi, Author's Note, dated September 20, 1894. pp[vii] and viii, List
of contents and of illustrations.

f. Text   pp[1] to 343, with printer's imprint (Spottiswoode) at foot of p 343.

g. Supplements   pp[1] to 24, Classified Catalogue of Works in General Literature dated
50,000–9/94 at foot of p 24.

h. Illustrations   There are 16 full page illustrations including the Frontispiece, all by
Arthur Layard. All have blank backs and are not included in the
pagination.

i. Errors   p vi is incorrectly numbered 'ii'. p 1, line 21. 'auctoineers' should read
'auctioneers'.

3 TECHNICAL

a. Format   Cr 8vo

b. Edges   All edges rough cut.

c. Collation   5; B to I × 8; K to U × 8; X and Y × 8; Z × 4; catalogue 12. The
illustrations are sewn into the gatherings as follows: Frontispiece; B
(facing p 17); C (facing p 23); D (facing p 35); F (facing p 75); H(2)
(facing pp 100 and 111); I (facing p 129); L (facing p 161); O (facing
p 207); R(2) (facing pp 248 and 252); S (facing p 260); T (facing
p 289); X(2) (facing pp 310 and 316). Total 205 leaves.

4 NUMBER OF COPIES IN FIRST EDITION AND DATE
10,000; 15 Oct 94. (10,023 copies printed Sep 94.)

5 EARLIER PUBLICATION IN MAGAZINE
Serial story in *Tit-Bits Weekly*, Vols XXV and XXVI, Dec 93 to Aug 94, Nos 636 to 670.

6 OTHER EDITIONS OF NOTE
a. An additional 7,502 copies were printed Sep 94 for Longmans Colonial Library. 2,021
of these were used for binding in cloth (2s.); the remainder were sewed.
b. Tauchnitz of Leipzig copyright edition, 1894, (Nos 3022–3).
c. First American Edition by Longmans, Green, and Co., New York, 1894.
d. 7,532 copies were printed Dec 96 for Longmans Silver Library.

7 NOTE
The *Tit-Bits* version of the story differs very slightly from the book version. In the book,
reference has been omitted to the appearance of the full moon which, when related to
other remarks about the moon's aspect in the same chapter (Ch 8) amounted (rather as in
the case *King Solomon's Mines*) to an astronomical impossibility. In addition, the text of
the book includes a note on p 115 which does not appear in the serial. On 17 Feb 1894, an
amusing letter appeared in *Tit-Bits*, signed 'A Much Abused Satellite', referring to the
moon error. Rider Haggard's reply, in an equally light vein, was printed in the same
magazine on 24 Feb.

F18   Joan Haste   1895

1 PUBLISHER   Longmans, Green, and Co., London.

2 IDENTIFICATION FEATURES
a. Binding   Blue cloth over bevelled edge boards. 120 × 190 mm.
b. Spine   JOAN / HASTE / [line] / H. Rider / Haggard / Longmans & Co. [All in gold.]
c. Front Cover   JOAN HASTE / by / H. Rider Haggard. [All in gold.]
d. End Papers   Plain black.
e. Preliminaries One blank leaf. p[i] Half title — JOAN HASTE; verso, list of 19 works by the same author. One page blank; verso, Frontispiece with tissue guard. p[iii] Title page — JOAN HASTE / by / H. Rider Haggard / Author of 'King Solomon's Mines' 'She' / 'Allan Quatermain' Etc. / 'Il y a page effrayante dans le livre des destinées / humaines; on y lit en tête ces mots — "les désirs accom- / plis." — Georges Sand / With 20 Illustrations By F.S. Wilson / London / Longmans, Green, and Co. / And New York / 1895 / All rights reserved; verso blank. p[v] Dedication to 'I.H.'; verso blank. pp vii and viii, Contents list. pp ix and x, List of illustrations.
f. Text   pp 1 to 425, with printer's imprint (Spottiswoode) at foot of p 425.
g. Supplements   One leaf blank. pp[1] to 24, Classified Catalogue of Works in General Literature dated July, 1895 on p[1] and 50,000–6/95 on p 24.
h. Illustrations There are 20 full page illustrations including the Frontispiece, all by F.S. Wilson. They have blank backs and are not included in the pagination.
i. Errors   None.

3 TECHNICAL
a. Format   Cr 8vo
b. Edges   All edges cut.
c. Collation   6; B to I × 8; K to U × 8; X to Z × 8; 2A to 2D × 8; 2E × 6; catalogue 12. The illustrations have been sewn into the gatherings as follows: Frontispiece; B (facing p 9); C (facing p 28); D(2) (facing pp 37 and 45); E(2) (facing pp 52 and 59); G (facing p 84); N (facing p 186); P (facing p 215); R (facing p 248); S (facing p 272); U (facing p 300); Z (facing p 346); 2A (facing p 356); 2B (facing p 378); 2C (facing p 396); 2D(2) (facing pp 402 and 408); 2E (facing p 412). Total 252 leaves.

4 NUMBER OF COPIES IN FIRST EDITION AND DATE
10,000; 12 Aug 95. (10,003 copies printed Jul 95).

5 EARLIER PUBLICATION IN MAGAZINE
Serial story in *The Pall Mall Magazine*, Vols 4, 5 and 6, Sep 94 to Jul 95, Nos 17 to 27.

6 OTHER EDITIONS OF NOTE
a. A Second Edition (I suspect actually a second issue of the First Edition) was put out by Longmans in 1895. 5,002 copies were printed Oct 95. This version is exactly like the First, except: (1). The verso of the half title lists only 18 Haggard works. Strangely, the First includes *Joan Haste* in the list; the Second does not. (2). The words 'Second

Edition' appear on the title page, above 'London'. (3). The catalogue at the end is dated 'August, 1895' on p[1] and '50,000−8/95' on p 24.

b. In Jul 95, Longmans printed an additional 7518 copies for the Longmans Colonial Library. 2,000 of these were used for binding in cloth (2*s.*); the remainder were sewed (1*s. 6d.*).

c. Tauchnitz of Leipzig copyright edition 1895, (Nos 3086−7).

d. George Newnes, Ltd, published a paperback version in 1907, in their 'Newnes Sixpenny Novels' series, No 128. It included 4 illustrations by Cyrus Cuneo.

e. First American Edition by Longmans, Green, and Co., New York, 1895.

7 NOTES

a. 'I.H.' in the dedication was Ida Hector, Haggard's secretary over many years.

b. In his autobiography, Haggard several times comments on the way that events of fact, about which he had no idea, often coincided with the ideas he imagined and created for the plots of his stories. *Joan Haste* was but one example: see below.

8 AN HAGGARD NOTE

'. . . While visting an old church in Suffolk I conceived the idea of my novel, "Joan Haste", . . . After reading it a connection of mine remarked that he had been much interested by the book, though he did not think that the A.−Z.'s, whom he knew well, would altogether appreciate such an accurate report of a passage in the family history whereof they did not often speak. . . . On further investigation it transpired that these A.−Z.'s were buried in the very churchyard where I had imagined my tale,. . . . It needs no great stretch of fancy to believe that in some subtle way the bones beneath the soil . . . had imparted some of their history to my mind . . .'

The Days of My Life
Vol II, p 103

F19   Heart of the World   1896

1 PUBLISHER   Longmans, Green, and Co., London.

2 IDENTIFICATION FEATURES

a. Binding	Blue cloth over bevelled edge boards. 120 × 190 mm.
b. Spine	HEART / OF THE / WORLD / [line] / H. Rider / Haggard / Longmans & Co. [All in gold.]
c. Front Cover	HEART OF THE WORLD / by / H. Rider Haggard. [All in gold.]
d. End Papers	Plain black, rather shiny.
e. Preliminaries	One page blank; verso, Frontispiece with tissue guard. Title page — HEART OF THE WORLD / by / H. Rider Haggard / Author of 'King Solomon's Mines' 'She' / 'Allan Quatermain' Etc. / Longmans, Green, and Co. / London, New York, and Bombay / 1896 / All rights reserved; verso blank. Dedication to Henry Rider Haggard of Butler, USA, dated Christmas Day, 1894; verso blank. Contents list; verso, list of illustrations.
f. Text	pp[1] to 347, with printer's imprint (Spottiswoode) at foot of p 347; verso, list of 19 works by the same author.
g. Supplements	pp[1] to 24, catalogue of Longmans publications, dated December 1895 on p[1].

h. Illustrations   There are 15 full page illustrations including the Frontispiece, all by Amy Sawyer. They all have blank backs and are not included in the pagination. They have been printed, however, as leaves integral to the gatherings.

i. Errors   p 271, line 1. 'phophecy' should read 'prophecy'.

3 TECHNICAL
a. Format   Cr 8vo
b. Edges   Top and bottom edges cut, fore edge rough cut.
c. Collation   4 (including Frontispiece); B to I × 8; K to U × 8; X to Z × 8; AA × 8; BB × 4. Total 192 leaves.

4 NUMBER OF COPIES IN FIRST EDITION AND DATE
10,000; 27 Mar 96. (10,003 copies printed Nov 95.)

5 EARLIER PUBLICATION IN MAGAZINE
Serial story in *Pearson's Weekly*, Vol 5, Aug 94 to Jan 95, Nos 212 to 236.

6 OTHER EDITIONS OF NOTE
a. First American Edition by Longmans, Green, and Co., New York, May 1895, well before the First English Edition.
b. Tauchnitz of Leipzig copyright edition, 1896, (Nos 3143−4).
c. In Mar 96, Longmans printed a further 7522 copies for a Longmans Colonial Library edition. The records indicate that only 5,000 covers were produced for this edition.

F20   The Wizard   1896

1 PUBLISHER   J.W. Arrowsmith, Bristol and London.

2 IDENTIFICATION FEATURES
a. Binding   Paperback. 104 × 164 mm.
b. Spine   THE WIZARD / H. Rider Haggard. [All in black.]
c. Front Cover   One Shilling / Christmas 1896 / ARROWSMITH ANNUAL [both words transfixed by arrows] / THE WIZARD / [vignette of Haggard] / H. Rider Haggard / Bristol: J.W. Arrowsmith, Quay Street. / London: Simpkin, Marshall, Hamilton, Kent & Co. Limited. [The above details are largely superimposed over smoke rising from a forge fire and anvil attended by a goblin. All printed in red and black.] (The back cover carries advertisements inside and out, as does the frontcover inside.)
d. End Papers   None.
e. Preliminaries   Four leaves of advertisements, partly illustrated. Title page — Copyright. Entered at Stationer's Hall [all underlined] / THE WIZARD / by / H. Rider Haggard / Author of / "She", "Allan Quatermain," "King Solomon's Mines" / Etc / [line] / Arrowsmith's Christmas Annual / 1896 / [line] / Bristol / J.W. Arrowsmith, Quay Street / London / Simpkin, Marshall, Hamilton, Kent and Company Limited. [All within a box of double lines; verso, advertisement. List of 20 works by the same author; verso, advertisement.] p[1] Dedication to Nada Burnham dated 6th July, 1896.; verso, advertisement. p[3] Contents list, with advertisement below; verso, advertisement.

f. Text   pp 5 to 208, with 'Printing Office of the Publisher' at bottom of p 208.
g. Supplements   8 leaves of advertisements, including 4 leaves Arrowsmith's Catalogue
                    of Books.
h. Illustrations None.
i. Errors   None.

3 TECHNICAL
a. Format   Fscp 8vo
b. Edges   All edges cut.
c. Collation   6; [1] 8; 2 to 14 × 8. Total 118 leaves.

4 NUMBER OF COPIES IN FIRST EDITION AND DATE
20,000; 29 Oct 96.

5 EARLIER PUBLICATION IN MAGAZINE
Serial story in *The African Review*, Vols VIII and IX, 4 Jul to 7 Nov 96. With 21
illustrations by Charles Kerr.

6 OTHER EDITIONS OF NOTE
a. An unknown number of the 20,000 copies printed for the Christmas Annual were
bound up in brown cloth, with title and author's name on the spine between a line at top
and bottom, all in gold; and the title and name on the front cover, in a single line border
at all edges, all in black. Charcoal end papers. There were two versions in this binding,
viz: (1) The Christmas Annual, bound up minus its original wrappers. Sold at 1*s.* 6*d.* (2)
An Arrowsmith's Bristol Library version, with the half-title listing, on verso, 20 works by
the same author. Title page, as for the Annual, except 'Arrowsmith's Christmas Annual'
on recto is replaced by the publisher's colophon, and the advertisement on verso is
replaced by 'Arrowsmith's Bristol Library/ Vol. LXX11.' in black letter between two
lines. Dedication to Nada Burnham; verso, advertisement. Contents page as for the
Annual; verso, advertisement. Text pp 5 to 208, followed by 32 pp of advertisements
(signatures 14 and 15.)
b. Tauchnitz of Leipzig copyright edition, 1897, (No 3191).
c. First American Edition by Longmans, Green, and Co, New York, 1896.
d. See also *Black Heart and White Heart* [F23]

F21   Dr. Therne   1898

1 PUBLISHER   Longmans, Green, and Co., London.

2 IDENTIFICATION FEATURES
a. Binding   Pale brown cloth. 122 × 191 mm.
b. Spine   [device] DR [device] / THERNE / [device] / H. Rider / Haggard /
                   Longmans & Co. [All in gold, between brown decoration at top and
                   bottom.]
c. Front Cover   DR. THERNE / H. Rider Haggard. [All in brown.]
d. End Papers   Patterned, brown, of swans, sailing ships and 1726, all entwined with
                   leafy twigs.
e. Preliminaries One leaf blank. p[i] Half title — DOCTOR THERNE; verso, list of 21
                   works by the same author. p[iii] Title page — DOCTOR THERNE /
                   by / H. Rider Haggard / Author of "She," "Allan Quatermain," Etc

/ Longmans, Green, and Co. / 39 Paternoster Row, London / New York and Bombay / 1898, verso; Copyright, 1898 / by H. Rider Haggard / [line] / All rights reserved. p[v] Dedication to the members of the Jenner Society; verso blank. pp[vii] and viii, Author's Note. p[ix] Contents list; verso blank.

f. Text   pp[1] to 253, with '17 asterisk' at foot of p 253, the verso of which is blank.

g. Supplements   One leaf, with 'Aberdeen University Press' on recto; verso blank.

h. Illustrations None.

i. Errors   p 96, line 12. 'issued' should read 'issue'.

3 TECHNICAL

a. Format   Cr 8vo

b. Edges   All edges cut.

c. Collation   [1] × 8; 2 to 16 × 8; 17 × 6. Total 134 leaves.

4 NUMBER OF COPIES IN FIRST EDITION AND DATE

10,000; 28 Nov 98. (10,000 copies printed Nov 98, for sale at 3*s*. 6*d*. each.)

5 EARLIER PUBLICATION IN MAGAZINE

None, but see para 7 below.

6 OTHER EDITIONS OF NOTE

a. An additional 5,000 copies were printed Nov 98 for a Longmans Colonial Library edition. 1800 of these were used for binding in cloth (2*s*.); the remainder were sewed (1*s*. 6*d*.)

b. Tauchnitz of Leipzig copyright edition, 1899 (No 3336).

c. First American Edition by Longmans, Green, and Co., New York, 1898.

d. George Newnes: London, brought out a 6*d*. edition in 1903, entitled *Doctor Therne, Anti-Vaccinist*. (pp 120). 200,000 copies were printed.

7 NOTES

a. The story was run as a serial in the magazine *The Dawn of the Day*, from Jan 1900 (No 265, p 1) to Dec 1900 (No 276, p 271). Three illustrations by W.S. Stacey appeared in each of the monthly parts. Due acknowledgement was made to Messrs. Longmans.

b. Scott refers to rare copies of the First Edition with plain white end papers, and states that such copies have rounded backs (spines) with the publisher's name thereon reduced to 'Longmans' (ie. '& Co' omitted). I have not seen such a copy. My two copies of the First Edition both have patterned end papers as described at para 2d above. One, however, has a rounded spine, the other being square backed. The square backed copy also differs from the other by including an Aberdeen University Press colophon instead of the words 'Aberdeen University Press' on the recto of the last leaf; and it is 4 mm thinner, perhaps being more tightly bound. The decoration at top and bottom of the spine is black, not brown. Finally, it has '1/6 L' on the inside front cover, stamped by rubber stamp. No conclusive evidence emerges to prove which binding is 'normal' and which 'variant'. I suspect that the round back binding is normal. Perhaps the square backed copies were bound up later and sold off cheap at 1*s*. 6*d*.

8 AN HAGGARD NOTE

'. . . my only novel with a purpose . . . appeared about a year previous to my journeyings in the Near East. It is called "Doctor Therne", and deals with the matter of the Anti-Vaccination craze — not, it may be thought, a very promising topic for romance. I was led to treat of it, however, by the dreadful things I had seen and knew of the ravages of smallpox in Mexico and elsewhere, and the fear, not yet realised, that they should repeat themselves in this country. . . . Although so different in matter and manner from my other works, this tale has been widely read, and will in due course appear in one of those sevenpenny editions which have become so popular in recent years. I dedicated it (without permission) to the Jenner Society. The Executive Committee of this Society on December 22, 1898, passed a warm and unanimous resolution thanking me for the work . . .'

The Days of My Life
Vol II, pp 139, 140.

F22   Swallow   1899

1 PUBLISHER   Longmans, Green, and Co., London.

2 IDENTIFICATION FEATURES
a. Binding   Blue cloth over bevelled edge boards. 120 × 190 mm.
b. Spine   SWALLOW / [line] / H. Rider / Haggard / Longmans & Co. [All in gold.]
c. Front Cover   SWALLOW / by / H. Rider Haggard. [All in gold.]
d. End Papers   Plain black.
e. Preliminaries   One leaf blank. p[i] Half title — SWALLOW; verso, list of 22 works by the same author. Blank page; verso, Frontispiece with tissue guard. p[iii] Title page — SWALLOW / A Tale of the Great Trek / by / H. Rider Haggard / Author of "She," "King Solomon's Mines," "Joan Haste," / "Allan Quatermain," "Heart of the World," Etc. / Longmans, Green, and Co. / 39 Paternoster Row, London / New York and Bombay / 1899; verso, — Copyright, 1898, by / H. Rider Haggard / [line] / All rights reserved. pp v and [vi] Dedication to Lieut.-Colonel Sir Marshal Clarke, R.A., K.C.M.G. pp[vii] and viii, Contents list. p[ix] List of illustrations; verso blank.
f. Text   pp[1] to 348, with printers imprint at the bottom of p 348.
g. Supplements   None.
h. Illustrations   There are 8 full page illustrations including the Frontispiece, all by Maurice Greiffenhagen. They all have blank backs, are unnumbered and are not included in the pagination.
i. Errors   p 107, line 21 and 22. These lines should be transposed.
                p 250, line 24. 'hes aid' should read 'he said'.

3 TECHNICAL
a. Format   Cr 8vo
b. Edges   All edges cut.
c. Collation   6; [1] to 21 × 8; 22 × 6. The illustrations are sewn into the gatherings as follows; Frontispiece; [1] (facing p 14); 4 (facing p 63); 9 (facing p 143); 12 (facing p 183); 16 (facing p 245); 20 (facing p 320); 21 (facing p 332). Total 188 leaves.

4 NUMBER OF COPIES IN FIRST EDITION AND DATE
10,000; 1 Mar 99. (10,000 copies printed Oct 98.)

5 EARLIER PUBLICATION IN MAGAZINE
Serial story in *The Graphic*, Vol 58, Jul to Oct 98, Nos 1492 to 1509. Illustrated by
W. Hatherell.

6 OTHER EDITIONS OF NOTE
a. Tauchnitz of Leipzig copyright edition, 1899, (Nos 3355–6).
b. First American Edition by Longmans, Green, and Co, New York, 1899.
c. Longmans Silver Library edition of 1921 states, in a bibliographical note: 'First
printed Jan 99; reprinted Apr 99. Colonial Edition Jan 99; reprinted Apr 99. Reissued in
The Silver Library Jul 01; reprinted Jun 07, Jan 11, Jul 16, Mar 21.'

F23   Black Heart and White Heart   1900

1 PUBLISHER   Longmans, Green, and Co., London.

2 IDENTIFICATION FEATURES
a. Binding	Blue cloth over bevelled edge boards. 120 × 190 mm.
b. Spine	BLACK HEART / AND / WHITE HEART / AND / OTHER STORIES / [line] / H. Rider Haggard / Longmans & Co. [All in gold.]
c. Front Cover	BLACK HEART / AND / WHITE HEART / HAGGARD. [All in gold.]
d. End Papers	Plain black.
e. Preliminaries	p[i] Half title — BLACK HEART AND WHITE HEART / AND OTHER STORIES; verso, list of 24 works by the same author. p[iii] blank; verso, Frontispiece with tissue guard. p[v] Title page — BLACK HEART AND WHITE HEART / AND OTHER STORIES / by / H. Rider Haggard / Author of / "She," "Allan Quatermain," "King Solomon's Mines," Etc. Etc. / Longmans, Green, and Co. / 39 Paternoster Row, London / New York and Bombay / 1900 ; verso blank. p[vii] Dedication to Nada Burnham; verso, Author's Note. pp[ix] and x, Contents list. pp[xi] and xii, List of illustrations. p[xiii] blank; verso, illustration.
f. Text	pp[1] to 414, with printer's imprint (Aberdeen University Press) at foot of p 414. The stories appear thus: pp[1] to 65, 'Black Heart and White Heart'; pp 67 to 232, 'Elissa'; or, 'The Doom of Zimbabwe'; pp 233 to 414, 'The Wizard'.
g. Supplements	None.
h. Illustrations	There are 34 full page illustrations including the Frontispiece and a repeat of it, not listed at p[xi], facing p 34. Charles Kerr illustrated 'Black Heart and White Heart' and 'The Wizard' (26, including the repeated Frontispiece) and F.H. Townsend provided 8 illustrations for 'Elissa'. They all have blank backs and all except the Frontispiece are not included in the pagination. They have all been printed, however, as leaves integral to the gatherings.
i. Errors	p[xi], line 7. '18' should read '16'.

3 TECHNICAL
a. Format	Cr 8vo

b. Edges   All edges cut.
c. Collation   6; 1 to 30 × 8. Total 246 leaves.

4 NUMBER OF COPIES IN FIRST EDITION AND DATE
10,000; 29 May 1900. (10,015 copies printed May 1900.)

5 EARLIER PUBLICATION IN MAGAZINE
a. 'Black Heart and White Heart' appeared in *The African Review*, New Year edition, Jan 1896. Illustrated by Charles Kerr.
b. 'Elissa' appeared as a serial story in *The Long Bow*, Vols I and II, Feb to Jun 1898, Nos 1 to 19. Illustrated by F.H. Townsend.
c. 'The Wizard' — see F20.

6 OTHER EDITIONS OF NOTE
a. An additional 5,000 copies were printed May 1900 for a Longmans Colonial Library edition. 1570 of these were used for binding in cloth (2*s.*); the remainder were sewed (1*s.* 6*d.*)
b. Tauchnitz of Leipzig copyright edition, 1900, (No 3440), containing only 'Black Heart and White Heart' and 'Elissa'.
c. First American Edition by Longmans, Green, and Co., New York, 1900. Published under the title 'Elissa' and contained only that title and 'Black Heart and White Heart'.

7 NOTE
The dedication to 'the Memory of the Child Nada Burnham' is taken from the original edition of *The Wizard*, though it is slightly amended for this later work.

F24   Lysbeth   1901

1 PUBLISHER   Longmans, Green, and Co., London.

2 IDENTIFICATION FEATURES
a. Binding   Blue cloth. 130 × 197 mm.
b. Spine   LYSBETH / A TALE OF / THE DUTCH / [line] / H. Rider / Haggard / Longmans & Co. [All in gold.]
c. Front Cover LYSBETH / [line] / H. Rider / Haggard [all in a box. All in gold.]
d. End Papers Plain black.
e. Preliminaries One leaf blank. p[i] Half title — LYSBETH / A Tale of the Dutch; verso, list of 24 works by the same author. Blank page; verso, Frontispiece with tissue guard. p[iii] Title page — LYSBETH / A TALE OF THE DUTCH / by / H. Rider Haggard / Author of "Jess," "King Solomon's Mines," / "Swallow," Etc., Etc. / With Twenty-Six Illustrations by / G.P. Jacomb Hood, R.I. / Longmans, Green, and Co. / 39 Paternoster Row, London / New York and Bombay / 1901; verso, — Copyright, 1900, by / H. Rider Haggard / Copyright, 1901, by / H. Rider Haggard / [line] / All rights reserved. p[v] Dedication to the memory of William the Silent of Nassau; verso blank. pp[vii] and viii, Authors Note. pp[ix] and x, Contents list. pp[xi] and xii, List of illustrations. p[xiii] Book the First / The Sowing; verso blank.
f. Text   pp[1] to 496, with printers imprint at bottom of p 496.
g. Supplements Two leaves advertising popular novels and tales. They are undated.

| *h. Illustrations* | The 26 illustrations by G.P. Jacomb Hood, R.I. include the Frontispiece. All have blank backs, are unnumbered and are not included in the pagination. |
| *i. Errors* | None. |

3 TECHNICAL

a. Format	Cr 8vo
b. Edges	All edges cut.
c. Collation	8; [1] × 8; 2 to 31 × 8; 2. The illustrations are sewn into the gatherings as follows: Frontispiece; 3 (facing p 38); 4 (facing p 62); 5 (facing p 78); 7 (facing p 98); 8 (facing p 117); 9 (facing p 134); 11 (facing p 166); 12 (facing p 181); 14(2) (facing pp 211 and 217); 16 (facing p 244); 17(2) (facing pp 259 and 273); 19 (facing p 304); 20 (facing p 315); 21 (facing p 336); 23 (facing p 354); 24 (facing p 370); 25 (facing p 388); 26 (facing p 407); 27 (facing p 428); 28 (facing p 443); 29 (facing p 452); 30 (facing p 473); 31 (facing p 494). Total 284 leaves.

4 NUMBER OF COPIES IN FIRST EDITION AND DATE
10,000; 11 Apr 01. (10,025 copies printed Mar 01.)

5 EARLIER PUBLICATION IN MAGAZINE
Serial story in *The Graphic*, Vols 62 and 63, Sep 1900 to Mar 01, Nos 1605 to 1631. Illustrated by Jacomb Hood.

6 OTHER EDITIONS OF NOTE
a. An additional 7,500 copies were printed Mar 01 for a Longmans Colonial Library edition. 1920 of these were used for binding in cloth (2*s.*); the remainder were sewed (1*s. 6d.*)
b. Tauchnitz of Leipzig copyright edition, 1901, (Nos 3502−3).
c. First American Edition by Longmans, Green, and Co., New York, 1901.

7 NOTE
In addition to the divisional title noted at para 2e above (p[xiii]), two more are included in the text, viz;
  a. p[125] Book the Second / The Ripening.
  b. p[363] Book the Third / The Harvesting.

8 AN HAGGARD NOTE
'. . . There are, roughly, two ways of writing an historical romance — the first to choose some notable and leading characters of the time to be treated, and by the help of history attempt to picture them as they were; the other, to make a study of that time and history with the country in which it was enacted, and from it to deduce the necessary characters. In the case of "Lysbeth" the author has attempted this second method . . .'
Extract from Author's Note to Lysbeth. p[vii]

F25   Pearl-Maiden   1903

1 PUBLISHER	Longmans, Green, and Co., London.

2 IDENTIFICATION FEATURES

a. Binding	Blue cloth. 125 × 198 mm.
b. Spine	PEARL- / MAIDEN / [line] / H. Rider / Haggard / Longmans & Co. [All in gold.]
c. Front Cover	PEARL- / MAIDEN / [line] / H. Rider / Haggard, [all in a box. All in gold.]
d. End Papers	Plain black.
e. Preliminaries	One leaf blank. Half title — PEARL-MAIDEN / A Tale of / The Fall of Jerusalem; verso, list of 26 works by the same author. Blank page; verso, Frontispiece with tissue guard. Title page — PEARL-MAIDEN / A Tale of / The Fall of Jerusalem / by / H. Rider Haggard / Author of "Jess," "She," "King Solomon's Mines," / "Lysbeth," Etc. / Longmans, Green, and Co. / 39 Paternoster Row, London / New York and Bombay / 1903. Verso — Copyright 1901 and 1902 / By H. Rider Haggard / [line] / All Rights Reserved. Dedication to Gladys Christian dated September 14, 1902; verso blank. One leaf containing Contents List. List of illustrations; verso blank.
f. Text	pp 1 to 463, with printers imprint at bottom of p 463, verso blank.
g. Supplements	Two leaves advertising popular novels and tales. They are undated.
h. Illustrations	There are 16 full page illustrations by Byam Shaw, including the Frontispiece. All have blank backs, are unnumbered and are not included in the pagination.
i. Errors	None.

3 TECHNICAL

a. Format	Cr 8vo
b. Edges	All edges cut.
c. Collation	6; 1 to 29 × 8; 2. The illustrations are sewn into the gatherings as follows: Frontispiece; 2 (facing p 33); 4 (facing p 57); 9 (facing p 132); 11 (facing p 163); 12 (facing p 191); 16(2) (facing pp 243 and 256); 20 (facing p 313); 21 (facing p 330); 22 (facing p 344); 23 (facing p 362); 24 (facing p 377); 25 (facing p 391); 27 (facing p 425); 29 (facing p 463). Total 256 leaves.

4 NUMBER OF COPIES IN FIRST EDITION AND DATE
10,000; 2 Mar 03. (10,000 printed Feb 03.)

5 EARLIER PUBLICATION IN MAGAZINE
Serial story in *The Graphic*, Vol 66, Jul to Dec 02, Nos 1701 to 1726. Illustrated by Byam Shaw.

6 OTHER EDITIONS OF NOTE
a. An additional 7,500 copies were printed Feb 03 for issue in a Longmans Colonial Library edition. 2600 of these were used for binding in cloth (2*s.*); the remainder were sewed (1*s.* 6*d.*).
b. In Nov 03 a further 3,000 copies were printed for the normal 6*s.* edition (comment:

the Second issue) and 2000 for the Colonial Library. 550 of the latter were bound in cloth.

c. Tauchnitz of Leipzig copyright edition, 1903, (Nos 3648–9).

d. First American Edition by Longmans, Green, and Co., New York, 1903.

F26 Stella Fregelius 1904

1 PUBLISHER Longmans, Green, and Co., London.

2 IDENTIFICATION FEATURES

a. *Binding* Blue cloth. 126 × 196 mm.

b. *Spine* STELLA / FREGELIUS / A Tale of / Three Destinies / [line] / H. Rider / Haggard / Longmans & Co. [All in gold.]

c. *Front Cover* STELLA / FREGELIUS / [line] / H. Rider / Haggard [all in a box. All in gold.]

d. *End Papers* Plain black.

e. *Preliminaries* One leaf blank. p[i] Half title — STELLA FREGELIUS / A Tale of Three Destinies; verso, list of 27 works by the same author. p[iii] Title page — STELLA FREGELIUS / A Tale of Three Destinies / by / H. Rider Haggard / "Felix qui potuit rerum cognoscere causas, / Atque metus omnes, et inexorabile fatum / Subjecit pedibus; strepitumque Acherontis avari." / Longmans, Green, and Co. / 39 Paternoster Row, London / New York and Bombay / 1904; verso blank. p[v] Dedication to John Berwick dated 25 August, 1903; verso blank. pp[vii] and viii, Author's Note. pp[ix] and x, Contents list.

f. *Text* pp 1 to 361, with printers imprint at bottom of p 361, verso blank.

g. *Supplements* One leaf advertising two new historical romances. The leaf is undated.

h. *Illustrations* None.

i. *Errors* None.

3 TECHNICAL

a. *Format* Cr 8vo

b. *Edges* All edges cut.

c. *Collation* 6; [1] to 22 × 8; 23 × 6. Total 188 leaves.

4 NUMBER OF COPIES IN FIRST EDITION AND DATE
10,000; 3 Feb 04. (10,000 copies were printed Jan 04.)

5 EARLIER PUBLICATION IN MAGAZINE
Serial story in *T.P.'s Weekly*, Vol I, Nov 1902 to Apr 1903, Nos 1 to 21.

6 OTHER EDITIONS OF NOTE

a. An additional 8,000 copies were printed Jan 04 for a Longmans Colonial Library edition. 2401 of these were used for binding in cloth (2s.); the remainder were sewed (1s. 6d.).

b. Tauchnitz of Leipzig copyright edition, 1904, (Nos 3720–1).

c. First American Edition by Longmans, Green, and Co., New York, Oct 1903, before the First English Edition.

7 NOTE
One interesting point in this work is the introduction of a primitive type radio, — an 'Aërophone' — at a time when the subject of radio experiments was in its infancy.

8 AN HAGGARD NOTE

'. . . The author feels that he owes some apology to his readers for his boldness in offering to them a modest story which is in no sense a romance of the character that perhaps they expect from him; . . . His excuse must be that, in the first instance, he wrote it purely to please himself and now publishes it in the hope that it may please some others. . . . . He may explain further that when he drafted this book, now some five years ago, instruments of the nature of the "aërophone" were not much talked of as they are to-day . . .'

From the Author's Note to *Stella Fregelius*, pp[vii] and viii

F27 The Brethren 1904

1 PUBLISHER   Cassell and Co., London.

2 IDENTIFICATION FEATURES

a. Binding   Red cloth. 126 × 199 mm.

b. Spine   [device of five dots] THE [device of five dots] / BRETHREN / [device of five dots] / H. Rider / Haggard / Cassell & Company / Limited. [All in gold.]

c. Front Cover   THE BRETHREN / [ornament] / H. Rider Haggard. [All in gold.]

d. End Papers   Patterned, light grey-brown, of crouching female archer with 'C & Co: Ld' beneath.

e. Preliminaries   p[i] Half title — THE BRETHREN; verso, list of 29 works by the same author. p[iii] Title page — THE / BRETHREN / by / H. Rider Haggard / Author of "King Solomon's Mines" / &c, &c. / Cassell and Company, Limited / London, Paris, New York / and Melbourne. MCMIV / All Rights Reserved; verso, a verse by Scott. p[v] Dedication to Mrs Maddison Green; verso blank. pp[vii] and viii, Contents list.

f. Text   p[1] Author's Note. pp[2] to 4, Prologue. pp[5] to 342, Text, with printers imprint at bottom of p 342.

g. Supplements   One leaf advertising new and popular novels, followed by pp[1] to 16, a catalogue of A Selection from Cassell & Company's Publications, dated 6G.−9.04. on p[1].

h. Illustrations   None.

i. Errors   None.

3 TECHNICAL

a. Format   Cr 8vo

b. Edges   All edges cut.

c. Collation   4; B to V × 8; W × 4; catalogue 8. (Unusually, the signatures include J, V and W). Total 184 leaves.

4 NUMBER OF COPIES IN FIRST EDITION AND DATE

15,000; 30 Sep 04.

5 EARLIER PUBLICATION IN MAGAZINE

Serial story in *Cassell's Magazine*, Dec 03 to Nov 04. Illustrated by H.R. Millar.

6 OTHER EDITIONS OF NOTE

a. Early editions noted in a bibliographical note in a One shilling edition dated 1912 are; First Edition Sep 04, Reprinted Oct 04, Feb 05, Apr 07, Feb 12.
Popular Edition Sep 07, Nov 07, Apr and Nov 08, Aug 09, Oct 11. One Shilling Edition Aug 10.

b. Tauchnitz of Leipzig copyright edition, 1904, (Nos 3775–6).

c. First American Edition by McClure, Phillips & Co., New York 1904.

7 NOTE

Mrs Maddison Green, to whom the book was dedicated, was Rider Haggard's sister, Ella, whose son accompanied Haggard to Cyprus and Palestine as his secretary. It was during this journey (1900) that Haggard conceived the idea of writing *The Brethren*.

8 AN HAGGARD NOTE

'. . . In the year 1903, which I spent at home, . . . I wrote a romance of chivalry called "The Brethren", of which the scene is laid in the Holy Land at the time of the Crusades. Personally it is a favourite with me, but my historical tales have never been quite so popular as are those which deal with African adventure.'

The Days of My Life
Vol II, p 154

F28   Ayesha   1905

1 PUBLISHER   Ward Lock and Co. Ltd., London.

2 IDENTIFICATION FEATURES

a. Binding	Blue cloth. 125 × 195 mm.
b. Spine	AYESHA / [small triangle] / H / Rider / Haggard / [decoration] / Ward• Lock• &• Co. [All in gold.]
c. Front Cover	AYESHA / [decoration] / H. Rider / Haggard. [All in gold, within panels formed by four horizontal and four vertical green lines.]
d. End Papers	Plain white.
e. Preliminaries	p[1] Half title — AYESHA / The Return of She; verso, list of 31 works by the same author. One blank page; verso, Frontispiece with tissue guard. p[3] Title page — AYESHA / The Return of She / by / H. Rider Haggard / Author of "She" Etc / [quotation from *She*, Silver Library Edition, p 227.] / London / Ward Lock & Co. Limited / 1905; verso blank. p 5, Dedication to Andrew Lang dated Ditchingham 1905; verso, blank. p 7, Author's Note; verso blank. pp 9 and 10, Contents list.
f. Text	pp 11 to 384, with printer's imprint at bottom of p 384.
g. Supplements	None.
h. Illustrations	There are 32 full page illustrations by Maurice Greiffenhagen, including the Frontispiece. All have blank backs, are unnumbered and are not included in the pagination.
i. Errors	p 49, line 7 from bottom. 'Khublighan' should read 'Khubilghan'. p 207, line 21. 'heirophant' should read 'hierophant'.

3 TECHNICAL

a. Format	Cr 8vo

b. *Edges*	All edges cut.
c. *Collation*	[A] × 8; B to I × 8; K to U × 8; X to Z × 8; AA × 8. The illustrations have been pasted into the gatherings as follows: Frontispiece; C(2) (facing pp 34 and 36); D(2) (facing pp 52 and 56); F(2) (facing pp 86 and 90); H(2) (facing pp 116 and 128); I (facing p 132); K (facing p 158); M(2) (facing pp 180 and 182); N (facing p 206); O (facing p 220); P(2) (facing pp 234 and 238); Q (facing p 256); R(4) (facing pp 258, 262, 264, and 268); S (facing p 280); T(3) (facing pp 290, 296 and 298); U (facing p 308); X (facing p 332); Y (facing p 350); Z(2) (facing pp 360 and 368); AA (facing p 380). Total 224 leaves.

4 NUMBER OF COPIES IN FIRST EDITION AND DATE
25,000; 6 Oct 1905.

5 EARLIER PUBLICATION IN MAGAZINE
Serial story in the *Windsor Magazine*, Vols 21 and 22, Dec 04 to Oct 05, Nos 120 to 130. Illustrated by Maurice Greiffenhagen.

6 OTHER EDITIONS OF NOTE
a. Tauchnitz of Leipzig copyright edition *Ayesha. The Return of 'She'*, 1905, (Nos 3848−9).
b. First American Edition by Doubleday, Page & Company, New York, 1905. (Scott remarks that the illustration facing p 252 in this edition has been misplaced in binding and should be facing p 263. I do not understand this remark; the illustration in question appears to be correctly sited where it is, both according to the List of Illustrations and to the text.)
c. Ward Lock and Co. Ltd. published a paperback edition in 1908, with a pictorial front cover (She against a background of symbolized flames) and a back cover advertising the *Windsor Magazine*. 'Illustrated by Maurice Greiffenhagen' has been added to the title page and 8 of his illustrations from the First Edition appear.

7 NOTES
a. There are two variant bindings, one without the decoration on the spine and front cover, and with a double line border in blue on the front cover: the other has the ornament on the front cover but not on the spine.
b. *She* had been dedicated to Andrew Lang, and Haggard repeated the compliment in this revival of his greatest heroine.

8 SOME HAGGARD NOTES
a. '. . . Not with a view of conciliating those who on principle object to sequels, but as a matter of fact, the Author wishes to say that he does not so regard this book. Rather does he venture to ask that it should be considered as the conclusion of an imaginative tragedy . . . it was always his desire to write . . .'

From Author's Note to *Ayesha*

b. '. . . This book "Ayesha" which was published while I was in the nursing home, is a sequel to "She", which, in obedience to my original plan, I had deliberately waited for twenty years to write.'

The Days of My Life
Vol II, p 203

F29   The Way of the Spirit   1906

1 PUBLISHER   Hutchinson and Co., London.

2 IDENTIFICATION FEATURES
a. Binding   Blue cloth. 120 × 195 mm.
b. Spine   THE / WAY / OF THE / SPIRIT / H. Rider / Haggard [all in a
                     single line box] / Hutchinson & Co. [All in gold.]
c. Front Cover   THE / WAY / OF THE / SPIRIT / H. Rider / Haggard. [All in a
                     single line box. All in gold.]
d. End Papers   Plain white.
e. Preliminaries   p[1] Half title — THE WAY OF THE SPIRIT; verso, list of 34 works
                     by the same author. p[3] Title page — THE WAY OF THE SPIRIT /
                     by / H. Rider Haggard / Author of "Jess," "Stella Fregelius," Etc. /
                     "Rejoice, O young man, in thy youth . . . and walk / in the ways of
                     thine heart, and in the sight of thine / eyes; but know thou that for all
                     these things God will / bring thee to judgement." / "To him that
                     overcometh will I give to eat of the / tree of life which is in the midst
                     of the paradise of God." / London / Hutchinson & Co. / Paternoster
                     Row / 1906; verso blank. p[5] Dedication to Rudyard Kipling, Esq
                     dated 14th August 1905; verso blank. p[7] Contents list; verso blank.
                     pp[9] and 10, Author's Note.
f. Text   pp 11 to 344, with printers imprint at bottom of p 344.
g. Supplements   Four leaves of advertisements, followed by pp[1] to [24] Messrs.
                     Hutchinson & Co.'s Preliminary Announcements for the Spring of
                     1906, dated London, February, 1906. on p[1].
h. Illustrations   None.
i. Errors   None.

3 TECHNICAL
a. Format   Cr 8vo
b. Edges   All edges cut.
c. Collation   [A] to I × 8; K to U × 8; X and Y × 8; catalogue 12. Total 188
                     leaves.

4 NUMBER OF COPIES IN FIRST EDITION AND DATE
15,000; 9 Mar 06. (The Hutchinson Catalogue in fact says '9 Mar *05*' but this is
impossible.)

5 EARLIER PUBLICATION IN MAGAZINE
None.

6 OTHER EDITIONS OF NOTE
a. Tauchnitz of Leipzig copyright edition 1906, (Nos 3883−4).
b. Hutchinson and Co. produced a paperback edition in about 1910.

7 NOTES
a. Early in 1904 Haggard went on holiday to Egypt, and the book *The Way of the Spirit*
was one result of his experiences there.
b. This is another of the stories in which an item of the plot, imagined by Haggard,
turned out to have some relation to facts previously unknown to him. See my note to
Joan Haste, (F18).

8 AN HAGGARD NOTE
'. . . On my return to England I wrote "The Way of the Spirit", an Anglo-Egyptian
book which is dedicated to Kipling, and one that interested him very much. Indeed he
and I hunted out the title together in the Bible, as that of "Renunciation", by which it
was first called, did not please him. . . .'

The Days of My Life
Vol II, p 159

F30   Benita   1906

1 PUBLISHER   Cassell and Co., London.

2 IDENTIFICATION FEATURES

a. Binding	Red cloth. 125 × 200 mm.
b. Spine	BENITA / An African / Romance / [dot] / H. Rider / Haggard / Cassell & Company / Limited. [All in gold.]
c. Front Cover	BENITA / An African Romance by / H. Rider Haggard. [All in gold.]
d. End Papers	Patterned, light grey-brown, of crouching female archer with 'C & Co: Ld' beneath.
e. Preliminaries	p[i] Half title — BENITA; verso, list of 35 works by the same author. One page blank; verso, Frontispiece with tissue guard. p[iii] Title page — BENITA [in red] / An African Romance / by / H. Rider Haggard / With Sixteen Illustrations by / Gordon Browne, R.I. / Cassell & Company, Limited [in red] / London, Paris, New York and / Melbourne. MCMVI / All Rights Reserved; verso blank. pp[v] and vi, Contents list. p[vii] List of illustrations; verso blank.
f. Text	pp[1] to 344, with printer's imprint at foot of p 344.
g. Supplements	pp[1] to 8, advertising New Fiction (glazed paper.) Followed by pp[1] to 8, a catalogue of A Selection from Cassell & Company's Publications. Each set of 8 pages is dated 7.06 on p[1].
h. Illustrations	There are 16 illustrations including the Frontispiece, all by Gordon Browne, R.I. They all have blank backs and are not included in the pagination.
i. Errors	None.
j. Dust Jacket	Plain off-white paper, with 'Benita / An African Romance By / H. Rider Haggard' at top.

3 TECHNICAL

a. Format	Cr 8vo
b. Edges	All edges cut.
c. Collation	4; B to W × 8; catalogue 4. (Unusually, the signatures include J, V and W). The illustrations have been pasted into the gatherings as follows: Frontispiece; D (facing p 42); E (facing p 52); F (facing p 70); G (facing p 92); H (facing p 108); I (facing p 126); K (facing p 150); N (facing p 204); O (facing p 210); P (facing p 226); Q (facing p 254); S(2) (facing pp 274 and 280); U (facing p 312); V (facing p 336). Total 200 leaves.

4 NUMBER OF COPIES IN FIRST EDITION AND DATE
15,000; 7 Sep 06.

5 EARLIER PUBLICATION IN MAGAZINE
Serial story in *Cassell's Magazine*, Dec 05 to May 06. Illustrated by Gordon Browne.

6 OTHER EDITIONS OF NOTE
a. Tauchnitz of Leipzig copyright edition 1907, (Nos 3950).
b. First American Edition by Longmans, Green, and Co., New York, 1906. Published under the title *The Spirit of Bambatse*.

7 NOTES
a. The advertisements for New Fiction referred to above (2g) include a portrait of Rider Haggard alongside the publishers blurb for *Benita*.
b. Haggard believed that the treasure seeking theme of this story had some foundation in fact: see his Note at p[1] of the book.

F31   Fair Margaret   1907

1 PUBLISHER   Hutchinson and Co., London.

2 IDENTIFICATION FEATURES
a. Binding   Blue cloth. 122 × 196 mm.
b. Spine   FAIR / MARGARET / H. Rider / Haggard [all in a single line box] / Hutchinson & Co. [All in gold.]
c. Front Cover   FAIR MARGARET / H. Rider Haggard. [All in a single line box. All in gold.]
d. End Papers   Plain white.
e. Preliminaries   p[i] Half title — FAIR MARGARET [in top right-hand corner]; verso, advertisement for the Second Edition of *The Way of the Spirit*. One blank page; verso, Frontispiece. p[iii] Title page — FAIR MARGARET / by / H. Rider Haggard / Author of / "King Solomon's Mines," "She," "Jess," etc. / With 15 illustrations by J.R. Skelton / London: Hutchinson & Co. / Paternoster Row [two ornaments] 1907; verso blank. pp v to vii, Contents list. p viii, List of illustrations.
f. Text   pp[1] to 374, with printer's imprint at bottom of p 374.
g. Supplements   One leaf advertising some recent novels, followed by pp 1 to [32] of Preliminary Announcements for the Autumn of 1907, dated August 1907 on p 1.
h. Illustrations   There are 15 illustrations including the Frontispiece, all by J.R. Skelton. The Frontispiece has a blank back. The remaining 14 illustrations are printed on seven leaves, back to back. They are unnumbered and are not included in the pagination.
i. Errors   None.

3 TECHNICAL
a. Format   Cr 8vo
b. Edges   All edges cut.
c. Collation   4; 1 to 23 × 8; 24 × 4; catalogue 16. The illustrations have been pasted into the gatherings as follows: Frontispiece; 4(2) (facing pp 64 and 65); 5(2) (facing pp 76 and 77); 10(2) (facing pp 146 and 147); 12(2) (facing pp 182 and 183); 15(2) (facing pp 228 and 229); 18(2)

(facing pp 282 and 283); 22(2) (facing pp 340 and 341). Total 216 leaves.

4 NUMBER OF COPIES IN FIRST EDITION AND DATE
15,000; 11 Sep 07.

5 EARLIER PUBLICATION IN MAGAZINE
Serial story in *The Lady's Realm*, Vols 21 and 22, Nov 06 to Oct 07. Illustrated by J.R. Skelton.

6 OTHER EDITIONS OF NOTE
a. Tauchnitz of Leipzig copyright edition 1907, (Nos 4004–5).
b. First American Edition by Longmans, Green, and Co., New York, 1907. Published under the title *Margaret*.

7 SOME HAGGARD NOTES
'. . . Perhaps the most curious example of a literary coincidence with which I have been personnally concerned is to be found in the case of my story, "Fair Margaret". . . . In that romance the name of the hero is Peter Brome. The father of this Peter Brome is represented in the tale as having been killed at Bosworth Field. . . . I received a letter from Colonel Brome Giles . . . asking me where I obtained the particulars concerning the said Peter Brome. I answered — out of my head. . . . All I can say is that the coincidence is extremely curious . . .'
b. '. . . From Egypt we went to Naples and from Naples to the south of Spain, which I now visited for the first time in preparation for a tale which I wrote afterwards and named "Fair Margaret".'

The Days of My Life
Vol II, pp 99–100, 159

F32   The Ghost Kings   1908

1 PUBLISHER   Cassell and Co., London.

2 IDENTIFICATION DETAILS
a. Binding	Blue cloth. 125 × 198 mm.
b. Spine	THE / GHOST / KINGS / [small leaf decoration] / H. Rider / Haggard / [Flower stem decoration] / Cassell / and Co. [All in gold.]
c. Front Cover	Flower stem decoration, bottom right. All in gold.
d. End Papers	Plain white.
e. Preliminaries	p[i] Half title — THE GHOST KINGS; verso, list of 36 works by the same author. One page blank; verso, Frontispiece with tissue guard. p[iii] Title page — THE GHOST KINGS / by / H. Rider Haggard / With Eight Illustrations By / A.C. Michael / Cassell and Company, Limited / London, Paris, New York, Toronto and Melbourne / MCMVIII; verso, blank except for All Rights Reserved at bottom. p[v] Contents list; verso, List of illustrations. pp[vii] and viii, Extract from letter.
f. Text	pp[1] to 376, with printer's imprint at foot of p 376.
g. Supplements	pp[1] to [8] Catalogue of Delightful Fiction, dated 8.08 at foot of p[1]. Printed in green.

h. Illustrations   There are 8 illustrations including the Frontispiece, all by A.C.
                     Michael. They all have blank backs, are unnumbered and are not
                     included in the pagination.

i. Errors   None.

3 TECHNICAL

a. Format   Cr 8vo

b. Edges   All edges cut.

c. Collation   4; B to X × 8; Y × 4; catalogue 4. (Unusually, the signatures include
                     J, V and W). The illustrations have been pasted into the gatherings as
                     follows: Frontispiece; C (facing p 24); E (facing p 60); K (facing
                     p 150); M (facing p 180); Q (facing p 244); R (facing p 272); X (facing
                     p 262). Total 200 leaves.

4 NUMBER OF COPIES IN FIRST EDITION AND DATE

15,000; 25 Sep 08.

5 EARLIER PUBLICATION IN MAGAZINE

Serial story in *Pearson's Magazine*, Vols XXIV and XXV, Oct 07 to Jun 08, Nos 142 to
150. Illustrated by A.C. Michael.

6 OTHER EDITIONS OF NOTE

a. First American Edition by Frank Lovell, New York, 1909. Published under the title
The Lady of the Heavens.

7 AN HAGGARD NOTE

'. . . When I escaped from that nursing home, very feeble and with much-shattered
nerves, I went to stay with my friend Lyne Stivens to recuperate, and thence for a day or
two to Kipling's. Here I remember we compounded the plot of "The Ghost Kings"
together, writing down our ideas in alternate sentences upon the same sheet of foolscap.'

The Days of My Life
Vol II, pp 207 and 208

F33   The Yellow God   1909

1 PUBLISHER   Cassell and Co., London.

2 IDENTIFICATION FEATURES

a. Binding   Blue-green cloth. 125 × 198 mm.

b. Spine   THE / YELLOW / GOD / [line] / H. Rider / Haggard / [line] /
                     [decoration in blind] / [line] / Cassell. [All within a single line box. All
                     in gold except decoration.]

c. Front Cover   THE YELLOW GOD / H. Rider Haggard. [All in black, within a
                     single line border in blind.]

d. End Papers   Plain white.

e. Preliminaries   Half title — THE YELLOW GOD / An Idol of Africa; verso, list of
                     38 works by the same author. One page blank; verso, coloured
                     Frontispiece with tissue guard. Title page — THE / YELLOW GOD /
                     . . An Idol of Africa . . / By H. Rider Haggard [all in a box] / With
                     Three Illustrations by / A.C. Michael / Cassell and Company, Limited
                     / London, New York, Toronto and Melbourne / 1909 [all within two

	single line boxes]; verso, blank except for All Rights Reserved at bottom. Contents page; verso blank. List of illustrations; verso blank.
f. Text	pp[1] to 352, with printer's imprint at foot of p 352.
g. Supplements	One page blank; verso, author's acknowledgement of another work entitled *The Yellow God.* Followed by pp[1] to [8] catalogue of Delightful Fiction, dated 10.08 on p[1], and printed in red and black.
h. Illustrations	There are 3 full page illustrations including the Frontispiece, all by A.C. Michael. They have blank backs, are unnumbered and are not included in the pagination.
i. Errors	None.

3 TECHNICAL

a. Format	Cr 8vo
b. Edges	All edges cut.
c. Collation	4; B to W × 8; 1; catalogue 4. The illustrations have been pasted in as follows: Frontispiece; I (facing p 122); U (facing p 316). J, V and W have been included in the signatures. Total 188 leaves.

4 NUMBER OF COPIES IN FIRST EDITION AND DATE
12,500; 5 Mar 09.

5 EARLIER PUBLICATION IN MAGAZINE
None.

6 OTHER EDITIONS OF NOTE
a. First American Edition by Cupples and Leon Co., New York, 1908.

F34   The Lady of Blossholme   1909

1 PUBLISHER   Hodder and Stoughton, London.

2 IDENTIFICATION FEATURES

a. Binding	Green cloth. 123 × 196 mm.
b. Spine	THE / LADY / OF / BLOSS- / HOLME / H. Rider / Haggard / Hodder & Stoughton. [All in gold except that T, L and B are in black.]
c. Front Cover	THE LADY OF / BLOSSHOLME / [coloured plate — 83 × 126 mm — pasted to cover between two vertical columns each with a lion at the top] / [line joining the two columns' bases] / H. Rider Haggard. [All in black except that T, L and B are in gold.]
d. End Papers	Plain white.
e. Preliminaries	p[i] Half title — THE LADY OF BLOSSHOLME; verso, list of 39 works by the same author. One page blank; verso, coloured Frontispiece with tissue guard. p[iii] Title page — THE / LADY OF BLOSSHOLME / by / H. Rider Haggard / Author of "She," "King Solomon's Mines," Etc / Hodder and Stoughton / London MCMIX; verso, Printer's imprint. pp v to vii, Contents list; p[viii] blank.
f. Text	pp[1] to 316, with printer's imprint at foot of p 316.
g. Supplements	None.
h. Illustrations	There are 5 full page coloured illustrations including the Frontispiece,

all by W. Paget. They all have blank backs, are unnumbered and are not included in the pagination.

i. Errors   p 79, line 16. 'very' should read 'every'.

3 TECHNICAL
a. Format   Cr 8vo
b. Edges   Top and fore edges cut, bottom edge uncut.
c. Collation   4; B to I × 8; K to U × 8; X × 6. The illustrations have been pasted in as follows: Frontispiece; H (facing p 102); M (facing p 164); O (facing p 202); S (facing p 258). Total 167 leaves.

4 NUMBER OF COPIES IN FIRST EDITION AND DATE
15,000; 15 Dec 09. (15,270 copies were ordered but only 15,190 were actually printed because half a ream of paper was damaged and could not be replaced in time. Of the 15,190, 775 were imprinted not only 'London   Hodder and Stoughton' but also 'Toronto   Henry Frowde'. All these copies were printed in Aug 09.)

5 EARLIER PUBLICATION IN MAGAZINE
Serial story in *The British Weekly*, Vols XLVI and XLVII, Jun to Nov 09, Nos 1182 to 1203.

6 OTHER EDITIONS OF NOTE
a. In January 1909, 100 proof copies were printed, folded and sewn in plain wrappers, with printed on them 'Advance Proof Copy'. All copies were trimmed and sent to Hodder and Stoughton.
b. In April 1909, 12 pulls of the corrected version of the proofs were sent to Hodder and Stoughton and 2 to Rider Haggard.
c. Tauchnitz of Leipzig copyright edition, 1909, (No 4158).
d. I have another edition in plain blue cloth, internally the same as the First Edition (including the error on p 79), but without illustrations and with date omitted from title page and 'New York   Toronto' added there, verso blank.

7 NOTE
The plate pasted to the front cover of the First Edition is a cut down version of the full page illustration facing p 102.

F35   Morning Star   1910

1 PUBLISHER   Cassell and Co., London.

2 IDENTIFICATION FEATURES
a. Binding   Red cloth. 125 × 197 mm.
b. Spine   MORNING / STAR / [star decoration] / H. Rider / Haggard / Cassell. [All in gold.]
c. Front Cover   MORNING STAR / H. Rider Haggard. [All in black, within a single line blind border at all edges.]
d. End Papers   Plain white.
e. Preliminaries   p[i] Half title — MORNING STAR; verso, list of 40 works by the same author. One page blank; verso, coloured Frontispiece with tissue guard. p[iii] Title page — MORNING STAR / by / H. Rider Haggard / With Three Illustrations by / A.C. Michael / Cassell and Company,

Ltd. / London, New York, Toronto & Melbourne / 1910; verso, All Rights Reserved [at foot of page] . p[v] Dedication to Dr Wallis Budge; verso blank. pp[vii] to x, Author's note. p[xi] Contents list; verso, List of illustrations.

f. Text   pp[1] to 308, with printer's imprint at foot of p 308.

g. Supplements   One leaf blank, followed by pp 1 to 16, a catalogue of new and recent fiction, dated 1/10 on p 16. Printed in black and red.

h. Illustrations There are 3 full page illustrations including the Frontispiece, all by A.C. Michael. They have blank backs, are unnumbered and are not included in the pagination. The Frontispiece and one other are coloured.

i. Errors   None.

3 TECHNICAL

a. Format   Cr 8vo

b. Edges   All edges cut.

c. Collation   6; B to S × 8 (J is included.) T × 10; 1 (blank leaf.); catalogue 8. The illustrations are pasted in as follows: Frontispiece; F (facing p 74); N (facing p 198). Total 172 leaves.

4 NUMBER OF COPIES IN FIRST EDITION AND DATE
13,500; 11 Mar 10.

5 EARLIER PUBLICATION IN MAGAZINE
Serial story in *The Christian World News of the Week*, Vols LIII and LIV, Oct 09 to Mar 10, Nos 2742 to 2762.

6 OTHER EDITIONS OF NOTE
a. Tauchnitz of Leipzig copyright edition 1910, (No 4186).
b. First American Edition by Longmans, Green, and Co., New York, 1910.

7 AN HAGGARD NOTE
'. . . Another of my early friends . . . is Dr Wallis Budge, (Sir E.W. Budge) the head of the Egyptian Department of the British Museum, to whom not long ago I dedicated my book "Morning Star", an attention that pleased him very much.'

The Days of My Life
Vol II, p 30

F36   Queen Sheba's Ring   1910

1 PUBLISHER   Eveleigh Nash, London.

2 IDENTIFICATION FEATURES

a. Binding   Red cloth. 121 × 195 mm.

b. Spine   QUEEN / SHEBA'S / RING / H. Rider / Haggard / Eveleigh Nash. [All in gold.]

c. Front Cover QUEEN SHEBA'S / RING / H. Rider Haggard. [All in gold. All within a double line box in blind, itself within a blind single line border.] (The rear cover has a publisher's device in blind.)

d. End Papers   Plain white.

e. Preliminaries p[i] Half title — QUEEN SHEBA'S / RING [top left; publisher's

device bottom right]; verso, list of 41 works by the same author. One
page blank; verso, coloured Frontispiece with tissue guard. p[iii] Title
page — QUEEN SHEBA'S RING / by / H. Rider Haggard /
Frontispiece by Cyrus Cuneo / London / Eveleigh Nash / Fawside
House / 1910; verso, All Rights Reserved, Including That of
Translation / Into Foreign Languages, Including the Scandinavian /
Copyright 1909 by H. Rider Haggard. p v, Contents list; verso, blank.

f. Text	pp 7 to 319; printer's imprint on verso, p 319.
g. Supplements	None.
h. Illustrations	Frontispiece only.
i. Errors	None.

3 TECHNICAL

a. Format	Cr 8vo
b. Edges	Top and fore edges cut, bottom edge uncut.
c. Collation	[A] × 8; B to I × 8; K to U × 8. Frontispiece is pasted into [A]. Total 161 leaves.

4 NUMBER OF COPIES IN FIRST EDITION AND DATE
7,600; Sep 10 (18,600 were actually printed, 7,600 with the Eveleigh Nash imprint, and
11,000 for a Colonial Edition with the imprint of Bell & Sons.)

5 EARLIER PUBLICATION IN MAGAZINE
Serial story in *Nash's Magazine*, Vol I, Apr to Nov 1909, Nos 1 to 8.

6 OTHER EDITIONS OF NOTE
a. The Colonial Edition (see 4 above.)
b. The book was reprinted for Eveleigh Nash in 1913, p 319.
c. Tauchnitz of Leipzig copyright edition 1910, (No 4222).
d. First American Edition by Doubleday, Page and Co., New York, 1910.

7 NOTE
Haggard originally selected *Maqueda* as the title for this work, but was advised by
Eveleigh Nash to change it to *Queen Sheba's Ring* because 'There's romance in the title
and women love a story about a ring'.

F37   Red Eve   1911

1 PUBLISHER   Hodder and Stoughton, London.

2 IDENTIFICATION FEATURES

a. Binding	Red cloth. 125 × 193 mm.
b. Spine	RED / EVE / H. Rider / Haggard / Hodder & / Stoughton. [All in gold.]
c. Front Cover	RED EVE / [coloured paste-on (82 × 89 mm cut-down version of Frontispiece) within a black border] / H. Rider Haggard. [Lettering all in gold.]
d. End Papers	Plain white.
e. Preliminaries	One blank leaf. p[i] Half title — RED EVE; verso, list of 43 works by the same author. One page blank; verso, coloured Frontispiece with tissue guard. p[iii] Title page — RED EVE / by / H. Rider Haggard /

Hodder and Stoughton / London, New York, Toronto; verso, printer's imprint (Richard Clay). p[v] Dedication to Dr. Jehu, F.G.S., St. Andrews, N.B., dated May 27, 1911; verso blank. pp vii to ix, Contents list; p[x] blank.

f. Text   pp[1] to 296, with printer's imprint at foot of p 296.

g. Supplements   A 16 page Selected List of Works in Fiction and General Literature, undated. On shiny paper.

h. Illustrations   There are 4 full page illustrations including the Frontispiece, all by A.C. Michael. They have blank backs and are not included in the pagination.

i. Errors   On p 227, lines 19 and 36 and p 252, line 25, a space has been omitted between two words in each line.

3 TECHNICAL

a. Format   Cr 8vo

b. Edges   Top and fore edges cut, bottom edge uncut.

c. Collation   6; B to I × 8; K to T × 8; U × 4; Catalogue 8. The illustrations have been pasted in as follows: Frontispiece; H (facing p 102); P (facing p 210); P (facing p 288). Total 166 leaves.

4 NUMBER OF COPIES IN FIRST EDITION AND DATE
13,500; 28 Aug 11.

5 EARLIER PUBLICATION IN MAGAZINE
Serial story in *The Red Magazine*, from Christmas Number, No 40, Vol VII, 1 Dec 10 to No 46, Vol VIII, 1 Mar 11. Published fortnightly. With 21 illustrations by Paul Hardy.

6 OTHER EDITIONS OF NOTE
a. In November 1910, 12 proof copies were compiled, stitched and trimmed in wrappers, and sent to Hodder and Stoughton.
b. In October 1911, 2000 copies were printed for the Second Edition. The style was the same as the First, with 'Second Edition' added to the title page.
c. Tauchnitz of Leipzig copyright edition, 1911, (No 4287).
d. First American Edition by Doubleday, Page & Co., New York, 1911.

7 NOTE
There is some evidence that Haggard co-operated with Rudyard Kipling over the selection of the name of Murgh for the central figure in this work.

8 AN HAGGARD NOTE
'. . . I made some good friends upon that Commission, notably that charming and able geologist, Professor Jehu (to whom I dedicated my tale "Red Eve"), who was my constant companion during those five years'. (Haggard is referring here to the Royal Commission on Coast Erosion and Afforestation, on which he served from 1906 to 1911.)

The Days of My Life
Vol II, p 225

F38 The Mahatma and the Hare 1911

1 PUBLISHER   Longmans, Green, and Co., London.

2 IDENTIFICATION FEATURES
a. Binding   Red cloth. 126 × 195 mm.
b. Spine   THE / MAHATMA / AND THE / HARE / `[device] / H. Rider /
           Haggard / Longmans; [all between two lines at top and two at bottom.
           All in gold.]
c. Front Cover   THE MAHATMA / AND / THE HARE / A Dream Story / H. Rider
           Haggard. [All within a frame with, at left, the silhouette to be found
           also facing p 21 (artist's name excepted). All in black.]
d. End Papers   Plain white.
e. Preliminaries   One leaf blank except for asterisk on recto. p[i] Half title — THE
           MAHATMA AND THE HARE; verso blank. p[iii] blank; verso,
           Frontispiece with tissue guard. p[v] Title page — THE MAHATMA
           AND / THE HARE / A Dream Story / by / H. Rider Haggard / With
           12 illustrations by W.T. Horton / and H.M. Brock, R.I. / Longmans,
           Green and Co. / 39 Paternoster Row, London / New York, Bombay,
           and Calcutta / 1911 / All Rights Reserved; verso blank. p[vi] Contents
           list; verso blank. p ix, list of illustrations; verso blank.
f. Text   pp[1] to [165]. Printer's imprint (Ballantyne Hanson and Co.) at foot
           of p[165], verso blank.
g. Supplements   One leaf blank.
h. Illustrations   6 illustrations, including the Frontispiece, by W.T. Horton and 6 by
           H.M. Brock. All have blank backs and are all included in the
           pagination.
i. Errors   None.

3 TECHNICAL
a. Format   Cr 8vo
b. Edges   Top and fore edges cut, bottom edge rough cut.
c. Collation   6; A to I × 8; K × 8; L × 4. The illustrations are printed as part of
           the signatures. Total 90 leaves.

4 NUMBER OF COPIES IN FIRST EDITION AND DATE
5,000; 16 Oct 11 (5003 copies printed Aug 1911.)

5 EARLIER PUBLICATION IN MAGAZINE
None.

6 OTHER EDITIONS OF NOTE
a. First American Edition by Henry Holt and Co., New York, Oct 1911.

7 AN HAGGARD NOTE
'. . . Years afterwards another dream about an animal came to me which I embodied in
the story called "The Mahatma and the Hare", a little book that, up to the present, has
no great public vogue. Largely, this is because so many of the papers neglected it as
though it were something improper. Their reason was, I think, that they feared to give
offence to that great section of their readers who, directly or indirectly, are interested in
sport, by extended notices of a parable which doubtless in its essence amounts to an
attack upon our habit of killing other creatures for amusement. . . .'

The Days of My Life
Vol II, pp 166 and 167

F39   Marie   1912

1 PUBLISHER	Cassell and Co., London.

2 IDENTIFICATION FEATURES

a. Binding	Red cloth. 123 × 195 mm.
b. Spine	MARIE / H. / Rider / Haggard [all within a leafy decoration] / Cassell. [All in gold.]
c. Front Cover	MARIE / H. / Rider / Haggard [all in a box within a single line border at all edges, all in blind.]
d. End Papers	Plain white.
e. Preliminaries	One leaf blank. p[i] Half title — MARIE; verso, list of 46 works by the same author. One page blank; verso, coloured Frontispiece with tissue guard. p[iii] Title page [glazed paper] — MARIE / by / H. Rider Haggard / [vignette] / Illustrated by A.C. Michael / Cassell and Company, Ltd / London, New York, Toronto and Melbourne / 1912; verso, All Rights Reserved [at foot of page]. pp[v] and vi, Dedication to Sir Henry Bulwer, G.C.M.G. p[vii], Preface; verso blank. pp[ix] to xii, Editor's Note. p[xiii] Contents list; verso blank. p[xv] List of illustrations; verso blank.
f. Text	pp[1] to 346, with printer's imprint at foot of p 346.
g. Supplements	One blank leaf.
h. Illustrations	There are 4 illustrations including the coloured Frontispiece, all by A.C. Michael. They all have blank backs, are unnumbered and are not included in the pagination. All on glazed paper.
i. Errors	None.
j. Dust Jacket	Large version of coloured frontispiece, showing Allan and Marie defending the farmhouse. With 'Marie / By / H. Rider Haggard' at bottom right.

3 TECHNICAL

a. Format	Cr 8vo
b. Edges	All edges cut.
c. Collation	9; B to V × 8, W × 6. (Unusually, the signatures include J, V and W.) The illustrations are pasted into the gatherings as follows: Frontispiece; I (facing p 124); O (facing p 218); W (facing p 340).

4 NUMBER OF COPIES IN FIRST EDITION AND DATE
6997; 25 Jan 12.

5 EARLIER PUBLICATION IN MAGAZINE
Serial story in *Cassell's Magazine*, Vol LIII, Sep 11 to Feb 12, Nos 1 to 6. Twenty illustrations and a repeated chapter headpiece, all by A.C. Michael.

6 OTHER EDITIONS OF NOTE
a. Tauchnitz of Leipzig copyright edition, 1912, (No 4317.)
b. First American Edition by Longmans, Green, and Co., New York, 1912.

F40   Child of Storm   1913

1 PUBLISHER   Cassell and Co., London.

2 IDENTIFICATION FEATURES

a. Binding   Red-brown cloth. 124 × 197 mm.

b. Spine   CHILD / OF / STORM / H. Rider / Haggard / Cassell. [All in gold.]

c. Front Cover   CHILD OF STORM / H. Rider Haggard. [All in blind within single line border at all edges, also in blind.]

d. End Papers   Plain white.

e. Preliminaries p[i] Half title — CHILD OF STORM; verso, list of 47 works by the same author. One page blank; verso, coloured Frontispiece with tissue guard. p[iii] Title page — CHILD OF STORM / By / H. Rider Haggard / With Illustrations by / A.C. Michael / [printer's ornament] / Cassell and Company, Ltd / London, New York, Toronto and Melbourne / 1913; verso blank. pp[v] to vii, Dedication to James Stuart, Esq., dated 12 October 1912. p[viii] blank. p[ix] Contents list; verso blank. p[xi] List of illustrations; verso blank. pp[xiii] to xvi, Author's note.

f. Text   pp[1] to 348, with printer's imprint (Cassell) at foot of p 348.

g. Supplements   One leaf blank, followed by a four page catalogue dated 1.13 on p[1].

h. Illustrations There are 3 illustrations including the coloured Frontispiece, all by A.C. Michael. Only the Frontispiece is coloured. All have blank backs and are not included in the pagination.

i. Errors   None.

j. Dust Jacket   Full page version of the coloured Frontispiece with, at the top, 'Child of Storm / H. Rider Haggard.'

3 TECHNICAL

a. Format   Cr 8vo

b. Edges   All edges cut.

c. Collation   [A] × 8; B to V × 8; W × 7; catalogue 2. (Signatures J, V and W are included.) The illustrations have been pasted into the signatures as follows: Frontispiece; D (facing p 34); S (facing p 282). Total 188 leaves.

4 NUMBER OF COPIES IN FIRST EDITION AND DATE
13,500; 23 Jan 13.

5 EARLIER PUBLICATION IN MAGAZINE
None.

6 OTHER EDITIONS OF NOTE
a. A 1*s*. Edition, 20,000 published in September 1914, in red cloth. The title page of this edition has '(Mameena)' printed below 'Child of Storm'. The dust jacket front is similar to that of the First Edition jacket. Some rare examples of the jacket are particularly interesting because they have a brown label pasted to the front, bearing in a single line box the words 'From which the Play / MAMEENA / has been adapted'.
b. Tauchnitz of Leipzig copyright edition, 1913, (No 4391).
c. First American Edition by Longmans, Green and Co., New York, 1911.

7 SOME HAGGARD NOTES

a. '. . . Osborn actually saw the battle of the Tugela, which took place between the rival princes Cetywayo and Umbelazi in 1856. . . . I have described this battle, in which and the subsequent rout tens of thousands of people perished, in a romance . . . under the title "Child of Storm".'

b. '. . . If I am asked what book of mine I think the best as a whole, I answer that one . . . to my mind is the most artistic. At any rate, to some extent, it satisfies my literary conscience. It is the book named "Child of Storm".'

The Days of My Life
Vol I, pp 76, 77; Vol II, p 207

F41   The Wanderer's Necklace   1914

1 PUBLISHER   Cassell and Co., London.

2 IDENTIFICATION FEATURES

a. Binding	Brown cloth. 122 × 197 mm.
b. Spine	THE / WANDERER'S / NECKLACE / H. Rider / Haggard / Cassell. [All in gold.]
c. Front Cover	THE WANDERER'S / NECKLACE / H. Rider Haggard. [Within a single line border at all edges. All in blind.]
d. End Papers	Plain white.
e. Preliminaries	p[i] Half title — THE WANDERER'S NECKLACE; verso, list of 48 works by the same author. One page blank; verso, coloured Frontispiece with tissue guard. p[iii] Title page — THE / WANDERER'S NECKLACE / by / H. Rider Haggard / With Four Illustrations by / A.C. Michael / Cassell and Company, Ltd / London, New York, Toronto and Melbourne / 1914; verso blank. p[v] Dedication to Sir Edgar Vincent, K.C.M.G., dated November 1913.; verso blank. pp[vii] and viii, Note by the Editor. pp[ix] and x, Contents list. p[xi] List of plates; verso blank.
f. Text	pp[1] to 328, with printer's imprint at foot of p 328. These pages include three divisional titles, viz: p[1] Book I / Aar; verso blank; p[93] Book II / Byzantium; verso blank; p[245] Book III / Egypt; verso blank.
g. Supplements	None.
h. Illustrations	There are four full page illustrations including the Frontispiece, all by A.C. Michael. They all have blank backs, are unnumbered and are not included in the pagination. They are on glazed paper.
i. Errors	The signature letter C is missing from p 17.

3 TECHNICAL

a. Format	Cr 8vo
b. Edges	All edges cut.
c. Collation	6; B to U × 8; V × 4. (Unusually, the signatures include J and V.) The illustrations have been pasted into the gatherings as follow: Frontispiece; J (facing p 144); M (facing p 192); T (facing p 300). Total 174 leaves.

4 NUMBER OF COPIES IN FIRST EDITION AND DATE
13,500; 29 Jan 14.

5 EARLIER PUBLICATION IN MAGAZINE
None.

6 OTHER EDITIONS OF NOTE
a. Tauchnitz of Leipzig Copyright edition, 1914, (No 4473).
b. First American Edition by Longmans, Green, and Co., New York, 1914.

F42   The Holy Flower   1915

1 PUBLISHER	Ward, Lock and Co. Ltd., London.

2 IDENTIFICATION FEATURES

a. Binding	Blue cloth. 122 × 193 mm.
b. Spine	THE / HOLY / FLOWER / [device] / H / Rider / Haggard / [flower decoration] / Ward. Lock. &. Co. [Lettering and device in gold, decoration in blind.]
c. Front Cover	THE / HOLY. FLOWER / [flower decoration] / H [device of three vertical dots] Rider / Haggard. [All in gold, within panels formed by four horizontal and four vertical lines in blind. A rough head appears on the flower.]
d. End Papers	Plain white.
e. Preliminaries	p[1] Half title — THE HOLY FLOWER; verso, list of 49 works by the same author. One page blank; verso, Frontispiece with tissue guard. p[3] Title page — THE / HOLY FLOWER / by / H. Rider Haggard / Illustrated by Maurice Greiffenhagen / Ward, Lock & Co., Limited / London, Melbourne and Toronto / 1915; verso blank. pp 5 and 6, Contents list. p 7, List of illustrations; verso blank.
f. Text	pp 9 to 368, with printer's imprint at foot of p 368.
g. Supplements	pp 1 to 16, catalogue of Popular Fiction, undated.
h. Illustrations	There are 16 full pages illustrations including the Frontispiece, all by Maurice Greiffenhagen. All have blank backs, are unnumbered and are not included in the pagination.
i. Errors	p 17, line 12. 'a me' should read 'at me'.
	p 29, line 29. 'out' should read 'our'.
	p 196, line 5 from bottom. 'enter' should read 'entered'.
	p 300, line 17. 'least' should read 'lest'.
	p 304, line 5 from bottom. 'carred' should read 'carried'.
	p 361, line 7 from bottom. 'I' has been omitted before 'think'.
j. Dust Jacket	White paper printed in colour. Spine — THE HOLY / FLOWER / [picture of a native with a spear] / 3/6 Net / Ward, Lock & Co. Ltd. Front — THE HOLY FLOWER / H. Rider Haggard [at top, above picture of a native before two white women with flowers between them.]

3 TECHNICAL

a. Format	Cr 8vo
b. Edges	All edges cut.

c. Collation	[A] × 8; B to I × 8; K to U × 8; X to Z × 8; catalogue 8. The illustrations are pasted in, not opposite the pages where the events depicted appear in the text (as noted on each illustration). Instead, in every case except the Frontispiece, they appear between the last and first pages of nearby signatures, as follows: Frontispiece; [A] (facing p 16); D (facing p 64); E (facing p 80); G (facing p 112); H (facing p 128); K (facing p 160); M (facing p 192); N (facing p 208); O (facing p 224); P (facing p 240); Q (facing p 256); R (facing p 272); U (facing p 320); X (facing p 336); Y (facing p 352). Total 208 leaves.

4 NUMBER OF COPIES IN FIRST EDITION AND DATE
14,000; 31 Mar 15.

5 EARLIER PUBLICATION IN MAGAZINE
Serial story in *The Windsor Magazine*, Vols XXXIX and XL, Dec 13 to Nov 14, Nos 228 to 239. Illustrated as First Edition.

6 OTHER EDITIONS OF NOTE
a. Thomas Nelson & Sons published an edition in 1915, in their Nelson's Continental Library series — No 2 in the series. pp 480.
b. First American Edition by Longmans, Green, and Co., New York, 1915. Published under the title *Allan and the Holy Flower*.

F43   The Ivory Child   1916

1 PUBLISHER   Cassell and Co., London.

2 IDENTIFICATION FEATURES

a. Binding	Brown cloth. 123 × 197 mm.
b. Spine	THE / IVORY / CHILD / H. Rider / Haggard / Cassell. [All in gold.]
c. Front Cover	THE / IVORY CHILD / H. Rider Haggard. [All within single line border at all edges. All in blind.]
d. End Papers	Plain white.
e. Preliminaries	Half title — THE IVORY CHILD; verso, list of 50 works by the same author. One page blank; verso, coloured Frontispiece. Title page — THE IVORY CHILD / by / H. Rider Haggard / With Four Illustrations by A.C. Michael / Cassell and Company, Ltd / London, New York, Toronto and Melbourne; verso, First Published 1916. Contents list; verso blank. List of plates; verso blank.
f. Text	pp[1] to 344, with printer's imprint at foot of p 344, together with 'F.135.1115'.
g. Supplements	None.
h. Illustrations	There are 4 full page illustrations including the Frontispiece, all by A.C. Michael. All have blank backs, are unnumbered and are not included in the pagination.
i. Errors	None.
j. Dust Jacket	White paper printed in colour. Across spine and front, a battle scene dominated by a huge elephant. Advertisement on back.

3 TECHNICAL
a. Format   Cr 8vo
b. Edges   All edges cut.
c. Collation   4; B to V × 8; W × 8. (The signatures include J, V and W.) The
                 illustrations have been pasted into the gatherings as follows:
                 Frontispiece; E (facing p 56); N (facing p 200); R (facing p 264). Total
                 180 leaves.

4 NUMBER OF COPIES IN FIRST EDITION AND DATE
13,500; 6 Jan 16.

5 EARLIER PUBLICATION IN MAGAZINE
Serial story in various newspapers, commencing Jan 1915.

6 OTHER EDITIONS OF NOTE
a. First American Edition by Longmans, Green and Co., 1916.

F44   Finished   1917

1 PUBLISHER   Ward, Lock and Co., Ltd., London.

2 IDENTIFICATION FEATURES
a. Binding   Green cloth. 123 × 194 mm.
b. Spine   FINISHED / [decoration — six triangles] / H. Rider / Haggard /
                  Ward. Lock. &. Co. [All in black.]
c. Front Cover FINISHED / [decoration — eight vertical lines in V shape] / H.
                  [device of three vertical dots] Rider / Haggard, [all in panels formed
                  by four horizontal and four vertical lines. All in black.]
d. End Papers   Plain white.
e. Preliminaries p[1] Half title — FINISHED; verso, list of 42 works by the same
                  author. One blank page; verso, Frontispiece. p[3] Title page —
                  FINISHED / by / H. Rider Haggard / Ward, Lock & Co., Limited /
                  London Melbourne and Toronto / 1917; verso blank. p[5] Dedication
                  to Colonel Theodore Roosevelt, dated May, 1917; verso blank. pp 7
                  and 8, Contents list. pp 9 to 11, Introduction, dated 1916 on p 11,
                  verso blank.
f. Text   pp 13 to 320, with printer's imprint at foot of p 320.
g. Supplements None.
h. Illustrations The Frontispiece is the only illustration. It is by A.C. Michael, and is
                  in monochrome, not in colour as stated by Scott.
i. Errors   None.
j. Dust Jacket White paper with Frontispiece reproduced in colour.

3 TECHNICAL
a. Format   Cr 8vo.
b. Edges   All edges cut.
c. Collation   8; B to I × 8; K to U × 8. With Frontispiece, total 161 leaves.

4 NUMBER OF COPIES IN FIRST EDITION AND DATE
15,000; 10 Aug 17.

5 EARLIER PUBLICATION IN MAGAZINE
None.

6 OTHER EDITIONS OF NOTE
a. First American Edition by Longmans, Green, and Co., New York, 1917.

F45 Love Eternal 1918

1 PUBLISHER Cassell and Co., London.

2 IDENTIFICATION FEATURES
a. Binding Blue cloth. 123 × 194 mm.
b. Spine LOVE / ETERNAL / H. Rider / Haggard / Cassell. [All in gold.]
c. Front Cover LOVE ETERNAL / H. Rider Haggard. [All within single line border at all edges. All in blind.]
d. End Papers Plain white.
e. Preliminaries Half title — LOVE ETERNAL; verso, list of 52 works by the same author. One page blank; verso, coloured Frontispiece. Title page — LOVE ETERNAL / by / H. Rider Haggard / [device] / Cassell and Company, Ltd / London, New York, Toronto and Melbourne; verso, First published 1918. Dedication to The Rev. Philip T. Bainbrigge, dated 1st March, 1918.; verso blank. Contents list; verso blank.
f. Text pp[1] to 344, with printer's imprint and 'F125,318' at foot of p 344.
g. Supplements None.
h. Illustrations The Frontispiece is the only illustration. It is in colour, and is the work of A.C. Michael.
i. Errors None.

3 TECHNICAL
a. Format Cr 8vo
b. Edges Top and fore edges cut, bottom edge rough cut.
c. Collation 8; B to V × 8. (The signatures include J and V.) With the Frontispiece, total 177 leaves.

4 NUMBER OF COPIES IN FIRST EDITION AND DATE
12,500; 4 Apr 18.

5 EARLIER PUBLICATION IN MAGAZINE
None.

6 OTHER EDITIONS OF NOTE
a. First American Edition by Longmans, Green, and Co., New York, 1918.

7 NOTE
Scott records a variant binding to the First Edition, viz: blue cloth, with black lettering and a pattern on the front cover similar to a Tudor rose.

F46   Moon of Israel   1918

1 PUBLISHER   John Murray, London.

2 IDENTIFICATION FEATURES

a. Binding   Blue cloth. 123 × 190 mm.

b. Spine   MOON / OF / ISRAEL / . / H. Rider / Haggard / John Murray. [All between a single line at top and bottom. All in black.]

c. Front Cover   MOON OF ISRAEL / . / H. Rider Haggard. [All within an ornamental box of a thick line enclosed in two thin lines. All in black.]

d. End Papers   Plain white.

e. Preliminaries   [For some unexplained reason, the first page appears to be p v. See para 7 below.]
p[v] Half title — MOON OF ISRAEL; verso, list of 53 works by the same author. p[vii] Title page — MOON OF ISRAEL / A Tale of the Exodus / By Sir H. Rider Haggard / Author of / "She," "Jess," "King Solomon's Mines" / Etc / London / John Murray, Albemarle Street, W. / 1918; verso, All rights reserved. pp ix and x, Author's Note with an intended dedication to Sir Gaston Maspero, K.C.M.G. pp xi and xii, Contents list.

f. Text   pp 1 to 328, with printer's imprint at foot of p 328.

g. Supplements   Four leaves, unnumbered and undated, of John Murray advertisements.

h. Illustrations   None.

i. Errors   p 55, line 1. 'ast' should read 'last'.
p 210, line 6. 'I' is missing from the start of the line.

j. Dust Jacket   Cream paper printed in colour. Front — MOON / OF ISRAEL / [a scene of travellers in front of pyramids lit by a full moon in a blue sky. Long-haired girl in foreground, right]. At bottom left — H. Rider / Haggard / Author of / Jess / 7/- net. [All printing in black except price, white in blue circle].

3 TECHNICAL

a. Format   Cr 8vo

b. Edges   All edges cut.

c. Collation   6; 2 to 21 × 8; 22 × 6. Total 172 leaves.

4 NUMBER OF COPIES IN FIRST EDITION AND DATE
10,000; 31 Oct 18.

5 EARLIER PUBLICATION IN MAGAZINE
Serial story in *The Cornhill Magazine*, Vols XLIV and XLV, Jan to Oct 1918, Nos 259 to 268.

6 OTHER EDITIONS OF NOTE
a. The book was reprinted by John Murray in November 1918, with the errors noted above amended, but November misspelt on p[viii].
b. First American Edition by Longmans, Green and Co., New York, 1918.
c. An Esperanto edition, published in 1928.

7 NOTE
a. The page numbering in this and one or two later volumes begins at p v. By strict

counting, the pasted down end paper could be regarded as comprising pp i and ii; the loose front end paper could be pp iii and iv. This peculiar artificiality seems clumsy to me.

F47 When the World Shook 1919

1 PUBLISHER Cassell and Co., London.

2 IDENTIFICATION FEATURES

a. Binding Yellow brown cloth. 122 × 194 mm.

b. Spine WHEN / THE / WORLD / SHOOK / H. Rider / Haggard / Cassell. [All in gold.]

c. Front Cover WHEN THE / WORLD SHOOK / H. Rider Haggard. [All within single line border at all edges. All in blind.]

d. End Papers Plain white.

e. Preliminaries p[i] Half title — WHEN THE WORLD SHOOK; verso, list of 54 works by the same author. p[iii] Title page — WHEN THE WORLD SHOOK / Being an Account of the Great Adventure / of Bastin, Bickley and Arbuthnot / by / H. Rider Haggard / [device] / Cassell and Company, Ltd / London, New York, Toronto and Melbourne; verso, First published 1919. p[v] Dedication to the Earl Curzon of Kedleston, K.G., dated 1918; verso blank. pp[vii] and viii, Contents list.

f. Text pp[1] to 347, with, verso p 347, printer's imprint and 'F140.219'.

g. Supplements None.

h. Illustrations Four charts of the stars are inserted at p 148.

i. Errors None.

j. Dust Jacket [Multi-coloured front showing the adventurers witnessing the release of Oro's powers to end the world.] [At top] When The / World Shook [in a creamy pink] / Being an account of the Great Adventure / of Bastin, Bickley and Arbuthnot [in red] / by H. Rider Haggard [in blue]. [White back with an advertisement for *The King's Widow* by Mrs. Baillie Reynolds.] [White spine] When / The World / Shook / H. Rider / Haggard / 7/- / net / Cassell [all in blue]. [Front flap, advertisement for Cassell's Brilliant Fiction. Back flap blank.]

3 TECHNICAL

a. Format Cr 8vo

b. Edges Top and fore edges cut, bottom edge uncut.

c. Collation 6; B to V × 8; W × 4. (The signatures include J, V and W.) The two leaves of illustrations have been sewn in between gatherings J and K (facing pp 148 and 149.) Total 180 leaves.

4 NUMBER OF COPIES IN FIRST EDITION AND DATE
14,000; 20 Mar 19.

5 EARLIER PUBLICATION IN MAGAZINE
Serial story in *The Quiver*, Vol 54, Nov 1918 to Apr 1919, Nos 1 to 6. Illustrated by A.C. Michael.

6 OTHER EDITIONS OF NOTE
a. First American Edition by Longmans, Green and Co., New York, 1919.

7 NOTES
a. The original title Haggard had in mind for this work was 'The Glittering Lady'. This later became 'Yva', the name of the book's heroine. Both were discarded in favour of the eventual title.
b. Lord Curzon helped to refute charges of plagiarism made against Haggard early in his career, and Haggard wished to dedicate a book to him for this reason.
c. An unknown number of copies of the First Edition were bound in a variant binding of red cloth, with cover details the same as in para 2 above.

F48   The Ancient Allan   1920

1 PUBLISHER   Cassell and Co., London.

2 IDENTIFICATION FEATURES
a. *Binding*   Yellow brown cloth. 122 × 194 mm.
b. *Spine*   THE / ANCIENT / ALLAN / H. Rider / Haggard / Cassell. [All in gold.]
c. *Front Cover*   [Picture of a seal (63 × 31 mm) pasted on] / THE / ANCIENT ALLAN / H. Rider Haggard [All within a single line border at all edges. All except picture in blind.]
d. *End Papers*   Plain white.
e. *Preliminaries*   One leaf blank. Half title — THE ANCIENT ALLAN; verso, list of 54 works by the same author. One page blank; verso, Frontispiece. Title page — THE ANCIENT ALLAN / by / H. Rider Haggard / With Eight Illustrations / Cassell and Company, Ltd / London, New York, Toronto and Melbourne; verso, First published 1920. Contents list; verso blank. List of illustrations; verso picture of The Little White Seal of the King of the East (picture the same as on front cover.)
f. *Text*   pp[1] to 310, with printer's imprint at foot of p 310 and 'F125.120'.
g. *Supplements*   None.
h. *Illustrations*   There are 8 illustrations including the Frontispiece, all by Albert Morrow. The picture of the seal is additional. All the full page illustrations have blank backs, are unnumbered and are not imcluded in the pagination.
i. *Errors*   None.

3 TECHNICAL
a. *Format*   Cr 8vo
b. *Edges*   Top and fore edges cut, bottom edge uncut.
c. *Collation*   [A] × 8; B to T × 8. (Signature J has been included.) The illustrations have been sewn into the gatherings as follows: Frontispiece; G (facing p 96); J (facing p 138); M (facing p 184); O (facing p 220); Q (facing p 256); R (facing p 268); S (facing p 288). Total 168 leaves.

4 NUMBER OF COPIES IN FIRST EDITION AND DATE
12,500; 12 Feb 20.

5 EARLIER PUBLICATION IN MAGAZINE
Serial story in *Cassell's Magazine*, Mar to Oct 1919, Nos 84 to 91. Illustrated by Albert Morrow.

6 OTHER EDITIONS OF NOTE
a. First American Edition by Longmans, Green and Co., New York, 1920.

F49   Smith and the Pharaohs   1920

1 PUBLISHER   J.W. Arrowsmith Ltd, Bristol and London.

2 IDENTIFICATION FEATURES

a. Binding   Light brown cloth. 120 × 188 mm.

b. Spine   SMITH / AND THE / PHARAOHS / H. Rider / Haggard / Arrowsmith / Bristol. [All between line at top and at bottom. All in black.]

c. Front Cover   SMITH AND THE / PHARAOHS / and Other Stories / H. Rider Haggard. [All within a single line border at all edges. All in black.]

d. End Papers   Plain white.

e. Preliminaries   p[1] Half title — SMITH AND THE PHARAOHS / AND OTHER TALES; verso, list of 56 works by the same author. p[3] Title pages — All rights reserved [underlined] / SMITH AND THE / PHARAOHS / AND OTHER TALES / By / H. Rider Haggard / Author of / "She," "Allan Quatermain," "King Solomon's Mines" / "The Wizard," Etc / [publisher's device] / J.W. Arrowsmith Ltd., Quay Street / London / Simpkin, Marshall, Hamilton, Kent & Company Limited / [line] / 1920; verso blank. p[5] Contents list; verso blank.

f. Text   pp 7 to [320], with 'Printing Office of the Publishers' at foot of p[320].

g. Supplements   None.

h. Illustrations   None.

i. Errors   p 48, line 23. 'truck' should read 'struck'.
p 58, line 26. 'Man-kau-ra' should read 'Men-kau-ra'

3 TECHNICAL

a. Format   Cr 8vo

b. Edges   All edges cut.

c. Collation   8; 2 to 20 × 8. Total 160 leaves.

4 NUMBER OF COPIES IN FIRST EDITION AND DATE
3,000; 4 Nov 20.

5 EARLIER PUBLICATION IN MAGAZINE
See 7 below.

6 OTHER EDITIONS OF NOTE
a. First American Edition by Longmans, Green and Co., New York, 1921.

7 NOTES
a. The contents of this book are:
(1) 'Smith and the Pharaohs', pp 7 to 74. This was first published as a serial story in

The Strand Magazine, Vols XLIV and XLV, Dec 1912 to Feb 1913, Nos 264 to 266. Illustrated by Alec Ball.

(2) 'Magepa the Buck', pp 75 to 93. This was first published in *Pears' Christmas Annual,* 1912, pp 1 to 4. It also appeared in *Princess Mary's Gift Book* in 1914 (pp 63 to 74).

(3) 'The Blue Curtains', pp 95 to 137. First published in *The Cornhill Magazine,* Vol VII, 1886, No 39. See also para 8 below.

(4) 'Little Flower', pp 139 to 230. First publication not traced.

(5) 'Only a Dream', pp 231 to 240. This first appeared as 'A Wedding Gift' in *Harry Furniss's Christmas Annual* 1905.

(6) 'Barbara Who Came Back', pp 241 to [320]. First published in *The Pall Mall Magazine,* Vol LI, Mar and Apr 1913, Nos 239 and 240.

b. Scott lists an alternative binding to that described above (2b and c), with decoration to top and foot of spine and to front cover.

8 AN HAGGARD NOTE
a. '. . . My Dear Sir, — Your paper "Bottles" has reached me as London Editor of Harper's . . . A. Lang (extract from letter dated 28 Mar 1885.) . . . What the paper "Bottles" may have been I am not now sure. I think however, that I can identify it with a short tale which subsequently appeared in a magazine, perhaps the Cornhill, under the title of "The Blue Curtains".'

The Days of My Life
Vol I, p 227

F50   She and Allan   1921

1 PUBLISHER   Hutchinson and Co., London.

2 IDENTIFICATION FEATURES
a. Binding   Red cloth. 122 × 190 mm.
b. Spine   SHE / AND / ALLAN / H. Rider / Haggard / Hutchinson. [All between two lines at top and two lines at bottom. All in black.]
c. Front Cover   Double line border at all edges, in blind.
d. End Papers   Plain white.
e. Preliminaries   p[i] Half title — SHE AND ALLAN; verso, list of 57 works by the same author. One page blank; verso, Frontispiece. p[iii] Title page — SHE AND ALLAN / By H. Rider Haggard [device of four dots] / Author of "She," "Ayesha," "The Return of She," / etc., etc. [row of seven devices each of four dots] / [double line] / With Eight Illustrations By / Maurice Greiffenhagen, A.R.A. / [double line] / London: Hutchinson & Co. / Paternoster Row [row of three devices each of four dots]; verso blank. pp[v] and vi, Contents list. p[vii] List of illustrations. pp[viii] to xii, Note by the Late Mr Allan Quatermain.
f. Text   p[13] to 303, with printer's imprint at foot of p 303, verso blank.
g. Supplements   pp[1] to [24] Catalogue of important New Books for the Spring, 1921, and a list of New Novels.
h. Illustrations   There are 8 illustrations including the Frontispiece, all by Maurice Greiffenhagen. All have blank backs, are unnumbered and are not included in the pagination.

i. Errors	As indicated at para 2e above, 'Ayesha' and 'The Return of She' have been printed as if they were separate books. They are, of course, one.

3 TECHNICAL
a. Format	Cr 8vo
b. Edges	All edges cut.
c. Collation	[A] × 8; B to I × 8; K to T × 8; catalogue 12. The illustrations have been sewn into the gatherings as follow: Frontispiece; [A] (facing p 15); D (facing p 53); I (facing p 142); O(2) (facing pp 210 and 219); R (facing p 268); T (facing p 297). Total 172 leaves.

4 NUMBER OF COPIES IN FIRST EDITION AND DATE
8,000; 14 Mar 21.

5 EARLIER PUBLICATION IN MAGAZINE
Serial story in *Hutchinson's Story Magazine*, Vols I and II, Jul 1919 to Mar 1920. Each episode has a note stating that the story has been abbreviated for serial purposes. The serial has the title 'She Meets Allan'. With 17 illustrations by Maurice Greiffenhagen, all but 7 signed.

6 OTHER EDITIONS OF NOTE
a. First American Edition by Longmans, Green and Co., New York, 1921.

F51   The Virgin of the Sun   1922

1 PUBLISHER   Cassell and Co., London.

2 IDENTIFICATION FEATURES
a. Binding	Light brown cloth. 122 × 195 mm.
b. Spine	THE / VIRGIN / OF THE / SUN / H. Rider / Haggard / [decoration] / Cassell [in a box. All between decoration at top and at bottom. All in brown.]
c. Front Cover	THE VIRGIN / OF THE SUN / H. Rider Haggard. [All within decorated border at all edges. All in brown.]
d. End Papers	Plain white.
e. Preliminaries	One leaf blank. Half title — THE VIRGIN OF THE SUN; verso, list of 57 works by the same author. Title page — THE VIRGIN OF / THE SUN / By / H. Rider Haggard / [ornament] / Cassell and Company, Limited / London, New York, Toronto and Melbourne; verso, First published 1922. Dedication to James Stanley Little, Esq, dated Oct. 24, 1921.; verso blank. Contents list; verso blank.
f. Text	pp 1 to 308, with printer's imprint and F. 110.1121 at foot of p 308.
g. Supplements	One leaf blank.
h. Illustrations	None.
i. Errors	None.

3 TECHNICAL
a. Format	Cr 8vo
b. Edges	Top and fore edges cut, bottom edge rough cut.
c. Collation	8; B to T × 8. (J is included in these signatures.) Total 160 leaves.

4 NUMBER OF COPIES IN FIRST EDITION AND DATE
11,000; 26 Jan 22.

5 EARLIER PUBLICATION IN MAGAZINE
None.

6 OTHER EDITIONS OF NOTE
a. First American Edition by Doubleday, Page and Co., New York, 1922.

7 NOTE
The brown printing on spine and front cover has a bluish tinge making it purplish on close examination.

F52   Wisdom's Daughter   1923

1 PUBLISHER   Hutchinson and Co., London.

2 IDENTIFICATION FEATURES

a. Binding   Red cloth. 121 × 195 mm.

b. Spine   WISDOM'S / DAUGHTER / H. Rider / Haggard / Hutchinson. [All between two lines at top and two at foot. All in black.]

c. Front Cover   WISDOM'S DAUGHTER / H. Rider Haggard. [All in black, within double line border at all edges, in blind.]

d. End Papers   Plain white.

e. Preliminaries   p[i] Half title — WISDOM'S DAUGHTER; verso, list of 59 works by the same author. p[iii] Title page — WISDOM'S DAUGHTER / The Life and Love Story of / She-Who-Must-Be-Obeyed [device of four dots] By / H. Rider Haggard Author of / "She," "Ayesha, The Return of She," etc. / [double line] / [device] / [double line] / London. Hutchinson & Co. / [device of four dots] Paternoster Row [device of four dots]; verso blank. p[v] Dedication to Andrew Lang, dated 1923; verso blank. p[vii] Editor's Note; verso blank. pp ix and x, Introductory. p xi Contents list; verso blank.

f. Text   pp 13 to 288, with printer's imprint at foot of p 288.

g. Supplements   40 pp of Hutchinson's Announcements for Spring 1923.

h. Illustrations   None.

i. Errors   p 51, line 6. 'heirophants' should read 'hierophants'.
p 52, line 13 from bottom. 'pourtrays' should read 'portrays'.
p 130, line 15 from bottom. 'alter' should read 'altar'.
p 133, line 13 from bottom. 'captian' should read 'captain'.

j. Dust Jacket   White paper printed in colour. Title at top. Picture of woman on a throne with a supplicating woman before her.

3 TECHNICAL

a. Format   Cr 8vo

b. Edges   Top and fore edge cut, bottom edge uncut.

c. Collation   [A] × 8; B to I × 8; K to S × 8; catalogue 20. Total 164 leaves.

4 NUMBER OF COPIES IN FIRST EDITION AND DATE
11,000; 9 Mar 23.

5 EARLIER PUBLICATION IN MAGAZINE

Serial story in *Hutchinson's Magazine*, Vols VI, VII and VIII, Mar 1922 to Mar 1923, Nos 33 to 45. With 14 illustrations by A.E. Jackson and 2 coloured front covers (Mar and Apr 22.)

6 OTHER EDITIONS OF NOTE

a. Tauchnitz of Leipzig copyright edition, 1923, (No 4602).

b. First American Edition by Doubleday, Page & Co., New York, 1923.

7 NOTE

The magazine serial, illustrated by A.E. Jackson, claims that 'There is more than mere adventure in Sir Rider Haggard's latest story, for there is a deep psychological significance for all who are able to see beneath the surface of things.'

F53   Heu-Heu   1924

1 PUBLISHER	Hutchinson and Co., London.

2 IDENTIFICATION FEATURES

a. Binding	Red cloth. 121 × 193 mm.
b. Spine	HEU-HEU / OR THE / MONSTER / H. Rider / Haggard [all within a box in blind.] / Hutchinson. [All within a black line at top and one at bottom. All lettering in black.]
c. Front Cover	HEU-HEU / OR THE MONSTER / H. Rider Haggard. [All in black, in a box in blind, itself within a single line border at all edges, in blind.]
d. End Papers	Plain white.
e. Preliminaries	pp[1] and [2] blank. p[3] Half title — HEU-HEU / OR / THE MONSTER; verso, list of 60 works by the same author. p[5] Title page — HEU-HEU, or The Monster / By H. Rider Haggard [device of four dots] / [double line] / [device] / London: Hutchinson & Co. / Paternoster Row; verso blank. p[7] Author's Note; verso blank. p[9] Contents list; verso blank.
f. Text	pp 11 to 286, with printer's imprint at foot of p 286.
g. Supplements	One blank leaf, followed by pp[1] to 48, catalogue, partly illustrated, of Hutchinson's New Novels for the Spring 1924.
h. Illustrations	None.
i. Errors	None.
j. Dust Jacket	White paper, printed in colour. The front shows a robed man and girl embracing, with a smoking volcano at rear. Title at top, in volcano's smoke. Author's name and 'How Allan Quatermain sought out beauty in distress amid peril and adventures in a strange land' at bottom. Advertisements for 3*s.* 6*d.* novels on back.

3 TECHNICAL

a. Format	Cr 8vo
b. Edges	All edges cut.
c. Collation	[A] × 8; B to I × 8; K to S × 8; catalogue 24. Total 168 leaves.

4 NUMBER OF COPIES IN FIRST EDITION AND DATE

10,000; 25 Jan 24.

5 EARLIER PUBLICATION IN MAGAZINE
Serial story in *Hutchinson's Magazine*, Vol 10, Jan to Mar 1924, Nos 55 to 57.

6 OTHER EDITIONS OF NOTE
a. Tauchnitz of Leipzig copyright edition 1924, (No 4627).
b. First American Edition by Doubleday, Page and Co., New York, 1924, (4 Apr).

F54   Queen of the Dawn   1925

1 PUBLISHER   Hutchinson and Co., London.

2 IDENTIFICATION FEATURES
a. Binding   Greeny-grey cloth. 120 × 193 mm.
b. Spine   QUEEN / OF THE / DAWN / H. Rider / Haggard / Hutchinson.
[All between one line at top and one at foot. All in black.]
c. Front Cover   QUEEN / OF THE DAWN / H. Rider Haggard [all in a panel with a single line border in blind] / [Two cartouches in a single line box all in a panel with a single line border in blind. (All the above lies within a single line border at all edges, in blind.) Lettering and box with cartouches all in·black.]
d. End Papers   Plain white.
e. Preliminaries   pp[1] and [2] blank. p[3] Half title — QUEEN OF THE DAWN; verso, list of 61 works by the same author. p[5] Title page — QUEEN OF THE DAWN / A Love Tale of Old Egypt [two devices, each of four dots] / By H. Rider Haggard / Author of "Heu-Heu, or The Monster," "Wisdom's / Daughter," etc. [four devices, each of four dots] / [thick and thin line] / [two cartouches with, under the left] "Beautiful ascendress of pyramids." [and, under the right] "Great mistress of the dawn." / London: Hutchinson & Co. / Paternoster Row; verso blank. p[7] Contents list; verso blank.
f. Text   pp[9] to 287, with Printer's imprint (Anchor Press) at foot of p 287, the verso of which is blank.
g. Supplements   pp[1] to 48, Brief notices of new books for the spring, 1925.
h. Illustrations   None.
i. Errors   p 11, line 12. 'sisturm' should read 'sistrum'.

3 TECHNICAL
a. Format   Cr 8vo
b. Edges   Top and fore edges cut, bottom edge rough cut.
c. Collation   [A] × 8; B to I × 8; K to S × 8; catalogue 24. Total 168 leaves.

4 NUMBER OF COPIES IN FIRST EDITION AND DATE
10,000; 8 Apr 25.

5 EARLIER PUBLICATION IN MAGAZINE
None.

6 OTHER EDITIONS OF NOTE
a. Tauchnitz of Leipzig copyright edition, 1925, (No 4686).
b. First American Edition by Doubleday, Page & Company, 1925.

F55   The Treasure of the Lake   1926

1 PUBLISHER   Hutchinson and Co., London.

2 IDENTIFICATION FEATURES

a. Binding   Blue cloth. 120 × 193 mm.

b. Spine   THE / TREASURE / OF / THE LAKE / • / H. Rider / Haggard [all
in a decorated double line box] / Hutchinson. [All between one line at
top and one at bottom. All in black.]

c. Front Cover   THE / TREASURE / OF THE LAKE / • / H. Rider Haggard [all in a
decorated double line box as on spine. All in black. All within a single
line border at all edges, in blind.]

d. End Papers   Plain white.

e. Preliminaries   p[v] Half title — THE TREASURE OF THE LAKE; verso, list of 61
works by the same author. p[vii] Title page — THE TREASURE OF
THE LAKE / By H. Rider Haggard [device of four dots] Author of /
"Wisdom's Daughter," "Queen of the Dawn," etc., etc. / [double
line, thick and thin] / [device] / London: / Hutchinson & Co.
(Publishers), Ltd. / Paternoster Row; verso blank. pp ix to xii, Preface
by Allan Quatermain. p[xiii] Contents list; verso blank.

f. Text   pp 15 to 288, with printer's imprint at foot of p 288.

g. Supplements   pp[1] to 16, brief notices of books of serious interest for the Autumn,
1926.

h. Illustrations   None.

i. Errors   p 57, line 15. 'your' should read 'you'.
p 90, line 3 from bottom. 'lian' should read 'liar'.
p 90, line 2 from bottom. 'car' should read 'can'.

j. Dust Jacket   White paper printed in blue. Upper half of cover pictures a man and
woman embracing, with title and author's name below.

3 TECHNICAL

a. Format   Cr 8vo

b. Edges   All edges cut.

c. Collation   6; B to I × 8; K to S × 8; catalogue 8. Total 150 leaves.

4 NUMBER OF COPIES IN FIRST EDITION AND DATE
7,000; 24 Sep 26.

5 EARLIER PUBLICATION IN MAGAZINE
Serial story in *Hutchinson's Adventure Story Magazine*, Feb to May, 1926.

6 OTHER EDITIONS OF NOTE
a. Tauchnitz of Leipzig copyright edition, 1926, (No 4755).
b. First American Edition by Doubleday, Page and Co., New York, 1926. Issued under
the title *Treasure of the Lake.*

7 NOTES
Scott lists two blank leaves after the catalogue at the end of the book. None of the copies
I have seen have such leaves and I think the one seen by Scott must have been unusual.
Certainly, from the collation, one would not expect any leaves at the end.

F56   Allan and the Ice Gods   1927

1 PUBLISHER   Hutchinson and Co., London.

2 IDENTIFICATION FEATURES

a. Binding   Red cloth. 122 × 195 mm.

b. Spine   ALLAN / AND THE / ICE / GODS / • / H. Rider / Haggard [all in a single line box with indented corners] / Hutchinson. [All within one line at top and one at bottom. All in black.]

c. Front Cover   ALLAN / AND THE / ICE GODS / • / H. Rider Haggard [all in a single line box as on spine. All in black. All within a single line border at all edges, in blind.]

d. End Papers   Plain white.

e. Preliminaries   p[v] Half title — ALLAN AND THE ICE GODS; verso, list of 62 works by the same author. p[vii] Title page — ALLAN / AND THE / ICE-GODS / A Tale of Beginnings / By / H. Rider Haggard / A fire mist and a planet, / A crystal and a shell, / A jelly fish and a Saurian / And caves where the cave men dwell; / Then a sense of law and beauty, / And a face turned from the cold, — / Some call it Evolution, / And others call it God. / William Herbert Carruth. / Hutchinson & Co. (Publishers), Ltd. / Paternoster Row. [All within a three line box with decorated, blunted corners]; verso blank. p ix, Contents list; verso blank.

f. Text   pp 11 to 287, with printer's imprint at foot of p 287.

g. Supplements   None.

h. Illustrations   None.

i. Errors   None.

3 TECHNICAL

a. Format   Cr 8vo

b. Edges   All edges cut.

c. Collation   6; B to I × 8; K to S × 8. Total 142 leaves.

4 NUMBER OF COPIES IN FIRST EDITION AND DATE
6,000; 20 May 27.

5 EARLIER PUBLICATION IN MAGAZINE
None.

6 OTHER EDITIONS OF NOTE
a. Tauchnitz of Leipzig copyright edition 1927 (No 4792).
b. First American Edition by Doubleday, Page and Co., New York, 1927.

7 NOTE
Haggard and Kipling worked together on the plot for this story.

F57   Mary of Marion Isle   1929

1 PUBLISHER   Hutchinson and Co., London.

2 IDENTIFICATION FEATURES

a. Binding   Grey cloth. 122 × 193 mm.

b. Spine   MARY OF / MARION / ISLE / H. Rider / Haggard / Hutchinson.
                     [All between thick and thin line at top and same at bottom. All in
                     black.]

c. Front Cover   MARY OF MARION ISLE / H. Rider Haggard. [All in black, within
                     a single line border at all edges in blind.]

d. End Papers   Plain white.

e. Preliminaries   One leaf blank. p[1] Half title — MARY OF MARION ISLE; verso,
                     list of 65 works by the same author. p[3] Title page — MARY OF
                     MARION / ISLE / by / H. Rider Haggard / Hutchinson & Co.
                     (Publishers) Limited / 34–36 Paternoster Row, London, E.C.; verso,
                     printer's imprint [at foot of page.] p[5] Contents list; verso blank.

f. Text   pp[7] to 286.

g. Supplements   pp[1] to 24, catalogue of Hutchinson's books for the Autumn, 1928.

h. Illustrations   None.

i. Errors   None.

j. Dust Jacket   White, printed in colour. Title (red and black) and author (red) at top.
                     Picture of girl waving at left. Back, list of 7s. 6d. novels. Spine, title
                     and author in black. Front flap, blurb. Rear flap, advertisement for
                     Rafael Sabatini books.

3 TECHNICAL

a. Format   Cr 8vo

b. Edges   All edges cut.

c. Collation   8; B to I × 8; K to S × 8; catalogue 12. Total 156 leaves.

4 NUMBER OF COPIES IN FIRST EDITION AND DATE
8,000; 4 Jan 29.

5 EARLIER PUBLICATION IN MAGAZINE
None.

6 OTHER EDITIONS OF NOTE
a. First American Edition by Doubleday, Doran and Co., New York, 1929, with the title
Marion Isle.

7 NOTE
Not all copies of the First Edition included the catalogue of Hutchinson's books.
Furthermore, not all of the copies printed were bound with covers as described above.
The later binding is also grey cloth, but it has two thin lines in black at top and bottom of
the spine and a double thin black line border at all edges of the front cover. Internally,
this issue is exactly as the first, but the dust jacket has a 49 mm wide red and yellow band
pasted around it saying 'Cheap 3/6d edition'.

F58   Belshazzar   1930

1 PUBLISHER   Stanley Paul & Co., Ltd., London.

2 IDENTIFICATION FEATURES

a. Binding   Light brown (pinkish) cloth. 122 × 192 mm.

b. Spine   BELSHAZZAR / H. Rider / Haggard / Stanley Paul. [All in black. All between two lines (thick and thin) at top and same at bottom, in blind.]

c. Front Cover   BELSHAZZAR / H. Rider Haggard. [All in black. All within a single line border at all edges, in blind.]

d. End Papers   Plain white.

e. Preliminaries   pp[1] and [2] blank. p[3] Half title — BLESHAZZAR; verso, list of 65 works by the same author. p[5] Title page — BELSHAZZAR / by / H. Rider Haggard / Author of / "King Solomon's Mines," "She," etc. / "In that night was Belshazzar the / King of the Chaldeans slain." / [publisher's device] / Stanley Paul & Co. (1928) Ltd. / Paternoster House, London, E.C.4.; verso, printer's imprint. p[7] Dedication to A. Cowan Guthrie, Esq., M.B.; verso blank. p[9] Contents list; verso blank.

f. Text   pp 11 to 285.

g. Supplements   One leaf blank, followed by pp 1 to 32, Stanley Paul & Co. (1928) Ltd. Autumn Announcements for 1930.

h. Illustrations   None.

i. Errors   None.

3 TECHNICAL

a. Format   Cr 8vo

b. Edges   All edges cut.

c. Collation   [A] × 8; B to I × 8; K to S × 8; catalogue 16. Total 160 leaves.

4 NUMBER OF COPIES IN FIRST EDITION AND DATE

2,500; 25 Sep 30.

5 EARLIER PUBLICATION IN MAGAZINE

None.

6 OTHER EDITIONS OF NOTE

a. First American Edition by Doubleday, Doran and Co., New York, 1930.

7 NOTE

This was Haggard's last novel, finished in late 1924 but not published until 1930. Haggard died on 14 May 1925.

2 Principal Works: Non-Fiction (NF)

NF1 Cetywayo and His White Neighbours 1882

1 PUBLISHER Trübner and Co., London.

2 IDENTIFICATION FEATURES
a. Binding Green cloth. 150 × 216 mm.
b. Spine CETYWAYO / AND HIS / WHITE NEIGHBOURS / [line] / H.R. Haggard / Trübner & Co. [All in gold, between three black lines at top and three at bottom.]
c. Front Cover Device of decorated, eight pointed star over a circle, in gold, between three black lines at top and three at bottom.
d. End Papers Brown.
e. Preliminaries One leaf blank. p[i] Half title — CETYWAYO / AND HIS WHITE NEIGHBOURS; verso, printer's imprint — Ballantyne Press / Ballantyne, Hanson and Co. / Edinburgh and London. p[iii] blank; verso, extracts from two speeches. p[v] Title page — CETYWAYO / AND / HIS WHITE NEIGHBOURS; / OR, / REMARKS ON RECENT EVENTS IN ZULULAND, / NATAL, AND THE TRANSVAAL. / by / H. Rider Haggard. / London: Trübner & Co., Ludgate Hill. / 1882 / (All Rights Reserved); verso blank. pp[vii] to xiii, Introduction dated [on p xiii] Windham Club, St. James' Square / June 1882; verso blank. pp[xv] to xix, Contents list; verso, List of Appendixes. p[xxi] CETYWAYO / AND HIS WHITE NEIGHBOURS; verso blank.
f. Text pp[1] to 294, with printer's imprint at foot of p 294.
g. Supplements One leaf blank.
h. Illustrations None.
i. Errors None.

3 TECHNICAL
a. Format Lge Cr 8vo.

b. Edges   All uncut.
c. Collation   4; b × 8; A to I × 8; K to S × 8; T × 4. Total 160 leaves.

4 NUMBER OF COPIES IN FIRST EDITION AND DATE
750; 22 Jun 1882 (750 copies printed Jun 82. 250 bound up in Jun, 27 in Feb, 50 in Mar, 50 in Apr, 150 in Jun/Jul, 100 in Sep, 125 in Dec.)

5 PREVIOUS PUBLICATION IN MAGAZINE
a. 'A Zulu War Dance' in *Gentleman's Magazine*, Jul 1877.
b. 'A Visit to Chief Secocoeni' in *Gentleman's Magazine*, Sep 1877. Both these magazine articles differ in part from the book versions.

6 OTHER EDITIONS OF NOTE
a. Trübner and Co. published a second edition in 1888 (1,000 copies), with an introduction added and two first edition appendixes removed.
b. The third edition appeared in 1889 (500 printed Nov 1889) and the fourth edition, with a new introduction, in 1891 (500 printed in Jul 1891).
c. There were several later editions, e.g. 1893 (500); 1896 (1,000); 1900 (500), etc.
d. In 1899, Kegan Paul, Trench and Trübner re-published part of the work under the title *The Last Boer War*. This has a further introductory passage by Haggard. See NF9.

7 NOTES
The contents of the first edition are:
  Cetywayo and the Zulu Settlement, pp 1–48.
  Natal and Responsible Government, pp 49–69.
  The Transvaal
      Ch I: Its Inhabitants; Laws and Customs, pp 70–87.
      Ch II: Events Preceding the Annexation, pp 88–109.
      Ch III: The Annexation, pp 110–39.
      Ch IV: The Transvaal Under British Rule, pp 140–67.
      Ch V: The Boer Rebellion, pp 168–97.
      Ch VI: The Retrocession of the Transvaal, pp 198–236.
  Appendixes
      I: The Potchefstroom Atrocities.
      II: Pledges Given By Mr. Gladstone's Government As To the Retention of The
          Transvaal.
      III: The Case of Indabezimbi.
      IV: A Boer Advertisement.
      V: 'Transvaal's' Letter to the 'Standard'.
      VI: A Visit to Chief Secocoeni.
      VII: A Zulu War Dance.

8 SOME HAGGARD NOTES
a. 'I accompanied Sir Henry [Bulwer] on a tour he made up-country and there saw a great war dance which was organised in his honour. I mention this because the first thing I wrote for publication was a description of this dance. I think that it appeared in the *Gentleman's Magazine*.'
b. '. . . A letter from Trübner and Co., dated May 18, 1882, informs me that my MS will make a volume of 320 pages "like the enclosed specimen" and "if you will send us a cheque for the sum of £50 sterling we will undertake to produce an edition of 750 copies".'

c. '. . . the book at this time proved a total failure. At this date (1883) an eager public had absorbed 154 copies of the work. Say Messrs Trübner "You will no doubt consider the account a most unsatisfactory one, as we do, seeing that we are out of pocket to the extent of £82−15−5d. Against this we hold the £50 advanced by you, but we fear that we are never likely to recover the balance." As it happened, however, Messrs Trübner did in the end recover their £32. When I became known through other works of a different character the edition sold out.'

The Days of My Life
Vol I, pp 57, 204−8

NF2   A Farmer's Year   1899

1 PUBLISHER   Longmans, Green, and Co., London.

2 IDENTIFICATION FEATURES

a. Binding   Blue cloth. 135 × 199 mm.

b. Spine   [Decoration] / A / FARMER'S / YEAR / [decoration] / H. Rider Haggard / Longmans & Co. [All in gold.]

c. Front Cover   A / FARMER'S / YEAR [all within a surrounding decoration] / H. Rider Haggard. [All in gold.]

d. End Papers   Plain black.

e. Preliminaries   p[i] Half title — A FARMER'S YEAR; verso, list of 22 works by the same author. One page blank; verso, Frontispiece with tissue guard. p[iii] Title page — A FARMER'S YEAR / Being / His Commonplace Book for 1898 / By / H. Rider Haggard / "Who minds to quote / Upon this note / May easily find enough: / What charge and pain, / To little gain, / Doth follow toiling plough. / "Yet farmer may / Thank God and say, / For yearly such good hap, / 'Well fare the plough / That sends enough / To stop so many a gap' " / Thomas Tusser, 1558 / With 2 Maps and 36 Illustrations / by G. Leon Little / Longmans, Green, and Co. / 39 Paternoster Row, London / New York and Bombay / 1899 / All rights reserved; verso blank. p[v] Dedication to Herbert Hartcup, Esq. dated 1899; verso blank. pp[vii] to xii, Author's Note. pp[xiii] to xviii, Contents list. pp[xix] and xx, List of illustrations.

f. Text   pp[1] to 489, including Appendix I (pp[459] to 469), Appendix II (pp 470 and 471) and Index (pp[473] to 489.) The verso of pp 471 and 489 are blank. The printer's imprint (Spottiswoode) appears at the foot of p 489.

g. Supplements   pp[1] to 32, Classified Catalogue of Works in General Literature, dated 50,000 — 9/98 on p 32.

h. Illustrations   There are 36 full page illustrations including the Frontispiece, all in brown monochrome, all by G. Leon Little. All have blank backs and are not included in the pagination.

i. Errors   p 392, line 9. 'Thurston' should read 'Thruston'. (This error is noted on p xx of the work.)

3 TECHNICAL

a. Format   Cr 8vo

b. Edges   All edges cut.

c. Collation   8; a × 2; B to I × 8; K to U × 8; X to Z × 8; AA to HH × 8; II ×
5; catalogue 16. The illustrations have been bound into the signatures
as follows: Frontispiece; B(2) (facing pp 4 and 10); C (facing p 21); D
(facing p 35); E(2) (facing pp 56 and 64); F (facing p 79); H(2) (facing
pp 104 and 110); I (facing p 124); K(2) (facing pp 133 and 140); L
(facing p 150); N (facing p 178); O (facing p 195); P (facing p 221);
Q(2) (facing pp 234 and 238); R (facing p 249); S (facing p 263); T
(facing p 277); U (facing p 302); X(2) (facing pp 307 and 312); Y
(facing p 325); Z (facing p 337); AA (facing p 365); BB(2) (facing
pp 375 and 381); CC (facing p 388); DD(2) (facing pp 401 and 411);
EE (facing p 420); FF (facing p 433); GG(2) (facing pp 453 and 458).
The above totals 37 illustrations, not 36 as stated on the title page. The
extra one is a facsimile engraving (noted above facing p 21), listed in
the List of Illustrations but not executed by Little.
The two maps are not additional leaves but are included in the text.
Total 308 leaves.

4 NUMBER OF COPIES IN FIRST EDITION AND DATE
3,000; 2 Oct 99. (3002 copies printed Sep 99, for sale at 36*s*. each.)

5 EARLIER PUBLICATION IN MAGAZINE
Serial in *Longmans Magazine*, Vols 32, 33 and 34, Nos 191 to 204, 1 Sep 98 to 1 Oct 99.

6 OTHER EDITIONS OF NOTE
a. Longmans published a large paper issue (Cr 4to) on the same date as the Cr 8vo
edition. Bound in light blue paper boards with white ribbed spine marked A /
FARMER'S / YEAR / H. Rider Haggard. Covers blank. Size 190 × 265 mm. The
contents are the same as the Cr 8vo issue, except:
   (1) Three lines of print on the title page are in red.
   (2) One leaf is added at the front to record the copy number.
   (3) The error on p 392 is corrected.
   (4) One leaf is added to the Index (pp 490 and 491).
   (5) End papers are white.
   (6) Higher quality (Bewick) paper is used.
   (7) Top edge is gilt, other edges uncut.
   (8) The illustrations comprise 10 photogravures and 26 half-tone plates.
300 copies were printed Sep 99, but the records are marked 'only 100 for sale'. Later, the
records note that 200 copies were 'wasted'. (It may be of interest that Copy No 17 is held
in the Norfolk Record Office, inscribed in Rider Haggard's hand writing 'Presented to
the Corporation of the City of Norwich by the Author. Ditchingham 9 September 1917.'
and signed. Copy No 100 is in the British Library.)
b. First American Edition by Longmans, Green, and Co., New York, 1899.
c. 3002 were printed for a new Cr 8vo edition Nov 99.
d. Longmans Silver Library included the work in an edition of 1906, with a Preface by
Haggard and a note on p 151. 1336 copies of a previous printing are noted in the records
as being transferred to the Silver Library Dec 05.

7 SOME HAGGARD NOTES
'. . . it came home to me that a great subject lay to my hand, that of the state of English
agriculture and of our rural population . . .'

b. '. . . First I wrote of a book that is called "A Farmer's Year," with the twofold purpose of setting down the struggles of those who were engaged in agriculture during that trying time, and of preserving for the benefit of future generations, if these should care to read them, a record of the circumstances of their lives and of the condition of their industry in England in the year 1898.'

The Days of My Life
Vol II, p 131, 132

NF3   The Last Boer War   1899

1 PUBLISHER   Kegan Paul, Trench, and Trübner, & Co., Ltd., London.

2 IDENTIFICATION FEATURES

a. Binding   Paper back, grey wrappers. 124 × 184 mm.

b. Spine   THE LAST BOER WAR. H. Rider Haggard. [All in black, printed along the length of the spine from bottom to top.]

c. Front Cover   Price One Shilling. / THE LAST BOER WAR [printed in an arc] / [picture of an armed Boer standing on a Union Jack, in grey, brown, blue and red wash] / By / H. Rider Haggard. / Kegan Paul, Trench, Trübner, & Co Ltd. [All lettering in black. Inside blank.] (The rear cover carries advertisements within a double line border, all in black. Inside blank.)

d. End Papers   None.

e. Preliminaries   One page blank except for asterisk at bottom right; verso blank. p[i] Half title — THE LAST BOER WAR; verso, extracts from three speeches. p[iii] Title page — THE LAST BOER WAR / By / H. Rider Haggard / London / Kegan Paul, Trench, Trübner & Co. Ltd / Paternoster House, Charing Cross Road / 1899; verso, list of 24 works by the same author, plus a sentence reserving the rights of translation and reproduction. pp v to xxv, Author's Note dated 9th October 1899 on p xxv and 14th October 1899 on p xx. p[xxvi] blank. pp[xxvii] to xxx, Contents list.

f. Text   pp 1 to 244, including Appendix I, II and III. Printer's imprint at foot of p 244.

g. Supplements   None.

h. Illustrations   None.

i. Errors   None.

j. Dust Jacket   None.

3 TECHNICAL

a. Format   Cr 8vo.

b. Edges   All edges cut.

c. Collation   [a] × 8; b × 8; A to I × 8; K to P × 8; Q × 2. Total 138 leaves.

4 NUMBER OF COPIES IN FIRST EDITION AND DATE
5,000; 20 Oct 99.

5 EARLIER PUBLICATION IN MAGAZINE
None.

6 OTHER EDITIONS OF NOTE

a. Several later editions were published, viz, Second (5,000 printed Oct 99), Third (5,000 printed Nov 99), Fourth (5,000 printed Nov 99); and Fifth, Sixth, Seventh (each 5,000 printed Jan 1900).

b. First American Edition by New Amsterdam Book Company, New York and London (Kegan Paul, Trench, Trübner & Co., Ltd.). Published under the title *A History of the Transvaal.*

7 AN HAGGARD NOTE

'. . . in 1899, at the time of the Boer War, that part of the book (ie. "Cetywayo and His White Neighbours") that deals with the Transvaal was republished at one shilling and sold to the extent of some thirty thousand copies.'

The Days of My Life
Vol I, pp 207, 208

NF4   A Winter Pilgrimage   1901

1 PUBLISHER   Longmans, Green and Co., London.

2 IDENTIFICATION FEATURES

a. Binding	Blue cloth, 141 × 228 mm.
b. Spine	A WINTER / PILGRIMAGE / IN PALESTINE, / ITALY / AND CYPRUS / H. Rider / Haggard / Longmans & Co. [All between two thin and one thick line at top and same at bottom. All in gold.]
c. Front Cover	Single line border in blind.
d. End Papers	Plain white.
e. Preliminaries	Two leaves blank. p[i] Half title — A WINTER PILGRIMAGE; verso, list of 25 works by the same author. One page blank; verso, Frontispiece with tissue guard. p[iii] Title page — A [in red] WINTER PILGRIMAGE / Being an Account of Travels through / Palestine, Italy, and the Island of / Cyprus, accomplished in the Year 1900 [device] / By / H. Rider Haggard [in red] / With Illustrations / Longmans, Green, and Co. [in red] / 39 Paternoster Row, London / New York and Bombay / 1901 / All rights reserved; verso blank. p[v] Dedication to Mr. & Mrs. Hart Bennett, dated 1901; verso blank. p vii, Contents list; p viii, List of illustrations.
f. Text	pp[1] to 355.
g. Supplements	pp[1] to 32, A Classified Catalogue of Works in General Literature, dated 10,000/4/01 on p 32, followed by two blank leaves.
h. Illustrations	31 photographs illustrate the text, 17 of which are full page, the remainder (14) two to a page. They all have blank backs and are not included in the pagination.
i. Errors	None.

3 TECHNICAL

a. Format	Demy 8vo
b. Edges	Top edge gilt, fore and bottom edges uncut.
c. Collation	6; A to I × 8; K to U × 8; X and Y × 8; Z × 2; catalogue 16; 2. The illustrations have been pasted into the gatherings as follows:

Frontispiece; A (facing p 17); B (facing p 20); D (facing p 65); E (facing p 75); F(2) (facing pp 88 and 91); G (facing p 112); I (facing p 139); K (facing p 153); L (facing p 176); M(3) (facing pp 178, 181 and 187); N (facing p 203); O(2) (facing pp 221 and 224); P (facing p 234); Q (facing p 246); R(2) (facing pp 270 and 272); S (facing p 279); T (facing p 292); U (facing p 308). Total 226 leaves.

4 NUMBER OF COPIES IN FIRST EDITION AND DATE
1,500; 7 Oct 01. (1,500 copies printed Jun 01.)

5 EARLIER PUBLICATION IN MAGAZINE
Serial in *The Queen*, Vols CIX, CX and CXI, Jan to Jun 1901 and Jul 1901 to Apr 1902, Nos 2819 to 2844 and Nos 2847 to 2885.

6 OTHER EDITIONS OF NOTE
a. First American Edition by Longmans, Green, and Co., New York, 1901.
b. The Second Impression of the First English Edition was issued in 1902, in the same form as the First, with a four page Silver Library catalogue preceding the General Literature catalogue which is dated 10,000/12/01 on p 32. 500 copies printed Jan 02.
c. Tauchnitz of Leipzig copyright edition, 1902, (Nos 3556−7).

7 NOTE
The two leaves at front and at rear of the book are part of the sheets folded to form the end papers. It is not clear why these extra pages were left to be bound in.

8 SOME HAGGARD NOTES
a. '. . . The Holy Land impressed me enormously,. . . . But of these matters I have written in the "Winter Pilgrimage" . . .'
b. '. . . By the way, this "Winter Pilgrimage" is, I think, unique in one respect: the first half of it was published serially after the last had already appeared. The managers of the *Queen* newspaper, who had agreed to bring out all that portion of the book which dealt with the Holy Land in this form, found the instalments so popular among their readers that they asked to be allowed to print the remainder, which dealt with Italy and Cyprus.'
The Days of My Life
Vol II, p 139.

NF5   Rural England   1902

1 PUBLISHER   Longmans, Green and Co., London.

2 IDENTIFICATION FEATURES
a. Binding   Two volumes. Blue cloth. 140 × 230 mm.
b. Spine   RURAL / ENGLAND / H. Rider / Haggard / Vol. I. [or II.] / Longmans & Co. [All between two lines at top and two at bottom. All in gold.]
c. Front Cover   Blank.
d. End Papers   Plain black.
e. Preliminaries
    Vol I   One leaf blank. p[i] Half title — RURAL ENGLAND / Vol. I.; verso, advertisement for 'A Farmer's Year'. One page blank; verso, Frontispiece with tissue guard. p[iii] Title page — RURAL

ENGLAND / Being an Account of / Agricultural and Social Researches Carried / Out in the Years 1901 & 1902 / By / H. Rider Haggard / 'I will make a man more precious than fine gold; even a man / than the golden wedge of Ophir.' — Isaiah / 'The highways were unoccupied . . . the inhabitants of the / villages ceased.' — Judges / In Two Volumes — Vol. I. / With 13 Maps and 46 Illustrations / From Photographs / Longmans, Green, and Co. / 39 Paternoster Row, London / New York and Bombay / 1902 / All rights reserved; verso blank. p[v] Dedication to Arthur H.D. Cochrane; verso blank. pp[vii] to xix, Introduction dated November 1902; p[xx] blank. p[xxi] Contents list, First Volume; verso blank. pp[xxiii] to xxv, list of illustrations, First Volume. p[xxvi] list of maps.

Vol II   As for Vol. I. up to Title page, except that Title page has 'Vol. II.' and '10 Maps and 29 Illustrations / From Photographs'. Then: p[v] Contents list, Second Volume; verso blank. pp[vii] and viii, list of illustrations, Second Volume. p[ix] list of maps.

f. Text
   Vol I   pp[1] to 584, with printer's imprint (Spottiswoode) at foot of p 584.
   Vol II   pp[1] to 623, including Index pp[577] to 623, with printer's imprint at foot of p 623, the verso of which is blank.

g. Supplements
   Vol I   pp[1] to 40, Longmans Classified Catalogue of Works in General Literature, dated 10,000/11/02 on p 40.
   Vol II   None.

h. Illustrations
   Vol I   46 photographs and 13 county maps.
   Vol II   29 photographs and 10 county maps. All have blank backs and are not included in the pagination.

i. Errors   None.

3 TECHNICAL
a. Format   Dmy 8vo
b. Edges   Top edges cut, fore and bottom edges rough cut.
c. Collation
   Vol I   8; a × 6; B to I × 8; K to U × 8; X to Z × 8; AA to II × 8; KK to OO × 8; PP × 4; catalogue 20. The illustrations and maps have been bound into the signatures as follows:
Illustrations
Frontispiece; B (facing p 8); D (facing p 44); F (facing p 77); G (facing p 93); H (facing p 108); I (facing p 118); L(2) (facing pp 147 and 157); O (facing p 196); Q(2) (facing pp 228 and 234); S (facing p 262); X (facing p 305); Z (facing p 345); AA(2) (facing pp 358 and 362); BB (facing p 372); CC(2) (facing pp 390 and 400); DD (facing p 412); FF (facing p 439); GG(2) (facing pp 461 and 463); HH(2) (facing pp 469 and 473); II (facing p 488); LL (facing p 528); MM(2) (facing pp 536 and 542); NN(2) (facing pp 551 and 559). (18 of the above are full page illustrations, and 28 are two to a page.)
Maps
B (facing p 1); H (facing p 104); K (facing p 137); M (facing p 175); Q

(facing p 225); S (facing p 257); T (facing p 287); Y (facing p 323); CC (facing p 389); DD (facing p 404); EE (facing p 422); FF (facing p 436); KK (facing p 509); Total 371 leaves.

Vol II   3; a × 2; B to I × 8; K to U × 8; X to Z × 8; AA to II × 8; KK to RR × 8. The illustrations and maps have been bound into the signatures as follows:

Illustrations

Frontispiece; B(2) (facing pp 12 and 16); C (facing p 28); D (facing p 42); E (facing p 64); G (facing p 88); I (facing p 124); L(2) (facing pp 146 and 152); N(2) (facing pp 182 and 188); O (facing p 204); Q (facing p 230); R (facing p 246); U (facing p 290); Y (facing p 322); Z (facing p 350); AA (facing p 360); CC (facing p 394); DD(2) (facing pp 405 and 406); GG (facing p 464); II (facing p 496). (19 of the above are full page illustrations, 10 are two to a page.)

Maps

B (facing p 1); G (facing p 95); I (facing p 122); K (facing p 144); R(2) (facing pp 245 and 254); T (facing p 282); U (facing p 300); BB (facing p 381); FF (facing p 448). Total 351 leaves.

4 NUMBER OF COPIES IN FIRST EDITION AND DATE

1500; 28 Nov 02. (1504 copies printed Nov 02, of which 250 were sent to New York. A ledger entry records that New York returned 100 copies in Apr 03.)

5 EARLIER PUBLICATION IN MAGAZINE

Part of this work was published in the *Daily Express* newspaper from 17 Apr to 3 Oct 01, under the title 'Back to the Land'. (The Norfolk Record Office holds copies of these articles, pasted on sheets of paper, annotated in Haggard's handwriting with corrections and additions.) Longmans 'Notes on Books' No CXCI, 29 Nov 02, states: 'Mr Haggard, by arrangement with the Daily Express, published a series of articles which appeared in 1901. The two volumes which are now published represent three or four times the bulk of the original articles, by the addition of matter for which it would have been impossible for a daily journal to fine space.' The *Yorkshire Post* also printed the same articles as in the *Express*, over the same period of time.

6 OTHER EDITIONS OF NOTE

a. A New Edition was produced by Longmans in 1906, for which 1001 copies were printed in Apr 06.

b. The First American Edition was made up of the 250 copies received from London; see para 4 above. They were available in America in Dec 02.

7 NOTES

a. A.H.D. Cochrane was Haggard's old friend from Transvaal days. He accompanied Haggard throughout his *Rural England* travels and recorded in note books the results of Haggard's observations, enquiries and interviews.

b. On 8 May 1903, Haggard delivered an address at a weekly evening meeting of the Royal Institution of Great Britain. His subject was 'Rural England'. The speech is recorded in a pamphlet of pp 15, Large Cr 8vo (177 × 203 mm). See PR7.

c. An article by Haggard appears in the *Windsor Magazine*, Vol XX, Nov 04, pp 643 to 648, entitled 'The Small Farmer in England'. It draws on 'Rural England' material and, by arrangement with Longmans, includes several of the illustrations from the book.

8 SOME HAGGARD NOTES

a. '. . . Of ''Rural England,'' the heaviest labour of all my laborious life, there is really not very much to say. . . . What a toil that was! First there were the long journeys; one of them took eight months without a break, though, happily, that summer was very different from this more disasterous year of cold and floods, 1912. Then there were the articles for the *Daily Express* and *Yorkshire Post*, which must be composed in my spare time, sometimes at midnight, of which I wrote more than fifty.

I do not think I could have completed the task at all without the assistance of my friend Mr. Arthur Cochrane, who took notes while I did the talking, and also helped very much in the preparation of the series of agricultural maps. These maps, I regret to say, it was found impossible to include in the cheaper edition because of the cost of reproducing them.'

b. '. . . the writing of the work itself . . . occupied the best part of another year of most incessant and careful application.'

The Days of My Life
Vol II, pp 140, 141

NF6 A Gardener's Year 1905

1 PUBLISHER Longmans, Green and Co., London.

2 IDENTIFICATION FEATURES

a. Binding	Blue cloth. 142 × 230 mm.
b. Spine	A / GARDENER'S / YEAR / H. Rider / Haggard / Longmans & Co. [All between two thin and one thick line at top and same at bottom. All in gold.]
c. Front Cover	Single line border in blind at all edges.
d. End Papers	Plain white.
e. Preliminaries	Two leaves blank. p[i] blank except for asterisk at bottom right; verso, list of 31 works by the same author. p[iii] Half title A GARDENER'S YEAR; verso, extracts from two works on gardens. One page blank; verso, Frontispiece with tissue guard. p[v] Title page — A GARDENER'S YEAR / By / H. Rider Haggard / With Plan and twenty-five Illustrations / Longmans, Green, and Co. / 39 Paternoster Row, London / New York and Bombay / 1905 / All rights reserved; verso blank. p[vii] Dedication to Mrs. Robert Mann, dated 16th August 1904; verso blank. p ix Contents list; verso blank. pp xi and xii, List of illustrations. One folded leaf of tracing paper with, on verso, a map of a garden.
f. Text	pp[1] to 404 (including Index pp 397 to 404), with printer's imprint at foot of p 404.
g. Supplements	pp[1] to 40, Classified Catalogue of Works in General Literature, dated 10,000/9/04 -A.U.P. on p 40. Then two blank leaves.
h. Illustrations	There are 25 photographs including the Frontispiece, as well as the map already listed above. All the photographs are full page except two which appear together on a page. All have blank backs and are not included in the pagination.
i. Errors	None.

3 TECHNICAL
a. Format   Demy 8vo
b. Edges   Top edge gilt, fore and bottom edges uncut.
c. Collation   8; A to I × 8; K to U × 8; X to Z × 8; 2A and 2B × 8; 2C × 2;
                   catalogue 20; 2. The illustrations have been pasted into the signatures
                   as follows: Frontispiece; map (p[1]); A (facing p 3); B (facing p 32); D
                   (facing p 55); E (facing p 69); G (facing p 105); I (facing p 137); K
                   (facing p 155); L(3) (facing pp 169, 173 and 175); M (facing p 186);
                   N(2) (facing pp 199 and 205); O (facing p 214); P (facing p 232); R
                   (facing p 264); S(2) (facing pp 277 and 289); T (facing p 301); U
                   (facing p 321); Y (facing p 339); Z (facing p 357); 2A (facing p 372).
                   Total 257 leaves.

4 NUMBER OF COPIES IN FIRST EDITION AND DATE
1,500; 13 Jan 05.

5 EARLIER PUBLICATION IN MAGAZINE
Serial in *The Queen*, Vols CXV and CXVI, Jan to Dec 1904, Nos 2976 to 3027.

6 OTHER EDITIONS OF NOTE
a. First American Edition by Longmans, Green, and Co., New York, 1905.

7 AN HAGGARD NOTE
'. . . In the year 1903, which I spent at home, I wrote another work of a rural character,
called "A Gardener's Year". This first appeared in the *Queen*, and was afterwards
brought out in a handsome volume of nearly four hundred pages by Messrs. Longman. It
went through two editions. . . .'

The Days of My Life
Vol II, p 154

NF7   Report on the Salvation Army Colonies 1905

1 PUBLISHER   His Majesty's Stationery Office, London.

2 IDENTIFICATION FEATURES
a. Binding   Wrappers. Blue paper, 199 × 319 mm.
b. Spine   Blank.
c. Front Cover   REPORT / ON THE / SALVATION ARMY COLONIES / In the
                   United States and at / Hadleigh, England, / by / Commissioner
                   H. Rider Haggard. / [double line] / Presented to both Houses of
                   Parliament by Command of His Majesty. / June, 1905. / [double line]
                   / [Royal Coat of Arms] / London: / Printed for His Majesty's
                   Stationery Office, / By Darling & Son, Ltd., 34–40 Bacon Street, E. /
                   [line] / And to be purchased, either directly or through any Bookseller,
                   from / Wyman and Sons, Ltd., Fetter Lane, E.C., / and 32, Abingdon
                   Street, Westminster, S.W.; / or Oliver & Boyd, Edinburgh; / or
                   E. Ponsonby, 116, Grafton Street, Dublin. / [line] / 1905 / Cd.2562.
                   [in square brackets] Price 8½d.
                   (The back cover is printed in the same way. The inside of both covers
                   carry lists of Parliamentary and Official publications.)

d. End Papers	None.
e. Preliminaries	p[i] Title page — (as frqnt cover); verso blank. pp[iii] to vi, Contents list. pp vii to viii, reprints of three letters between the Colonial Office and Rider Haggard.
f. Text	pp[1] to 74, including statistical tables pp 72 to 74. Divided into 38 items dated between 11 Mar 05 and 5 May 05.

3 TECHNICAL

a. Format	Lge Dmy 4to
b. Edges	All edges cut.
c. Collation	Total 41 leaves.

4 NUMBER OF COPIES IN FIRST EDITION AND DATE
2500; Jun 05.

5 EARLIER PUBLICATION IN MAGAZINE
None.

6 OTHER EDITIONS OF NOTE
a. See *The Poor and The Land* (NF8)
b. See also the report of a speech made by Rider Haggard to the Canadian Club, Ottowa, Mar 05, reprinted in *The Days of My Life* (qv), p 261 onwards in Vol II, made during his travels compiling evidence for this report on the Salvation Army Colonies.

NF8　　　The Poor and the Land　　　1905

1 PUBLISHER　　　Longmans, Green, and Co., London.

2 IDENTIFICATION FEATURES

a. Binding	Issued in two bindings. Red cloth. 125 × 196 mm. Also paperback — red paper wrappers.
b. Spine	Cloth — THE / POOR / AND THE / LAND / H. Rider / Haggard / Longmans. [All between two lines at top and two at bottom. All in black.] Paperback — None.
c. Front Cover	Cloth — THE POOR / AND / THE LAND / H. Rider Haggard. [All within a single line border at all edges. All in black.] Paperback — has a reproduction of the title page, with added below the date: Price One Shilling and Sixpence in Paper / and Two Shillings in Cloth.
d. End Papers	Cloth — plain white. Paperback — none.
e. Preliminaries	Cloth — One blank leaf. p[i] Half title — THE POOR AND THE LAND; verso, list of three works by the same author. One page blank; verso, Frontispiece with tissue guard. p[iii] Title page — THE / POOR AND THE LAND / Being a Report on the / Salvation Army Colonies / in the United States and at / Hadleigh, England / with / Scheme of / National Land Settlement / and an Introduction / by / H. Rider Haggard / Author of "Rural England," etc. / With Twelve Illustrations / Longmans, Green, And Co. / 39 Paternoster Row,

London / New York and Bombay / 1905; verso blank. pp v to xxx, Introduction dated 1st July, 1905. pp xxxi to xxxvi, Contents list. p xxxvii, list of illustrations; verso blank. pp xxxix to xli, Colonial Office letters (2) and a Haggard letter, numbered I to III; p xlii blank. Paperback — the same.

f. Text pp 1 to 144, including tables of statistics pp 141 to 144.

g. Supplements pp 145 to 157, Some Press Opinions. The printer's imprint (Aberdeen University Press) appears at foot of p 157, the verso of which is blank, followed by one blank leaf. (Same for both bindings.)

h. Illustrations There are 12 illustrations including the Frontispiece, all from photographs. They all appear two to a page, with blank backs; they are not included in the pagination. (Same for both bindings.)

i. Errors p xxxvii has the final 'i' missing, being printed as xxxvi. (Same for both bindings.)

3 TECHNICAL

a. Format Cr 8vo

b. Edges All edges cut.

c. Collation 8; b × 8; c × 4; d × 2; 1 to 10 × 8. The illustrations have been bound into the signatures as follows: Frontispiece; 3 (facing p 38); 5 (facing p 67); 6 (facing p 83); 7 (facing p 104); 9 (facing p 141). Total 108 leaves. Same for both bindings.

4 NUMBER OF COPIES IN FIRST EDITION AND DATE

5,000; 18 Aug 05. (5,000 copies were printed Aug 05, of which 2997 were used for binding in cloth (2s.); the remainder were sewed (1s. 6d.). 676 copies of the cloth bound edition were sold to New York.)

5 EARLIER PUBLICATION IN MAGAZINE

None.

6 OTHER EDITIONS OF NOTE

a. See *Report on the Salvation Army Colonies* (NF7)

b. The First American Edition was made up of the 676 copies received from London; see para 4 above. They were available in America in Sep 05.

7 NOTES

a. Longmans 'Notes on Books' No CCI, Nov 05, states: 'In February of the present year, on the initiative of the Rhodes Trustees, who contributed a sum of money to meet expenses, Mr Haggard was nominated a Commissioner by the Secretary of State for the Colonies and despatched to the United States for the purpose of inspecting three land settlements which have been established in that country by the charitable and social organisation known as the Salvation Army. Mr Haggard's report appeared as a Blue Book in due course, but he thinks that the general public will be more likely to read it if put in a more convenient form. This is done in the volume now published, which contains, besides the text of the report, an introduction by Mr Haggard.'

NF9   Regeneration   1910

1 PUBLISHER   Longmans, Green & Co., London.

2 IDENTIFICATION FEATURES
a. Binding   Dark red cloth. 132 × 200 mm.
b. Spine   REGENER / ATION / [device of four small squares] / H. Rider /
                    Haggard / Longmans, / Green & Co. [All between design at top and
                    bottom. All in gold.]
c. Front Cover   REGENERATION / H. Rider Haggard. [All in blind.]
d. End Papers   Plain white.
e. Preliminaries p[1] Half title — REGENERATION: verso, list of non-fiction works
                    by same author. One page blank; verso, Frontispiece. p[3] Title page
                    — REGENERATION / Being an Account of the Social / Work of the
                    Salvation Army / in Great Britian / by / H. Rider Haggard /
                    Longmans, Green & Co. / Paternoster Row, London, E.C. / 1910;
                    verso, Dedication to the Officers and Soldiers of the Salvation Army,
                    dated November 1910. [5] Contents list; verso, Author's Note.
f. Text   pp[7] to 234.
g. Supplements   pp[235] and [236], appeals for funds; pp[237] to 256, Appendix A —
                    Notes on the Army's Future, by Bramwell Booth; pp[257] to 259,
                    Appendix B —. The Salvation Army's Articles of War; pp[260] and
                    [261], Appendix C — Balance Sheet for the Year Ending 30 Sep 09;
                    p[262], Figures for Darkest England Scheme; pp[263] and 264, Index,
                    with printer's imprint at foot of p 264.
h. Illustrations Six photographs, including the Frontispiece. They all have blank backs
                    and are not included in the pagination.
i. Errors   None.

3 TECHNICAL
a. Format   Cr 8vo.
b. Edges   All edges cut.
c. Collation   [A] × 8; B to I × 8; K to Q × 8; R × 4. The photographs have been
                    pasted into the gatherings as follows: Frontispiece; C (facing p 48); E
                    (facing p[80]); G (facing p[112]); K (facing p 160); O (facing p[218]).
                    Total 138 leaves.

4 NUMBER OF COPIES IN FIRST EDITION AND DATE
3476 (but see note below); 16 Dec 10. (The records indicate that 3476 copies were printed
in the accounting period Dec 1910 to Jun 1911, and 416 more in 1912. The relative ease
with which copies can still be found makes these figures suspect.)

5 EARLIER PUBLICATION IN MAGAZINE
None.

6 OTHER EDITIONS OF NOTE
First American Edition by Longmans, Green, and Co., New York, 1910.

7 SOME HAGGARD NOTES
a. '. . . Whilst I was engaged upon this Commission (Note: ie. Coast Erosion) I
undertook another piece of work. One day General Booth sent an officer to me to ask if I
would write a report upon the social efforts and institution of the Salvation Army, for

which it would be prepared to pay a fee, to be arranged. I answered that I had no time, and that in any case I would not touch their money. Ultimately, however, I made the time and undertook the task as a labour of love, on the condition that they should pay the out-of-pocket expenses. It took me about three months in all, including the travelling to various cities in England and Scotland. As a result, I published my book "Regeneration", of the copyright of which I made the Army a present. I do not suppose that this has proved a valuable gift, as, to find a large sale, such books must be of the ultra-"sensational" order, which mine was not.'

b. '. . . "Regeneration" was extremely well received by scores of papers, both here and in America; thus I remember *The Times* gave it a leading article.'

The Days of My Life
pp 215, 216, 219

NF10 Rural Denmark 1911

1 PUBLISHER Longmans, Green, and Co., London.

2 IDENTIFICATION FEATURES

a. Binding Blue cloth. 142 × 230 mm.

b. Spine RURAL / DENMARK / H. Rider / Haggard / Longmans & Co. [All in gold.]

c. Front Cover Single line border in blind at all edges.

d. End Papers Plain white.

e. Preliminaries p[i] Half title — RURAL DENMARK / AND ITS LESSONS; verso, list of 8 non-fiction works by the same author. One page blank; verso, Frontispiece with tissue guard. p[iii] Title page — RURAL DENMARK / AND ITS LESSONS / By / H. Rider Haggard / "Get wisdom, get understanding; / Yea, with all thou hast gotten get understanding." / With 28 Illustrations / Longmans, Green and Co. / 39 Paternoster Row, London / New York, Bombay and Calcutta / 1911 / All rights reserved; verso blank. p[v] Dedication to The Farmers of Denmark, dated March 1911; verso blank. pp vii and viii, Authors Note. pp ix and x, Contents list. p xi, List of illustrations; verso blank.

f. Text pp[l] to 335, including Appendixes A to F and Index. Printer's imprint at foot of p 335.

g. Supplements None.

h. Illustrations There are 28 photographs including the Frontispiece. All have blank backs and are not included in the pagination. 4 are full page, the remainder, two to a page.

i. Errors None.

3 TECHNICAL

a. Format Demy 8vo

b. Edges Top edge cut, fore edge uncut, bottom edge rough cut.

c. Collation 6; A to I × 8; K to U × 8; X × 8. The illustrations have been pasted into the gatherings as follows: Frontispiece; A (facing p 17); B (facing p 22); C(2) (facing pp 37 and 40); D (facing p 64); F (facing p 88); G(3) (facing pp 104, 107 and 111); H(2) (facing pp 115 and 120); I(2) (facing pp 131 and 138); K(2) (facing pp 153 and 156). Total 190 leaves.

4 NUMBER OF COPIES IN FIRST EDITION AND DATE
1,500; 6 Apr 11.

5 EARLIER PUBLICATION IN MAGAZINE
Extracts published in *The Times* newspaper Feb to Mar 1911, namely:
- I.   The State of Small Holdings, 22 Feb, p 10.
- II. Eggs and a Dairy, 27 Feb, p 13.
- III. A Great Farm, 6 Mar, p 13.
- IV. Comments on Co-operation, 13 Mar, p 13. 22 Mar, p 7.

6 OTHER EDITIONS OF NOTE
a. First American Edition by Longmans, Green, and Co., New York, 1911.
b. A Silver Library edition, 1912.

NF11   The After-War Settlement and   1916
Employment of Ex-Servicemen

1 PUBLISHER	Saint Catherine Press, London, for the Royal Colonial Institute.

2 IDENTIFICATION FEATURES

a. Binding   Unbound pamphlet sewn in white paper wrappers. Also some bound in blue boards, 137 × 220 mm.

b. Spine   Blank.

c. End Papers   Wrappers — none.
Boards — plain white.

d. Front Cover Wrappers — The After-War Settlement / & Employment of Ex-Service / Men in the Overseas Dominions / Report to the Royal Colonial Institute / by / Sir Rider Haggard / 1916 / Published for the / Royal Colonial Institute / By the Saint Catherine Press / Stamford Street / London, S.E. / Price Sixpence Net. [All in black.] (The front cover is p[1]; verso, Royal Colonial Institute address in single line box.)
Boards — printed exactly as wrappers cover.

e. Preliminaries Wrappers — none.
Boards — the front cover of the wrappers version becomes the title page, p[1].

f. Text   Wrappers and Boards — pp 3 to [68], including Appendixes A to J, pp 41 to [68], with printer's imprint (W.H. Smith, The Arden Press) at foot of p[68]. (In wrappers version, p[68] is the back cover.)

g. Supplements Wrappers and Boards — none.

h. Illustrations Wrappers and Boards — none.

i. Errors   Wrappers and Boards — none.

j. Dust Jacket Wrappers and Boards — none.

3 TECHNICAL

a. Format   Lge Cr 8vo

b. Edges   All edges cut.

c. Collation   No signatures. 34 leaves.

4 NUMBER OF COPIES IN FIRST EDITION AND DATE
There is a record that 5174 in wrappers and 105 in boards were distributed but the
number printed is not clear. Published August 1916.

5 EARLIER PUBLICATION IN MAGAZINE
None.

6 OTHER EDITIONS OF NOTE
None.

7 NOTES
a. This slim volume belies the enormous amount of time and travelling devoted by Rider
Haggard to finding the views of Dominions' officials and preparing the report. He
travelled to and within South Africa (Feb and Mar 16), Australia (Apr and May), New
Zealand (May and Jun) and Canada (Jun and Jul 16), sounding out government views on
allowing British ex-servicemen to settle in the Dominions.

NF12   The Days of My Life   1926

1 PUBLISHER   Longmans, Green, and Co., London.

2 IDENTIFICATION FEATURES
a. Binding   Two volumes. Red cloth. 150 × 240 mm.
b. Spine   THE / DAYS OF / MY LIFE / H. Rider / Haggard / Vol. I [or II.] /
                     Longmans. [All between two lines at top and two at bottom. All in
                     gold.]
c. Front Cover   THE DAYS OF MY LIFE / H. Rider Haggard / Volume I [or II]. [All
                     in blind, within a single line border at all edges in blind.]
d. End Papers   Plain white.
e. Preliminaries
    Vol I   One leaf blank. p[i] Half title — THE DAYS OF MY LIFE; verso
                     blank. One page blank; verso, Frontispiece with tissue guard. p[iii]
                     Title page — THE / DAYS OF MY LIFE / An Autobiography / By /
                     Sir H. Rider Haggard / Author of 'King Solomon's Mines,' 'She,'
                     'Rural England,' Etc. / Edited by / C.J. Longman / With Illustrations
                     / In Two Volumes / Volume I / Longmans, Green and Co. Ltd. / 39
                     Paternoster Row, London, E.C.4 / New York, Toronto / Bombay,
                     Calcutta and Madras / 1926; verso, Made in Great Britain. All rights
                     reserved. p[v], Dedication to Haggard's wife and son, dated Midnight,
                     Whit Sunday, 1912; verso blank. [Stub of Frontispiece]. pp vii to x,
                     Preface, dated July 1926 on p x. pp xi to xiii, Contents list of Vol. I.
                     p[xiv] blank. p xv, list of illustrations in Vol. I.; verso blank. pp xvii
                     to xxv, Introduction, dated August 10, 1911 on p xxv, the verso of
                     which is blank.
    Vol II   Same as Vol I up to verso of title page, except for Volume number
                     changed to Vol II. Then — pp v to vii, Contents list of Vol II. [Stub
                     of Frontispiece appears between pp vi and vii, and verso of p vii is
                     blank]. p ix, List of illustrations in Vol II; verso blank.
f. Text
    Vol I   pp [1] to 294.

Vol II	pp[1] to 286, including Index pp 273 to 286, with printer's imprint at foot of p 286.
g. *Supplements*	One blank leaf, in each volume.
h.. *Illustrations*	
Vol I	There are 11 illustrations including the Frontispiece, all with blank backs. They are not included in the pagination. (Only 9 are listed on pxv because two pages each carry two illustrations.)
Vol II	There are 7 illustrations including the Frontispiece, as listed on p ix. All have blank backs and are not included in the pagination.
i. *Errors*	None.
j. *Dust Jacket*	Cream paper. Spine — THE / DAYS OF / MY LIFE / Sir / Rider Haggard / Volume I [or II] / Longmans. Front — THE / DAYS OF MY LIFE [above a head and shoulders photograph of Haggard, by Histed. Haggard's facsimile signature bottom right]. Back — list of 27 works by Haggard. Front flap — Two Vols / 28/- / net.

3 TECHNICAL

a. *Format*	Med 8vo
b. *Edges*	Top edges cut, fore and bottom edges rough cut.
c. *Collation*	
Vol.I	6; b × 8; B to I × 8; K to T × 8; U × 4. The illustrations have been pasted into the gatherings as follows: Frontispiece; B (facing p 16); C (facing p 33); F (facing p 73); H (facing p 112); N (facing p 193); P (facing p 224); Q (facing p 241); S (facing p 272). Total 171 leaves.
Vol II	6; B to I × 8; K to T × 8. The illustrations have been pasted into the gatherings as follows: Frontispiece; C (facing p 32); E (facing p 65); F (facing p 80); I (facing p 120); K (facing p 144); O (facing p 208). Total 157 leaves.

4 NUMBER OF COPIES IN FIRST EDITION AND DATE
3,000; 7 Oct 26.

5 EARLIER PUBLICATION IN MAGAZINE
Serial (abridged version of book) in *The Strand Magazine*, Vols 71 and 72, Apr to Oct 26, Nos 424 to 430.

6 OTHER EDITIONS OF NOTE
None, but see *A Note on Religion*, (NF13).

7 NOTE
'. . . Henry Rider Haggard was born on June 22, 1856, and died on May 14, 1925. The present work covers the first fifty-six years of his life, commencing with his earliest recollections and ending on September 25, 1912. On that day he wrote to me: "I have just written the last word of 'The Days of My Life', and thankful I am to have done with that book. Whenever I can find time and opportunity I wish to add 'A Note on Religion,' which, when done, if ever, I will send to you." This "note" he sent me on January 24, 1913. By his wish the entire MS. was sealed up and put away in Messrs. Longmans' safe, and was seen no more till after his death, when it was opened by me in the presence of one of his executors.'

From C. J. Longman's Preface to
The Days of My Life, p vii

NF13   A Note on Religion   1927

1 PUBLISHER   Longmans, Green, and Co., Ltd., London.

2 IDENTITICATION FEATURES

a. Binding   Paperback. Dark blue wrappers. 107 × 167 mm.
b. Spine   Blank.
c. Front Cover   A NOTE ON / RELIGION / Sir H. Rider Haggard. [All in black.]
d. End Papers   None.
e. Preliminaries   Half title — A NOTE ON RELIGION ; verso blank. Title page — A
                      NOTE ON / RELIGION / By / H. Rider Haggard / Author of
                      "She," "Allan Quatermain," / "The Days of My Life" etc. /
                      Longmans, Green and Co. Ltd / 39 Paternoster Row, London, E.C.4
                      / New York, Toronto / Bombay, Calcutta and Madras / 1927; verso,
                      printer's imprint (Burleigh). Preface; verso blank .
f. Text   pp[1] to 42.
g. Supplements   None.
h. Illustrations   None.
i. Errors   None.
j. Dust Jacket   None.

3 TECHNICAL

a. Format   Fcap 8vo
b. Edges   All edges cut.
c. Collation   [A] × 8; B and C × 8. Total 24 leaves.

4 NUMBER OF COPIES IN FIRST EDITION AND DATE

2,000; Jul 27. (2018 copies were printed Jun 27, for sale at 1s. each.)

5 NOTE

This is a separately printed and bound version of the chapter with the same title to be
found in Haggard's autobiography *The Days of My Life*, (NF12)

3 Pamphlets and Reports (PR)

PR1   An Heroic Effort   1893

A small pamphlet to advertise and seek support for the work of the Universities' Mission to Central Africa. It reproduces in print a speech made by Rider Haggard on 26 April 1893 at Norwich on behalf of the Mission. The front cover reads:

AN / HEROIC EFFORT / [decoration of shield and native weapons] / H. Rider
Haggard. [All within a double line border. All in black. The lettering is Black Letter.]
Size 79 × 123 mm. Printed on cream paper, pp [1] to [16], the first and last pages being the front and back covers. The text includes three portraits (Dr. Livingstone p [3], Bishop Mackenzie p 5 and Bishop Stoere p 13), decoration of foliage and palm-trees, and is enclosed on each page within a single line border in red. p 15 has at bottom 'H. Rider Haggard. / April 26, 1893'. p 16 has printer's imprint (Butler and Tanner) at foot. The whole is stapled together.

The pamphlet was reprinted in 1901, 04, and 10. It was also reproduced as a leaflet (a fly-sheet folded once), with 'April 26, 1893. H. Rider Haggard' at the foot of the second page.

PR2   Church and State   1895

A 24 page pamphlet, written by Rider Haggard at the request of Edward Benson, Archbishop of Canterbury, in defence of the Established Church of Wales. The front cover reads:

Church and State / New Style. / An Appeal to the Laity. / By / H. Rider Haggard. /
ccc 29.
p[1] (the title page) reads:

Church and State / (New Style). / [line] / An Appeal to the Laity / By / H. Rider
Haggard. / [line] / [beginning of text].
There follows pp 2 to 24 with, on p 24:

H. Rider Haggard. / January, 1895. / [line] / McCorquodale & Co., Limited,
Cardington Street, London, N.W.
Bound in light blue wrappers. Edges cut. Cr 8vo. 124 × 184 mm. Published Mar 95.

'. . . To adopt a convenient metaphor, the tree of this disendowment agitation has
four great roots through which it sucks its strength from the soil of our social and
political system, namely: (1) Greed, (2) Partisan Spleen, (3) Envy, and (4) Religious
Infidelity.
   These are the forces arrayed against the Church, . . .'

AN HAGGARD NOTE
'. . . many years ago I was responsible for a pamphlet called "Church and State", which
I composed in defence of the Established Church of Wales that was then, as now,
threatened with disendowment. This was undertaken at the request of the late Edward
Benson, Archbishop of Canterbury, who wrote to me at some length in August 1894,
giving me the various points on which he thought stress should be laid.'

The Days of My Life
Vol II, p 219

(The Library at Lambeth Palace holds two Haggard letters from the correspondence
described above, but no copy of the pamphlet which is now extremely elusive.)

Parliamentary Electioneering Material   1895

Haggard's first chance of entering Parliament occurred in 1893, when he was asked if he
would contest King's Lynn. He declined, but later regretted it. A couple of years later the
question arose again. By this time he was 'utterly weary of a retired life and of the writing
of books' from which he wanted to escape. He therefore agreed to contest the East
Norfolk constituency for the Conservatives. Two items of his electioneering material were
printed and therefore qualify for inclusion herein. These are:

PR3   East Norfolk Representation   1895

A Broadsheet 572 × 428 mm, headed:
   From the 'Norfolk Weekly Standard and Argus', March 23, 1895. / [line] / EAST
   NORFOLK / REPRESENTATION / [line] / Mr. Rider Haggard the / Unionist and Agri-
   cultural / Candidate / [line] / Meeting at Norwich.
There follows 6 columns of text, covering Haggard's selection as candidate, his speeches
of 16 and 19 Mar, and copies of articles about Haggard taken from various publications.
The imprint at the foot of the sheet reads 'Printed and published at the Office of the
"Norfolk Weekly Standard and Argus," Norwich.'

PR4   Lord Kimberly in Norfolk   1895

A 4 page pamphlet, 127 × 210 mm, comprising pp 3 of text, with imprint at foot of p 3
'Printed and published by the East Norfolk Printing Co., Gt. Yarmouth'.
The pamphlet reproduces Haggard's letter to *The Times*, dated 15 Apr 95, and was issued
on 20 Apr 95.

PR5   Speeches of the Earl of Iddesleigh   1895
and Mr. Rider Haggard

At the annual meeting of the National Society for the Prevention of Cruelty to Children, held in the Mansion House on 14 May 1895 in the presence of the Lord Mayor, Rider Haggard seconded the resolution moved by The Earl of Iddesleigh, 'That this Meeting of the National Society for the Prevention of Cruelty to Children, representing Great Britain and Ireland, having regard alike to the interests of the unhappy children of the country, and to the country's domestic and social welfare, would respectfully impress upon the Magistrates of the land the importance of their supporting the Society's endeavour to enforce upon neglectful parents the discharge of parental duty.'

The speeches were reproduced in the form of a pamphlet, the front page of which reads:

National Society For The Prevention Of / Cruelty To Children. / Incorporated By Royal Charter. / [line] / Patron — The Queen. / [line] / The Society's Supporters. / No. 8. / [line] / Speeches / of / The Earl of Iddesleigh, / and / Mr. Rider Haggard. / London: / Published for the Society by [all in Black Letter] / Kegan Paul, Trench, Trübner & Co., / Paternoster House, Charing Cross Road, W.C. / 1895.

154 × 236 mm. pp[1] (front cover as above) to [12] (back cover). p[2] The Object of the Society, signed Benjamin Waugh, Director, Central Office, 7, Harpur Street, London, W.C. pp[3] to 5, Earl of Iddesleigh's speech. pp 6 to 9 , Rider Haggard's speech. p[10] List of Objects of the Society. p[11] list of speeches. p[12] list of patrons and committee members.

A story told by Haggard in his speech is clearly the basis for his story 'Magepa the Buck', in *Smith and the Pharaohs* (F49).

PR6   A Visit to the Victoria Hospital   1897

A 16 page pamphlet to promote donations to the hospital. 117 × 181 mm. The front cover reads:

A VISIT / TO THE / VICTORIA HOSPITAL / by / H. Rider Haggard. [Printed all in green. Verso, drawing of the hospital in 1897.] pp[1] to 13, text. p 14, list of patrons, officers and an appeal for funds. The last leaf is a detachable subscription form, verso blank. There are 6 illustrations included, counting as one that of two girls on the rear cover, in green, with printer's imprint at foot.

The pamphlet is dated on p 13, 'H. Rider Haggard. / 19th October, 1897'.

NOTE

The hospital referred to in this pamphlet was the Victoria Hospital for Children, Tite Street, Chelsea, London, SW1. In August 1922, the Chairman of the hospital's Committee of Management put his name to a long resume of the history of the hospital which was itself published as a pamphlet — 'Victoria Hospital for Children. An Epitome'. Sir H. Rider Haggard is included in the list of 30 Vice-Presidents. The following extract is taken from p 39:

'. . . Sir H. Rider Haggard, when pleading the cause of the Victoria Hospital for Children in 1897, wrote "It has been a hand to mouth existence, an existence in which Faith, Hope and Charity — especially Charity — have proved the sustaining powers". Those words are no less the same today.'

PR7   Rural England   1903

'Rural England' was the subject of a speech by Rider Haggard at the Royal Institution of
Great Britain on 8 May 1903. It was printed in pamphlet form, apparently before the day
of the speech. The front cover reads:

> (Confidential till delivered on Evening of May 8.) [all underlined] / Royal Institute of
> Great Britain [in Black Letter] [line] / Weekly Evening Meeting, / Friday, May 8, 1903. /
> [blank] in the Chair. / Rural England. [text begins]

Size 177 × 203 mm, Large Cr 8vo, pp 1 (front cover) to 15 (verso blank). Initialled at
end (H.R.H.).

EXTRACT

'The subject (Rural England) upon which I have the honour to address you is so vast . . .
I must confine myself to certain aspects . . . the difficult and debated question of
smallholdings . . . (and) the present position of the agricultural labourer, the very
important matter of rural housing, and the palliatives that I propose for some existing
evils'.

(The Chairman at the Meeting was, in fact, Sir James Crichton Browne, MD, LL.D,
FRS, Treasurer and Vice-President of the Royal Institution.)

PR8   The Housing of Working Classes Acts   1906
Amendment Bill

A Government Committee was set up to consider legislation about housing. The object of
the Bill referred to the Committee was stated to be to facilitate the housing of the
working classes in the rural districts; but it was mainly confined to amending existing
legislation.

Rider Haggard gave evidence before the Committee because of his knowledge of rural
housing matters gained, *inter alia*, during his research before writing *Rural England*.

The results of the Committee's work were published in The Housing of Working
Classes Acts Amendments Bill (Report and Special Report). London 1906. pp cxxiv, 467.
Haggard's evidence appears on pp 107 to 121.

PR9   The Real Wealth of England   1908

A small pamphlet to advertise and seek donations for Dr. Barnardo's Homes. It
reproduces a speech made by Rider Haggard at an At Home held on behalf of Dr.
Barnardo's Homes by Lady Pearson, at Carlton House Terrace, London, on 15 Nov 07.
The front cover reads:

> DR. BARNARDOS . HOMES / National Incorporated Association / Founder: The Late
> Dr. Barnardo / [portrait of Rider Haggard within a circle] / [Photo by Wilkinson,
> Norwich.] / THE REAL WEALTH OF / ENGLAND. / By H. Rider Haggard. / 18 to 26,
> Stepney Causeway, London, E. [All except the last line superimposed upon a decorative
> background. All within a single line border at all edges. All in blank.]

Size 76 × 121 mm. Printed on white paper, pp[1] to 20, the first and last pages being the
front and back covers. The text runs from pp 2 to 20, with the printer's imprint (Ward

Lock) at foot of p 20. The imprint reads 'W.L. & Co., 20,000. – 3/1/08'. The text on each page is printed within a single line border at all edges in black with, at top of left-hand pages, a running title in Black Letter and, at top of right-hand pages, the author's name, also in Black Letter.

The pamphlet was reprinted in 1909, with 'A.20m. 28/4/09' at foot of p 20.

PR10 The Royal Commission   1907 – 1911
on Coast Erosion

In 1906, Rider Haggard wrote to Lloyd George, who was then President of the Board of Trade, to give his views on one method of preventing coast erosion, in the light of a proposed Royal Commission on the whole subject. Lloyd George asked Haggard to come to see him and, subsequently, Haggard was appointed a member of the Commission, of which Mr Ivor Guest (later Lord Ashby St. Ledgers) was Chairman. It became apparent after about a year that the Commission's subject was too superficial and that it needed wider scope. Accordingly, the Chairman and Haggard suggested that the question of afforestation should be added to the terms of reference. The Government pressed for an interim report and this was drafted by Haggard, among others. The Commissioners visited many parts of the coast in Great Britain and Ireland, keeping Haggard extremely busy.

The full title of the Commission and its Terms of Reference were:

Royal Commission Appointed to Enquire Into and to Report on Certain Questions Affecting Coast Erosion and the Reclamation of Tidal Lands (and, added later) Afforestation in the United Kingdom.

To enquire and report:

a. As to the encroachment of the sea in various parts of the coast of the United Kingdom and the damage which has been or is likely to be caused thereby; and what measures are desirable for the prevention of such damage.

b. Whether any further powers should be conferred upon local Authorities and owners of property with a view to the adoption of effective and systematic schemes for the protection of the Coast and the banks of tidal rivers.

c. Whether any alteration of the law is desirable as regards the management and control of the foreshore.

d. Whether further facilities should be given for the reclamation of tidal lands.

e. (Added under a later Warrant dated March 1908) Whether in connection with reclaimed lands or otherwise, it is desirable to make an experiment in afforestation as a means of increasing employment during periods of depression in the labour market, and if so by what authority and under what conditions such experiment should be conducted.

The Commission's reports comprise three volumes, as follows:

Vol. I.	Part I.	First Report. Cd. 3683. 1907.
	Part II.	Minutes of Evidence and Appendices Thereto. Cd. 3684. 1907.
Vol. II.	Part I.	Second Report. Cd. 4460. 1909.
	Part II.	Minutes of Evidence and Appendices Thereto. Cd. 4461. 1909.
Vol. III.	Part I.	Final Report. Cd. 5708. 1911.
	Part II.	Minutes of Evidence and Appendices Thereto. Cd. 5709. 1911.

Each volume in wrappers; each 211 × 333 mm.

PR11   Letters to the Right Honourable   1913 – 1914
Lewis Harcourt

While engaged as a Commissioner with the Dominions Royal Commission (see PR13)
Rider Haggard appears to have had a remit by letter from the Colonial Secretary, Lewis
Harcourt, to report his personal views on the state of affairs in the various Dominions
visited. Haggard's reports were made in a series of letters as follows, and were thereafter
printed for the Colonial Office:

1 AUSTRALIA AND NEW ZEALAND
   Printed confidentially for the use of the Colonial Office. [underlined] / Australian /
   No. 217. / Confidential. [underlined] / Letters / to / The Right Hon. Lewis Harcourt
   / from / Sir Rider Haggard / Relating to his visit to Australia and New Zealand as a
   Member of the Dominions Royal Commission. / [line] / Colonial Office, / August
   1913. pp[1] [front cover] to 22 [back cover]. Wrappers. 207 × 317 mm.
   Letter relating to New Zealand, written aboard SS *Meheno*, on passage from Aukland
   to Sydney, dated 27th March 1913.
   Letter relating to Australia, written aboard SS *Mooltan*, dated at the head 27th May
   1913 and signed, in the Red Sea, 14th June 1913.

2 SOUTHERN AFRICA
   Printed confidentially for the use of the Colonial Office. [underlined] / African
   (South) / No. 1024. / Confidential. [underlined] / Letter / to / The Right Hon. Lewis
   Harcourt / from / Sir Rider Haggard / Relating to his visit to Rhodesia and Zululand. /
   [line] / Colonial Office, / July 1914. pp[1] (front cover) to 18 (back cover). Wrappers. 197
   × 317 mm.
   Letter relating to Rhodesia and Zululand, written aboard SS *Gaika*, signed and dated in
   the Red Sea, 1st June 1914.

3 CANADA
   Haggard anticipated writing a similar report after visiting Canada with the Royal
   Commission, but I have not been able to trace it. Perhaps he found that the war
   altered circumstances so much that such a letter was no longer worthwhile.

EXTRACTS
Letter relating to Australia:
   '. . . To sum up, the assets of Australia are her vast territories, her extraordinary
   fertility, her climate, her insular position . . . and her membership of the British
   Empire which throws over her the cloak of its protection. Her dangers are: a
   population that is quite insignificant when compared with the area that it has to
   occupy: the fact that this small population is largely gathered in cities . . . and thirdly,
   such peril as may lie in the possible ultimate triumph of a selfish and untutored
   democracy, determined to have its share of the good things of this world, by fair
   means or foul, and to respect agreements for so long only as they minister to its aims
   and desires. Etc, etc.'

Letter relating to Southern Africa:
   'Dear Mr. Harcourt,
      With reference to your letter to me of the 29th October 1913, I have now to state
      . . . that at the conclusion of the South African sittings of the Dominions Royal
      Commission I went to Rhodesia. For some days I stayed . . . at Buluwayo. Thence I

journeyed to Salisbury . . . after which I travelled to Victoria to visit the great
Zimbabwe ruins. . . . Returning to Durban, I made a journey of 400 miles through
Zululand. . . . etc, etc.'

(This letter covered particularly the agricultural potential of Rhodesia and the
misfortunes of the Zulus. The letter is revealing once again of Haggard's respect for
and sympathy with the Zulu people and he recommends that white rule should be more
enlightened.)

PR12   A Call to Arms   1914

This is a four page pamphlet, reproducing a speech made by Rider Haggard at a
recruiting meeting at Bungay on 4 September 1914. The front page reads:
    A CALL TO ARMS [underlined] / To the Men of East Anglia [underlined] /
By / H. Rider Haggard / [line] / [followed by the text].
Size 142 × 222 mm (Dmy 8vo.) Text pp 1 to 4, with printer's imprint (Richard Clay) at
foot of p 4.

    The printer's records show that 10,000 copies were printed in Sep 1914, to Haggard's
order, thus: '14 Sep 14. 10,000. Call to Arms. Demy 8vo. Set up as copy herewith & send
two proofs each to Sir Rider Haggard, Ditchingham House and Miss Long, The Grove,
Ditchingham. Print and fold immediately Sir Rider Haggard returns his proofs.'

Extract from The Surrey Herald dated Friday, October 30 1914
    'A Call to Arms. The following spirited Call to Arms by Mr Rider Haggard to the men of
East Anglia is made public here, as recruits are urgently required for the New Army. In a
speech he has just made at a recruiting meeting Sir Rider Haggard asked:-
    WHAT ARE WE FIGHTING FOR?
What is the position? Why is this nation, for the first time for a hundred years, plunged in
a great European war? I will tell you why we are fighting. We are fighting for honour
(cheers). Belgium was about to be wickedly violated and wrecked by a hostile host.
Belgium relied upon us — upon our plighted word. Were we to abandon Belgium? Were
we to abandon France? Never! Etc, etc . . .'

PR13   The Dominions Royal   1912–1917
                 Commission

In January 1912, Rider Haggard was invited to be one of the British Commissioners on
the Royal Commission on the Natural Resources, Trade, and Legislation of Certain
Portions of His Majesty's Dominions, set up by the Imperial Conference of 1911, to visit
the various Dominions and to report upon them. Haggard felt grateful and honoured to
be summoned to this duty and, despite the inevitable personal and family inconvenience it
would involve, he accepted at once. The work required visits by the Commissioners to
Australia, New Zealand, South Africa, Canada and Newfoundland and their findings,
arguments and recommendations were published in a series of HMSO reports between
1912 and 1917. These were:

Reports
    First Interim Report 1912, Cd. 6515.
    Second Interim Report 1914, Cd. 7210.

Third Interim Report 1914, Cd. 7505.
Fourth Interim Report 1915, Cd. 7711.
Fifth Interim Report 1917, Cd. 8457.
Final Report 1917, Cd. 8462.
Minutes of Evidence and Papers Laid Before the Commission
London, 1912 — Migration, Cd. 6516; Natural Resources, Trade and Legislation,
    Cd. 6517.
New Zealand, 1913, Cd. 7170.
Australia, 1913, Part I, Cd. 7171; Part II, Cd. 7172.
London, 1913, Cd. 7173; January 1914, Cd. 7351.
Union of South Africa, 1914, Part I, Cd. 7706; Part II, Cd. 7707.
London, June and July, 1914, Cd. 7710.
Newfoundland, 1914, Cd. 7898.
Maritime Provinces of Canada, 1914, Cd. 7971.
Central and Western Provinces of Canada, 1916, Part I, Cd. 8458; Part II, Cd. 8459.
London, 1914–1917, Cd. 8460.
Miscellaneous
Memorandum and Tables as to the Food and Raw Material Requirements of the
    United Kingdom, 1915, Cd. 8123.
Memorandum and Tables as to the Trade Statistics and Trade of the Self-governing
    Dominions, 1916, Cd. 8156.
Memoranda and Tables as to the Chief Harbours of the British Empire and certain
    Foreign Countries, and as to the Suez and Panama Canals, 1917, Cd. 8416.

These twenty-four volumes were produced in wrappers, each 211 × 333 mm.

The Commissioners signing the report were:
United Kingdom: Lord D'Abernon K.C.M.G., Chairman; Sir H. Rider Haggard
(Norfolk) ; Mr. T. Garnett (Lancashire); Sir A.E. Bateman K.C.M.G. (London); Sir
W. Lorimer (Scotland); Mr. J. Tatlow (Ireland).
Canada: The Rt Hon Sir G.E. Foster K.C.M.G.
New Zealand: Mr. J.R. Sinclair.
Newfoundland: The Hon Sir E.K. Bowring.
Union of South Africa: Sir J.W.S. Langerman.

PR14   The Royal Commission on Public   1912
Records

The Royal Commission on Public Records was appointed to inquire into and report on
the state of the Public Records and Local Records of a Public Nature of England and
Wales. Rider Haggard gave evidence on his own volition, in a written statement on which
he was questioned before the Commissioners at Scotland House, Victoria Embankment,
London, on the Ninth day of their hearings, Thursday 27 July 1911. Haggard said, *inter
alia*;
    '. . . The main point I wish to lay before the Royal Commission is that the State
    Papers generally known, I believe, as the Publications of the Rolls Series, and more
    particularly the Callendars of State Papers, are very expensive to buy and very difficult
    to obtain otherwise.' . . . 'In writing certain tales, notably one named "Fair Margaret"

which deals with the time of Henry VIII and the relations between England and Spain at that period, and another named "The Lady of Blossholme" which is woven round the question of the suppression of the monasteries in the time of Henry VIII, I had occasion to read through all the available State documents of those epochs. Having come to the conclusion from a somewhat extensive perusal of histories that many, if not most of them, are but little to be trusted, since they are only too frequently coloured by the individual views or prejudices of the writer, at times to the point of falsehood, I was anxious to get at the facts for myself.'

Haggard then went on to suggest that the printing of the records he referred to should be subsidized so that they could be sold more cheaply.

The above was published in a Blue Book, *Royal Commission on Public Records, (Minutes of Evidence with Appendices and Index)*, Vol I, Part III. Cd. 6396. 1912. (see pp 101 and 102 for Haggard's evidence.)

PR15　　　The Salvation Army　　　　　　1920

A four page pamphlet carrying an appeal written by Rider Haggard on behalf of the Salvation Army. The front cover reads:

THE SALVATION ARMY / An Appeal / By Sir Rider Haggard, K.B.E. / [line] / [text]. Lge Cr 8vo, 133 × 209 mm. Signed and dated on p 4 'H. Rider Haggard. / 11th January, 1920.'

4 The African Review (AR)

In his autobiography, Haggard states:

'. . . I became co-director of a weekly paper called the "African Review", which some years ago was absorbed by another journal. It was a very good paper of its sort — too good for the market to which it appealed — and run on the most straightforward lines. The end of these activities was that, greatly daring, I entered into a partnership with my fellow-director, who was a financier in the African market. . . . My City labours endured but for nine months, after which time I was delivered. During those tumultuous days I toiled in a fine office in London, where thousands were talked of as of no account. It was the period of the great African boom, and the business machine hummed merrily. . . . But it was all much too speculative and nerve-racking for me, while the burden of those companies weighed upon my mind heavily. At last came a time when my partner, an excellent and very able gentleman in his own way and one for whom I retain the most friendly feelings, announced that he meant to depart to South Africa for a year or so, leaving me to conduct all the extremely intricate affairs with which he was connected. This was too much for me, and then and there I had the presence of mind to strike. . . . . Of course there was some difficulty, as under the deed of partnership I was bound for a period. But, when he saw that I was determined to go, my partner behaved very well and kindly signed a dissolution.'

The Days of My Life
Vol II, pp 110, 111, 119, 120

The African Review of Mining, Finance and Commerce was indeed a high quality weeekly, printed on high grade, thick paper and covering African affairs in great detail. The interior layout was not particularly logical, with the list of contents normally to be found tucked away somewhere in the middle pages.

From Vol III, No 76, Saturday, May 5, 1894, each issue bore at the top of the front cover 'The African Review / Conducted by H. Rider Haggard and W.A. Wills.' The previous issue (No 75, Saturday, April 28, 1894) ran a leading article entitled 'Mr. Rider Haggard Joins the Management of The African Review' and included a photograph of Haggard in it.

The last issue to carry Rider Haggard's name on the front cover was Vol V, No 120, Saturday, March 9, 1895, though the journal carried on for a long time thereafter. It can be assumed that Haggard wrote or had a hand in many of the articles appearing in the journal during his co-directorship. The following have been identified because they are signed with his name or initials.

1894

AR1 3 Feb [Letter] 'South African Independence'. Replying to the question 'Will South Africa Declare Her Independence?'

AR2 5 May [Article] 'The Bride of England', (On Swaziland); p 577.

AR3 26 May [Review] *Federal Britain* by F.P. de Labilliere; p 685.

AR4 9 Jun ' "Elephant Smashing" and Lion Shooting'. A review of *Travels and Adventures in the Congo Free State and Its Big Game Shooting* by Bula N'zau, and *Five Months Sport in Somali Land* by Lord Wolverton; pp 762 and 763.

AR5 23 Jun [Review] *Man Hunting in the Desert* by Captain Alfred E. Haynes, RE; p 842.

AR6 30 Jun [Review] *The Camel — Its Uses and Management* by Major Arthur Glyn Leonard, and *With Edged Tools* by Henry Seton Merriman; pp 877 and 878.

AR7 7 Jul 'South Africa'. A review of *The Story of the Nations* by C.M. Theal; p 10.

AR8 28 Jul [Review] *Sierra Leone After a Hundred Years* by The Right Reverend E.G. Ingham, DD, Bishop of Sierra Leone, and *Tales of a Nomad; or, Sport and Strife* by Charles Montague; p 124.

AR9 8 Sep 'Some Charming Verses'. A review of *Songs from Dreamland* by May Kendall; p 334.

AR10 22 Sep 'A Man's View of Woman'. A review of *Woman: The Predominant Partner* by Sir Edward Sullivan, Bart., p 407.

Two items in 1895 may be by Haggard, though they are unsigned:

AR11 12 Jan 'The Late Sir Theophilus Shepstone', in the *African Statesmen* series, No XLIII.

AR12 19 Jan 'The Late Sir Bartle Frere'. A review of *The Life and Correspondence of Sir Bartle Frere* by John Martineau.

(Haggard knew both these men well and would probably have wished to write on them.)

1896

AR13 19 Sep 'The Death of Majajie'. Haggard denies that Majajie inspired the idea of *She*.

1898

AR14 19 Feb 'The Transvaal Judicial Crisis — A Chat With H. Rider Haggard'; p 271.

It should also be noted that the following Haggard books were published as serial stores in *The African Review*:

Black Heart and White Heart, New Year Number, Jan 1896, pp[1] to 19. Illustrated by Charles Kerr.
The Wizard, Vols 8 and 9, Nos 189–207, 4 Jul–7 Nov 1896. Illustrated by Charles Kerr.

Similarly, several Haggard speeches are printed in issues of the journal from 1894 onwards. These are listed in section 7.

5 Miscellaneous Writings (M)

1877

M1   May   'The Transvaal', *Macmillan's Magazine*, vol 36, pp 71–9.
M2   Jul   'A Zulu War Dance', *The Gentleman's Magazine*, vol 241, no 1759, pp 94–107. (See also NF1)
M3   Sep   'A Visit to Chief Secocoeni', *The Gentleman's Magazine*, vol 241, no 1761, pp 302–18. (See also NF1)

1882

M4   28 Sep   'Under Which King, Beyonian', *The South African*, p 3.
M5   5 Oct   'Recent History of the Transvaal', *The South African*, p 3. Also a review of *Cetewayo and His White Neighbours*, p 5.
M6   12 Oct   'The Restoration of Cetewayo', *The South African*, pp 2 and 3. Note the changed spelling of 'Cetewayo' from the First Edition
M7   19 Oct   'Some Aspects of the Native Question in Natal', *The South African*, p 3.
M8   26 Oct   'Colonists and the Mother Country', *The South African*, p 3.
M9   9 Nov   'The Prospects of Confederation in South Africa', *The South African*, p 5.

1885

M10   'Hunter Quatermain's Story', in *In A Good Cause* (see F11).

1886

M11   Feb   'Long Odds', *Macmillan's Magazine*, vol 53, no 316, pp 289–97. See also F11.
M12   1 Sep   'The Sea Serpent of Marazion', *Over Land and Sea*.
M13   Sep   'The Blue Curtains', *The Cornhill Magazine*, vol 7, New Series, no 39, pp 310–36. (See also F49).

1887

M14	Feb	'About Fiction', *The Contemporary Review*, pp 172–80.
M15	27 May	'Books Which Have Influenced Me', *The British Weekly*, p 53. (Later reprinted in *British Weekly Extras*, no 1).

Haggard says he was more stirred by poetry than by prose.

M16	Jun	'Our Position in Cyprus', *The Contemporary Review*, vol 51, pp 878–86.

An argument against the payment of tribute by Britain to Turkey in respect of Cyprus, which had come under British jurisdiction in 1878.

M17	Oct–Dec	'A Tale of Three Lions', *Atalanta Mazagine*, vol 1, nos 1–3. (See also F11).
M18	Nov	'On Going Back', *Longmans Magazine*, vol 11, no 61, pp 61–6.

Haggard revisits Garsington village, Oxford, though the name of the village is not revealed. See also F6.

M19	Nov	'An Olive Branch From America', *The Nineteenth Century*, no 6, pp 601–24.

Concerning the vexed question of copyright in America.

1888

M20	Mar	'Suggested Prologue to a Dramatised Version of *She*', *Longmans Magazine*, vol 11, no 65, pp 492–7. (See F4 for details).
M21	18 Aug	'The Wreck of the *Copeland*', *Illustrated London News*, vol 93, no 2574, pp 194–5, with two illustrations.

An account of a real shipwreck endured by Haggard (see F14). It was republished in America by George Munro, New York, in his Seaside Library Pocket Edition. The title of this issue was 'My Fellow Laborer', another Haggard item previously printed in Collier's magazine *Once a Week*, but not published in England. See Appendix 1, under George Munro.

1889

M22	Dec	'About Fishing in Iceland', *Remington's Annual*.

1890

M23	Jan	'The Fate of Swaziland', *The New Review*, vol 2, no 8, pp 64–75.
M24	May	'In Memoriam', preface to *Life and Its Author, An Essay in Verse* by Rider Haggard's mother, Ella.

The preface is dated 5 Feb 90. The work was printed and published in May 1890 in an edition of 500 copies.

M25	29 Nov	'Golf For Duffers', *The Graphic*, p 610.

1893

M26	Mar	'My First Book — *Dawn*', *The Idler*, pp 279–91

This article, with similar articles by other authors, was republished in a collection, published as *My First Book* in 1894, edited by Jerome K. Jerome.

M27   8 Jul   'Sompesu', *South Africa*, pp 76–7.
                A memorial to Sir Theophilus Shepstone, who died 23 June 1893.
                Preceded by a leading article 'Mr Rider Haggard's Tribute', p. 74.

M28   Oct   'The Tale of Isandhlwana and Rorkes Drift', in *The True Story
                Book*, edited by Andrew Lang.

M29   23 Oct   'The Matabele', *The Pall Mall Gazette*, pp 1 and 2.

M30   26 Oct   'The War in South Africa — The Matabele', *The Pall Mall Budget*,
                pp 1676–8.
                This is another printing of M29, with one paragraph omitted.

1894

M31   4 Aug   'Should There Be An Examination For M.P.'s?', *Pearson's
                Weekly*, p 45.
                Haggard one of several contributors.

M32   Aug   'The Patterson Embassy to Lobengula', in *The Downfall of
                Lobengula: The Cause, History and Effects of the Matabele War*,
                by W.A. Wills and L.T. Collingbridge.

M33   Oct   Introduction to *A Strange Career — Life and Adventures of John
                Gladwyn Jebb*, by his widow.
                The introduction is dated 21 Aug 94, Jebb having died on 18 Aug
                1894. See also F16.

1895

M34   Apr   'The Canadian Copyright Act', *The Contemporary Review*, vol 67,
                p 482. Hall Caine and contributors.
                One of a series of remarks by various authors, concerning
                copyright in Canada.

M35   Oct   'Wilson's Last Fight', in *The Red True Story Book*, edited by
                Andrew Land, pp 1–18.
                Describes the death of Major Wilson and his patrol, 4 Dec 1893.

1896

M36   Preface to *In Monomopata*, by The Hon. A. Wilmot.
                The preface is dated 1 May 1896.

1897

M37   Apr   'The Output of Authors. Some Interesting Confessions of Popular
                Authors', *Pearson's Magazine*, p 459.

M38   24 Apr   'In the Transvaal of 1877', *The Golden Penny*, pp 396–7 and
       and 1 May 420–1. With two illustrations.

1898

M39   2 Feb–   'Elissa; or, The Doom of Zimbabwe', *The Long Bow*, vols 1 and 2,
       8 Jun   nos 1–19. (See also F23).

M40   Jun   'Sunday Newspapers', *Daily Mail*.

M41   10 Jun   'Sick and Dying Soldiers — Plea for Convalescent Homes',
                Morning Post, p 5.

1899

M42 'Good Luck to Gardening and the Gardeners', in *One and All Gardening Annual 1899*. (See also NF6 where this item is reproduced.)

M43 'The Ghost'.

At Christmas 1899, the author Stephen Crane, then living at Brede Place, Brede, East Sussex, gave a house party. As part of the festivities, Crane prepared a play (a comedy) entitled 'The Ghost', to be enacted by his guests as a village entertainment. He induced a number of famous authors, including Rider Haggard, not only to contribute to the content of the play but also to have their names printed in the programme under 'Written by'. The respective contributions are not recorded but they may have been as little as one word ('it', 'they', 'you'). The play was performed in Brede School House on the evening of 28 Dec 1899 and was reported in the *Sussex Express, Surrey Standard & Kent Mail*, 5 Jan 1900.

See the *Bulletin of the New York Public Library*, vol 56, no 12, Dec 1952: ' "The Ghost" at Brede Place', by J.D. Gordon. (BA287)

1900

M44 Dec 'An Incident in African History', *Windsor Magazine*, pp 112–19. With seven photographs and one drawing by R. Caton Woodville.

Haggard describes his early days with the Pretoria Horse.

1902

M45 Dec 'Lost on the Veld', *Windsor Magazine*, pp 185–94, with four illustrations by G. Montbard. Reprinted from *Youth's Companion*, New York 25 Sep 1902.

1904

M46 23 Apr 'Egypt Today. The Land of Cleopatra. I. Port Said and Cairo', *Daily Mail*.

M47 30 Apr 'Egypt Today. The Land of Cleopatra. II. England in Egypt', *Daily Mail*.

M48 7 May 'Egypt Today. The Land of Cleopatra. III. A Sudanese Object Lesson', *Daily Mail*.

M49 21 May 'The Giant Dam. A Miracle in the Land of the Pharoah' (*sic*), *Daily Mail*.

M50 4 Jun 'The Debris of Majesty. Plundering the Graves of Kings', *Daily Mail*.

M51 22 Jul 'The Trade in the Dead', *Daily Mail*.

M52 Oct 'Case L. 1139. Dream', *Journal of the Society for Psychical Research*; and *The Times*, 21 Jul.

'On the night of Saturday, July 9, I went to bed about 12.30, and suffered what I took to be a nightmare . . . etc, etc.' Haggard dreamed that his dog was dying and it transpired that the animal had in fact been killed.

M53	Nov	'Have We Lived on Earth Before? Shall We live on Earth Again?', *The London Magazine*, pp 403–6.

One of a series of articles on the subject, by various authors.

| M54 | Nov | Introduction to *The King's Homeland, Sandringham and North-West Norfolk*, by W.A. Dutt. |

Haggard's introduction is dated 1 Sep 04.

| M55 | Nov | 'The Small Farmer in England', *The Windsor Magazine*, vol 20, pp 643–8. (See also NF5). |

| M56 | 11 Mar | 'Orchid Hunting in America', *The Saturday Review*, p 316. |

A review of *Bog-Trotting for Orchids*, by Grace Greylock Niles. Unsigned.

| M57 | 22 Apr | 'A South African Worthy', *The Saturday Review*, p 530. |

A review of *The Life and Times of Sir Richard Southey, K.C.M.G.*, by The Hon. Alexander Wilmot. Unsigned.

| M58 | | 'A Soldier and a Gentleman', in *The Bravest Deed I Ever Saw*, edited by Alfred H. Miles. |

A short extract from *Cetywayo and His White Neighbours* (pp 147 and 148 of the First Edition, see NF1) sandwiched into a chapter dealing mainly with Cecil Rhodes.

| M59 | Oct | Introduction to *Garden City and Agriculture, How to Solve the Problem of Rural Depopulation*, by Thomas Adams. |

| M60 | 21 Dec | 'A Millionaire's Gift', *The Standard*, p 7. |

Concerning a gift to the Salvation Army in Birmingham.

| M61 | Dec | 'A Wedding Gift', in *Harry Furniss' Christmas Annual*, pp 63–9. Illustrated by Harry Furniss. See also F49. |

1906

| M62 | 5 May | 'An English Garden', *Black and White*, p 614. |
| M63 | 19 May | 'Mr. Rider Haggard on the Zulus. The Story of a Rebellious People', *The Illustrated London News*, pp 710–12. |

| M64 | 2 Jun | 'Wiser Than Solomon', *The Saturday Review*, pp 693–4. |

A review of *Mediaeval Rhodesia*, by David Randall Maciver.

| M65 | Jun | 'Thebes of a Hundred Gates', *Pall Mall Magazine*, pp 688–96. With 10 photographs. |

| M66 | 3 Aug | 'Land Reform', *The Times Literary Supplement*, p 270. |

A review of *Land Reform*, by The Rt. Hon Jesse Collings, MP.

| M67 | 1 Sep | 'Vanishing East Anglia', *The Saturday Review*, pp 263–4. |

A review of *Wild Life in East Anglia*, by W.A. Dutt.

| M68 | 27 Oct | 'The Poison of Dr. Leyds and the Antidote of Mr. Rider Haggard', *South Africa*, pp 246–9. |

A review of *The First Annexation of the Transvaal*, by Dr. W.J. Leyds.

'Mr Haggard Indignantly Exposes the Wickedness of Charges Against His Former Chief, Sir Theophilus Shepstone.'

1907

| M69 | Jan | 'The Book of 1906 Which Has Interested Me Most', *The Bookman*, p 162. |

M70	2 Mar	'The Careless Children', *The Saturday Review*, pp 265–6.
		A review of *Savage Childhood*, by Dudley Kidd. Signed.
M71	18 May	'The Mysteries of the Black Man's Mind', *The Saturday Review*, pp 622–3.
		A review of *At the Back of the Black Man's Mind*, by R.E. Dennett. Unsigned.
M72	15 June	'Smallholdings', *The Country Gentleman*.
M73	15 Jun	'Miss Jebb on Smallholdings', *Country Life*, pp xlviii and 1.
		A review of *Small Holdings of England*, by L. Jebb.
M74	Jul Summer Number	'The Real *King Solomon's Mines*', *Cassell's Magazine*, pp 144–51 With six illustrations by W. Russell Flint.
M75	Aug	'Pearson's Fresh Air Fund — Some Appreciations', *Pearson's Magazine*, vol 24, no 140, p 180.
M76	14 Sep	'The English Peasantry', *The Blackburn Times*, p 3.
M77	7 Dec	'Jock of the Bushveld', *The Saturday Review*, p iv.
		A review of *Jock of the Bushveld*, by Sir Percy Fitzpatrick. Unsigned.

1908

M78	Jun	'The Zulus: The Finest Savage Race in the World', *The Pall Mall Magazine*, pp 764–70.
M79	Sep	'A Few Prefaratory Remarks' to *The Case for the Goat*, by 'Home Counties' (J.W. Robertson-Scott).
M80	Nov	'Authors At Work. The Disadvantages of Working in London and Out Of It', *The Bookman*, p 86.

1909

M81	16 Sep	'The Culbin Sands', *Pearson's Weekly*, p 246.

1910

M82	Jan	'The Romance of the Ancient Nile', *The Windsor Magazine*, pp 259–66.
M83	15 Dec	'A Remarkable Service', *The Christian*, p 24.

1911

M84	18 Jan	'Sex and the Short Story', *The Bystander*, p 113.
		'In my opinion, it is not at all necessary that a short story should contain a sex interest . . .'
M85	5 Apr	'Novelist on Wheat', *The Daily Mirror*.
M86	20 Oct	'Crematorium for Books', *The Daily Express*, p 5.
		Impossible to limit the output of books.

1912

M87	11 Oct	'An Egyptian Date Farm. The Financial Aspect', *The Times*, p 5.
M88	Dec	'Magepa the Buck', *Pears Christmas Annual*, pp 1–4.
		See also F49.

1913

| M89 | Mar and April | 'Barbara Who Came Back', *Pall Mall Magazine*, vol 51, nos 239–240. |
| | | See also F49. |

1914

| M90 | Dec | 'The Desolation of Belgium', in *King Albert's Book*, produced by *The Daily Telegraph* in conjunction with *The Glasgow Herald* and Hodder and Stoughton. |
| | | 'The desolation of Belgium is perhaps the most appalling world-crime since the wrecking of the Netherlands by Alva. etc. etc.' |

1915

| M91 | 15 Mar | 'On the Land. Old Problems and New Ways', *The Times*, p 3. |
| M92 | 27 Nov | 'The Solace of Books. Sir Rider Haggard's Message to "The Independent" ', *The Sheffield Independent* , p 4. |

1916

| M93 | 16 Sep and 16 Dec | 'Empire Land Settlement', *United Empire* (the Royal Colonial Institute journal — supplement, pp 616–21, 784–91. |
| M94 | Dec | 'A Journey Through Zululand', *The Windsor Magazine*, pp 85–90. |

1918

| M95 | 3 Aug | 'Pelmanism', *The Sphere*, p iii. |

1919

| M96 | Dec | 'The Hill of Death', *The Windsor Magazine*, pp 53–60. |
| | | Concerning the murder of Piet Retief and his party in 1838, and Haggard's visit to Dingaan's kraal in 1914. With seven photographs. |

1920

M97		Introduction to the *Norfolk Roll of Honour, 1914–18*.
		The Introduction is dated Christmas Day 1919.
M98	Sep	'Imperial and Racial Aspects', in *The Control of Parenthood*, edited by Sir James Marchant.

1921

M99	17 Jan	'The Boy Scouts Association. What it is', *The Daily Telegraph* and other newspapers.
M100	23 Dec	'England's Suffering Childhood. "We Must Save the Children" ', *The Church Family Newspaper*, p 13.
		An appeal on behalf of sick and crippled children.

1922

M101   15 Aug   'My Favourite Holiday', *The Daily Despatch*, p 6.

1923

M102   23 Feb   'Let Tutankhamen Rest in His Tomb', *The Daily Chronicle*, p 7.

1924

M103   Contribution to *The British Legion Album*, compiled by E. Lonsdale Deighton in aid of Field Marshal Earl Haig's appeal for ex-servicemen.
An extract from Chapter 24 of *Ayesha* (see F28).

6 Letters to Newspapers and Periodicals (L)

1882

L1	13 Mar	'The Peace of South Africa', *Standard*, p 3.
L2	23 Mar	'Our Policy in South Africa', *Standard*, p 2.
L3	10 Apr	'Cetewayo', *Standard*, p 6.
L4	11 Apr	'Should We Abandon South Africa?', *St. James's Gazette*.
L5	30 Apr	'The News From Natal', *Standard*.
L6	24 Jun	'Conditions in Zululand', *Standard*.
L7	2 Aug	'The Future in Zululand', *Standard*.
L8	18 Aug	'The Restoration of Cetewayo', *Standard*.
L9	6 Nov	'The News From Transvaal', *Standard*.

1883

L10	12 Mar	'The Transvaal', *Standard*.

1885

L11	3 Nov	'Hydrophobia', *The Times*, p 10.

1886

L12	28 Apr	'The Land Question', *The Times*, p 4.
L13	10 Jul	'Fact and Fiction', *Athenaeum*, p 50.

1887

L14	22 Jan	'She', *Spectator*, pp 110–11.
L15	27 Apr	'Mr. Rider Haggard and His Critics', *The Times*, p 6.
L16	25 Sep	'Repudiating authorship of *Me*', *New York Times*, p 1. See F4, note 7d.
L17	11 Oct	'American Copyright', *The Times*, p 7.

| L18 | 17 Dec | 'Delagoa Bay Railway', *The Times*, p 8. |
| L19 | 27 Dec | 'Delagoa Bay Railway', *The Times*, p 6. |

1889

L20	25 Oct	'Hydrophobia and Muzzling', *The Times*, p 3.
L21	25 Dec	'The Mummy at St. Mary Woolmoth's', *The Times*, p 7.
L22	27 Dec	'Mummies', *The Times*, p 4.

1890

L23	5 Jun	'American Copyright', *The Times*, p 8.
		On the American pirated edition of *Beatrice*, see F12.
L24	10 Nov	'Mr. Herbert Ward and Mr. Stanley', *The Times*, p 10.
		On Stanley's Rear Column.

1892

| L25 | 19 Dec | 'A New Argument Against Cremation', *The Times*, p 12. |

1893

L26	12 Oct	'Lobengula', *The Times*, p 6.
L27	19 Oct	'Lobengula', *The Times*, p 10.
L28	6 Nov	'The New Sentiment', *The Times*, p 8.
L29	25 Dec	'Wanted — Imagination', *The Times*, p 5.
L30	28 Dec	'The Fate of Captain Patterson's Party', *The Times*, p 6.

1894

L31	17 Jan	'Mr. Rider Haggard and the Immuring of Nuns', *Pall Mall Gazette*, pp 1–2.
		Previous letters also copied.
L32	31 Jan	'The Immuring of Nuns', *Pall Mall Gazette*, p 11.
L33	19 Apr	'The Immuring of Nuns', *Pall Mall Gazette*, p 3.
L34	27 Jul	'The Three-Volume Novel', *The Times*, p ll.
L35	30 Oct	'The Adventures of John Gladwyn Jebb', *The Times*, p 10.

1895

L36	2 Jan	'Agriculture in Norfolk', *The Times*, p 3.
L37	8 Jan	'Agriculture in Norfolk', *The Times*, p 14.
L38	25 Jan	'Agriculture in Norfolk', *The Times*, p 15.
L39	16 Feb	'The Nelson Bazaar', *The Times*, p 17.
L40	20 Mar	'Everything Peaceful', *The Times*, p 11.
L41	25 Mar	'Mr. Rider Haggard and Protection', *Westminster Gazette*, p 3.
L42	17 Apr	'Lord Kimberley in Norfolk', *The Times*, p 8.
L43	25 May	'The East Norfolk Election', *Eastern Evening News*.
L44	1 Jun	'Mr. Rider Haggard and Local Veto', *Yarmouth Gazette*, p 8.
		On drink.
L45	11 Jun	'Explanation by Mr. Rider Haggard', *Eastern Evening News*.

L46	20 Jul	'Mr. Rider Haggard's Speech at Horsford, July 12, 1895', *Norfolk Gazette*.
L47	23 Jul	'The East Norfolk Election', *The Times*, p 8.
L48	29 Jul	'The East Norfolk Election', *The Times*, p 7.

1896

L49	2 Jan	'The Transvaal Crisis', *The Times*, p 4.
L50	13 Jan	'The Transvaal Crisis', *The Times*, p 11.
L51	14 Mar	'Jameson's Surrender', *The Times*, p 10.
L52	5 Nov	'Rinderpest in South Africa', *The Times*, p 11.

1898

L53	6 Sep	'A Transvaal "Myth" ', *Westminster Gazette*, p 2.
L54	14 Sep	'Mr. Rider Haggard and Agriculture', *North British Agriculturist*, p 583.
L55	7 Dec	'The Labourer Leaving the Land', *Eastern Daily Express*.
L56	8 Dec	'The Labourer Leaving the Land', *Eastern Daily Express*.
L57	10 Dec	'Dr. Therne', *Spectator*, p 867.
		Haggard answers criticism (see BA98) that vaccination is not a subject suitable for fiction writers.

1899

L58	6 Jan	'The Scarcity of Woodcocks', *Globe*, p 6.
L59	9 Jan	'Mr. Rider Haggard and Dr. Neufeld', *The Times*, p 12.
L60	16 Feb	'Lenten Lore', *Globe*, p 6.
L61	22 Feb	'Mr. Rider Haggard on Vaccination', *East Anglian Daily Times*, p 7.
L62	13 May	'Mr. Haggard and the Labourer', *Westminster Gazette*, p 3.
L63	1 Jul	'The South African Crisis — An Appeal', *The Times*, p 16.
L64	8 Sep	'Commandant-General Joubert and Mr. H. Rider Haggard', *The Times*, p 8.
L65	6 Oct	'A Contradiction', *East Anglian Daily Times*, p 7.
L66	25 Oct	'The War', *The Times*, p 7.
L67	22 Dec	'Farming in 1900', *The Times*, p 13.

1900

L68	1 Jan	'Farming in 1899', *The Times*, p 3.
L69	5 May	'Settlement of Soldiers in South Africa', *The Times*, p 15.
L70	3 Sep	'Mr. Rider Haggard on Town and Country', *East Anglian Daily Times*, p 5.
L71	2 Oct	'1881 and 1900', *The Times*, p 12.

1901

L72	1 Jan	'Farming in 1900', *The Times*, p 13.
L73	22 Jun	'The Flight of the Ploughman', *Spectator*, p 917.
		Intention to publish *Rural England* (see NF5).

| L74 | 8 Nov | 'Small Holdings', *The Times*, p 12. |
| L75 | 25 Nov | 'Mr. Rider Haggard and Small Holdings', *Mark Lane Express*, p 683. |

> Another letter in support of Haggard appears on the same page.

1902

| L76 | 2 Sep | 'Religious Difficulties', *Daily Express*, p 4. |
| L77 | 29 Dec | 'Rural England', *Morning Post*, p 6. |

1903

L78	21 Jan	'Rural England', *Guardian*, p 102.
L79	3 Feb	'British Agriculture', *The Times*, p 4.
L80	4 Feb	'Rural England', *The Times*, p 8.
L81	21 Feb	'The Cobden Club on Agriculture', *Saturday Review*, pp 229–30.
L82	11 Jun	'Agricultural Distress', *The Times*, p 12.
L83	24 Jun	'The Motor Problem', *The Times*, p 6.
L84	16 Dec	'Fiscal Policy and Agriculture', *The Times*, p 10.

1904

L85	5 May	'Rural Depopulation', *The Times*, p 10.
L86	21 Jul	'Telepathy (?) Between a Human Being and a Dog', *The Times*.
L87	9 Aug	'Telepathy', *The Times*, p 11.
L88	6 Aug	'Mr. Rider Haggard's Dream', *Spectator*, pp 187–8.

> Answering criticism.

L89	10 Sep	'The Housing Problem in the Country', *Spectator*, p 359.
L90	5 Nov	'The Deserted Country — Small Holdings', *Speaker*, pp 127–9.
L91	30 Dec	'One Sided Copyright from America', *Standard*, p 3.

1905

L92	19 Jan	'A Gardener's Year', *Daily Mail*.
L93	13 Feb	'Cheap Cottages', *Daily Mail*.
L94	25 Aug	'The Deserted Village', *The Times*, p 8.
L95	7 Oct	'The Chinese in South Africa', *Spectator*, p 522.

> Unrest among workmen caused by poor living conditions.

1906

L96	2 Jan	'Peasant or Pheasant', *Morning Leader*, p 4.
L97	6 Jan	'The Decrease of Population and the Land', *The Times*, p 13.
L98	12 Mar	'The New Land Tenure Bill', *The Times*, p 7.
L99	3 May	'Agriculturists and Parcel Post', *The Times*, p 15.
L100	4 Jul	'Small Holdings', *The Times*, p 14.
L101	19 Jul	'The Unemployed and Waste City Lands', *The Times*, p 4.
L102	5 Sep	'Landgrabbing at Plaistow', *The Times*, p 11.
L103	22 Nov	'The Land Tenure Bill', *The Times*, p 11.

1907

L104	1 Jan	'New Year's Greetings', *Daily Express*.
L105	19 Feb	'Publishers and the Public', *The Times*, p 4.
L106	27 Apr	'The Book That Has Interested Me Most', *The Reader*, p 3.
		Haggard letter in facsimile, naming Sir Oliver Lodge's work *On his Catechism*.
L107	29 Apr	'The Government and the Land', *The Times*, p 11.
L108	8 May	'The Government and the Land', *The Times*, p 5.
L109	8 Jun	'Agriculture in Yorkshire', *Spectator*, pp 903–4.
L110	12 Aug	'A Plea for the Sitting Tenant', *The Times*, p 8.
L111	19 Oct	'A Literary Coincidence', *Spectator*, p 565.
L112	5 Dec	'The Proposed Agricultural Party', *The Times*, p 6.

1908

L113	2 Apr	'The Drink Trade and Common Sense', *The Times*, p 8.
L114	18 Aug	'Sparrows', *The Times*, p 6.
L115	5 Sep	'Sparrows, Rats and Humanity', *The Times*, p 8.
L116	26 Nov	'The Letters of Queen Victoria', *The Times*, p 10.

1909

L117	13 Apr	'The Late Sir Marshal Clarke', *The Times*, p 9.
L118	28 Aug	'Land Banks for the People', *Daily Express*, p 1.
L119	27 Nov	'Agriculture', *The Times*, p 13.

1910

L120	18 Feb	'Rat Plague', *The Times*, p 13.
L121	11 Mar	'South Africa', *The Times*, p 12.
L122	25 Apr	'Why?', *The Times*, p 8.
		The high cost of elections.
L123	12 Jul	'Why Not?', *The Times*, p 14.
L124	16 Aug	'Agriculture', *The Times*, p 12.

1911

L125	25 Feb	' "Jess" Cottage', *South Africa*.
L126	22 Mar	'Rural Denmark — Butter Trade', *The Times*, p 7.
L127	3 Apr	'Rural Denmark', *The Times*, p 13.
L128	3 Apr	'Insurance (Industrial) Bill', *The Times*, p 13.
L129	6 Jun	'The Copyright Bill', *The Times*, p 7.

1912

L130	21 Jan	'Open Minds on Divorce Reform', *Weekly Budget*.
		Haggard letter in facsimile.
L131	1 Jun	'Congratulations', *Agricultural Economist*, p 168.
L132	24 Jul	'Sea Serpent Off Kessingland', *Eastern Daily Press*.
L133	28 Oct	'The New Interest in Country Life', *Daily Mail*.

1913

| L134 | 16 Aug | 'Umslopogaas and Makokel. Sir Rider Haggard on Zulu Types', *The Times*, p 5. |

1914

L135	18 Jul	'On Marconi's intention to talk across the Atlantic', *New York Times*, p 1.
L136	10 Oct	'The Death of Mark Haggard', *The Times*, p 9.
L137	18 Oct	'On the loyalty of the Boers to England', *New York Times*.

1915

L138	22 Oct	'Raids by Air. Zeppelins Against Zeppelins', *The Times*, p 9.
L139	29 Nov	'Women's Work on the Land', *The Times*, p 3.
L140	9 Dec	'Women on the Land. Town Girls' Unfitness for Farm Work', *The Times*, p 11.

1916

L141	7 Feb	'Soldiers as Settlers', *The Times*, p 9.
L142	10 Feb	'Soldier Settlers. The Future of Rural England', *The Times*, p 9.
L143	28 Dec	'Mr. Wilson's Note. British Publicity', *The Times*, p 7.

1917

L144	22 Feb	'Home Produce', *The Times*, p 7.
L145	11 Apr	'The Milk Supply', *The Times*, p 9.
L146	13 Jun	'Corn Production Bill', *The Times*, p 9.
L147	9 Oct	'A Protest and a Plea. Farmers and Meat', *The Times*, p 10.
L148	12 Dec	'Jerusalem', *The Times*, p 7.

1918

L149	22 Feb	'Pig Breeding. A Subject for Municipal Enterprise', *The Times*, p 8.
L150	5 Nov	'The German Colonies. Interests of the Dominions', *The Times*, p 10.
L151	19 Nov	'Light — More Light! Village Life; reconstruction and use of electricity', *The Times*, p 9.

1919

L152	8 Jan	'A Great American. Tributes to the Late Mr. Roosevelt', *The Times*, p 4.
L153	10 Mar	'Shut the Door', *The Times*, p 8. Exclusion of Russian Bolsheviks.
L154	11 Apr	'The Ex-Kaiser', *The Times*, p 8. Punishment for war responsibilities.
L155	10 May	'Ex-Servicemen Abroad. Warnings From California', *The Times*, p 8.
L156	16 May	'Edith Cavell', *The Times*, p 14.

L157	8 Jul	'The Ex-Kaiser. Uncertainties of Trial', *The Times*, p 8.
L158	5 Nov	'British Authors and Film Industry', *The Times*, p 8.
L159	19 Nov	'Horrors on the Film. Limits of Publicity', *The Times*, p 8.

1920

L160	24 Jan	'The British Museum', *The Times*, p 8.
L161	7 Feb	'Air Exploration and Empire', *The Times*, p 8.
L162	3 Mar	'The Liberty League. A Campaign Against Bolshevism', *The Times*, p 12.
L163	10 Jun	'Is the Day of Novels Past?', *Daily Express*, p 4.
L164	27 Jul	'A Plea for the Castle Museum', *Eastern Daily Press*.

1921

L165	21 Apr	'Films and Tyranny of Happy Endings', *The Times*, p 8.
L166	8 Aug	'Land and Its Burden. The Evil of Grinding Taxation', *The Times*, p 9.
L167	19 Dec	'Ireland and the Transvaal', *Morning Post*, p 6.

1922

L168	31 Mar	'Boy Emigrants', *The Times*, p 8.
L169	28 Oct	'Labour Party Programme', *The Times*, p 11.
L170	19 Dec	'Egyptian Find', *The Times*, p 11.

1923

L171	13 Feb	'King Tutankhamen. Reburial in Great Pyramid', *The Times*, p 13.
L172	2 Apr	'The Norfolk Dispute. A Truce While there is Time', *The Times*, p 9.
L173	1 May	'Liberalism and Land Reform', *The Times*, p 15.
L174	4 Jul	'Small Holdings. Influence of Heredity', *The Times*, p 10.

1924

L175	14 Jun	'Country Houses for Sale. Empty East Anglian Mansions', *The Times*, p 11.
L176	30 Jul	'Loans From the British Museum. Respect for Donor's Wishes', *The Times*, p 8.
L177	29 Oct	'Zinovieff Letter. Mr. Macdonald and a "Political Plot" ', *The Times*, p 15.

7 Selected Reports Of Haggard's Speeches (S)

My criterion for including items in this list is the likely value researchers will find from studying the reports in detail.

1885

S1	Feb	'The South Norfolk Election', *Eastern Daily Press*.
S2	17 Jul	'The South African Question', *Eastern Daily Press*.

1894

S3	24 Apr	'Mr. Rider Haggard on Anglo-Africa', *Daily Telegraph*, p 3.
S4	28 Apr	'The Zululand Mission. Mr. Rider Haggard on Polygamy', *The African Review*, pp 541–4.

1895

S5	16 Mar	'East Norfolk Representation. Mr. Rider Haggard, The Unionist Candidate', *Eastern Daily Press*. See PR3
S6	18 Mar	'Norfolk (Eastern Division)', *The Times*, p 7.
S7	20 Apr	'Mr. H. Rider Haggard at Sprowston', *Norfolk Daily Chronicle*, p 10.
S8	23 Apr	'Mr. Rider Haggard at Thorpe', *Eastern Daily Press*.
S9	4 May	'Regent Ward·Conservative Association, Yarmouth', *Yarmouth Advertiser*.
S10	4 May	'The Universities' Mission to Central Africa', *Norfolk Chronicle*, p 2.
S11	9 May	'Printer's Pension, Almshouses and Orphan Asylum', *The Sun*.
S12	15 May	'Saviours of the Children', *Morning Post*.
S13	31 May	'The "Haggard" Dinner', *Literary World*.
S14	14 Jun	'Representation of East Norfolk', *Norfolk Daily Standard*. Electioneering.

S15	15 Jun	'Representation at East Norfolk', *Norfolk Daily Standard*. Electioneering.
S16	20 Jul	'Mr. Rider Haggard at Horsford' and 'Mr. Rider Haggard at Drayton', *Norfolk Chronicle*, p 8. Two electioneering speeches.
S17	20 Jul	'Scene at North Walsham', *Norfolk Standard*. Electioneering.
S18	19 Sep	'The African Trust Ltd', *Pall Mall Gazette*.

1896

S19	18 Jan	'The Barrett-Browning Memorial Insititue', *Gloucester Journal*.
S20	14 Mar	'Mr. Rider Haggard on the Jameson Surrender', *The Times*, p 10.
	7 Mar	'Mr. Rider Haggard on the Jameson Surrender', *African Review*, pp 475–6.
S21	25 Jul	'The South African Association', *African Review*, p 246.

1898

S22	18 Feb	'The Society of Authors', *The Times*, p 12.
S23	21 May	'Mr. Rudyard Kipling at the Anglo-African Writers' Club', *African Review*, pp 311–12.
S24	25 Jun	'Anglo-African Writers' Club', *African Review*, pp 516–18. Welcoming Ex Chief Justice Kotze.
S25	10 Sep	'S.P.G. Women's Mission Association', *Norfolk Chronicle*, p 8.
S26	5 Dec	'Norfolk Chamber of Agriculture', *Eastern Daily Press*, p 7. On labourers' wages.
S27	22 Dec	'Anglo-African Writers' Club', *The Times*, p 8. Reprinted in *African Review*, on 24 Dec, p 499. Welcoming Professor Bryce.

1899

S28	17 Jan	'Sir George Goldie on Nigeria', *The Times*, p 10.
S29	4 Feb	'The Vaccination Question', *Eastern Daily Press*, p 3. A Haggard letter read out at a meeting.
S30	22 Apr	'Anglo-African Writers' Club', *African Review*, pp 128–9. Welcoming Lionel Phillips.
S31	9 May	'A Vanishing Population', *The Times*, p 3.
S32	31 May	'Central and Associated Chambers of Agriculture', *The Times*, p 12. On shrinking rural population.
S33	22 Jun	'Wymondham Market Cross. History and Fiction', *Eastern Daily Press*, p 6.
S34	3 Aug	'New Library at Norwich. Mr. Rider Haggard on the Boom', *Eastern Daily Press*, p 5.
S35	15 Aug	'Primrose League Fete at Earsham', *East Suffolk Gazette*, p[5]. Transvaal.

S36	21 Oct	'Anglo-African Writers' Club', *African Review*, p 84.
		Welcoming J.P. Fitzpatrick

1900

S37	16 Jun	'Anglo-African Writers' Club', *The Times*, p 18.
		Welcoming Captain Lambton, R.N.
S38	22 Jun	'S.P.G. Bicentenary at Norwich', *East Anglian Daily Times*, p 5.
		On South African problems.
S39	2 Jul	'St. Augustine's College Commemoration, Canterbury', *Kentish Observer*.
S40	21 Jul	'East Suffolk Prize Scheme', *Norfolk Chronicle*, p 12.
		On rural depopulation.
S41	23 Sep	'The Authors' Club', *Daily News*.
		Conan Doyle present.

1901

S42	24 Jan	'Missionary Exhibition at Bungay', *Eastern Daily Press*, p 7.
S43	6 Nov	'Associated Chambers of Agriculture', *The Times*, p 10.
		On rural depopulation. See also further reports in *The Times* on 7 Nov, p 9; 8 Nov, p 12.
S44	6 Nov	'Rural Depopulation', *The Globe*.
		Leading article referring to S43.
S45	30 Nov	'Mr. Rider Haggard on Agriculture', *East Anglian Daily Times*, p 5.

1902

S46	2 Feb	'The Rural Exodus', *Morning Post*.
S47	8 Apr	'Dinner to Sir H. Johnston', *The Times*, p 8.
S48	19 Jun	'New Village Hall at Scarning', *Eastern Daily Press*, p 9.
		On rural exodus.
S49	2 Aug	'At the Authors' Club', *African Review*, p 174.
		Welcoming the guests, who included Conan Doyle.

1903

S50	19 Jan	'Proposed Agricultural Post', *Eastern Daily Press*, p 5.
S51	4 Mar	'Central and Associated Chambers of Agriculture', *The Times*, p 13.
		Parcels post.
S52	18 Mar	'East Suffolk Chamber of Agriculture', *East Anglian Daily Times*, p 2.
		Agricultural post.
S53	3 Apr	'Mr. Rider Haggard in York', *Yorkshire Herald*.
		On parcels post.
S54	5 May	'Land and the Unemployed', *The Times*, p 10.
S55	11 May	'A Homer for an Ephah', *St. James's Gazette*.
		Comment on Haggard's Royal Institution speech. See PR7
S56	13 Jun	'Imperial South African Association', *The Times*, p 8.

S57	13 Aug	'The Primrose League', *Eastern Morning Gazette*.
		On fiscal policy.
S58	17 Oct	'Framlingham Farmers' Club', *East Anglian Daily Times*, p 5. ·
		On farming programme.
S59	23 Oct	'Colchester Oyster Feast', *East Anglian Daily Times*, p 5.
		On novelists.
S60	4 Nov	'Central Chamber of Agriculture', *East Anglian Daily Times*, p 2.
		On fiscal policy.
S61	10 Dec	'Central and Associated Chambers of Agriculture', *The Times*,
		p 12.
		On preferential tariffs.
S62	11 Dec	'Bungay Farmers' Club', *East Anglian Daily Times*, p 5.
		On fiscal campaign.

1904

S63	15 Jan	'Garden City Association', *The Times*, p 8.
S64	3 Feb	'Central and Associated Chambers of Agriculture', *The Times*, p 4.
S65	28 Jul	'Mr. Rider Haggard and Chinese Labour in South Africa', *Eastern Daily Press*, p 8.
S66	12 Sep	'Mr. Rider Haggard on Smallholdings', *The Times*, p 8.
S67	22 Oct	'Mr. Rider Haggard on Agriculture', *The Times*, p 9.
S68	27 Oct	'Mr. Rider Haggard on Rural Housing', *The Times*, p 9.
S69	25 Nov	'The Housing Problem', *Western Morning News*.

1905

S70	11 Jan	'Mr. Rider Haggard in York', *Yorkshire Herald*.
		On smallholdings.
S71	3 Jun	'Craft Masonry, Honor and Generosity Lodge', *The Freemason*.
S72	15 Jul	'Garden City Association', *The Times*, p 14.
S73	Jul	'Lyceum Club First Anniversary', *The Lyceum*.
S74	7 Nov	'Emptying the Land', *Standard*.
		On rural depopulation.
S75	12 Dec	'The Poor and Land Settlement', *The Times*, p 4.

1906

S76	11 Jan	'South Norfolk', *Eastern Daily Press*, p 8.
		On Chinese labour.
S77	3 Feb	'Our Falling Birth Rate', *The Times*, p 4.
S78	17 Mar	'Garden City Association', *The Times*, p 13.
S79	4 Jul	'Neglected Land of England', *The Times*, p 14.
S80	7 Aug	'Mr. Rider Haggard on the Transvaal Constitution', *The Times*, p 8.
S81	20 Dec	'Mr. Rider Haggard on War', *Evening Mail*.

1907

| S82 | 13 Mar | 'Co-operative Smallholdings', *Morning Post*. |
| S83 | 2 May | 'The Housing of the Poor', *The Times*, p 3. |

S84	27 Jun	'Mr. Rider Haggard and Superstition', *Daily Telegraph*, p 12.
S85	26 Oct	'Town Planning Conference', *The Times*, p 8.
S86	16 Nov	'Mr. Rider Haggard and Destitutes', *The Times*, p 5.
		Later printed in *The Real Wealth of England* (see PR9)

1908

| S87 | 10 Jan | 'Mr. Rider Haggard and Smallholdings', *The Times*, p 7. |
| S88 | 13 Mar | 'Mr. Haggard and Children's Legislation', *The Times*, p 17. |

1909

S89	7 Jan	'Opening of Bungay "Chaucer" Institute', *Eastern Daily Press*, p 3.
S90	1 Mar	'Afforestation. Mr. Rider Haggard's Views', *The Times*, p 16.
S91	23 Mar	'Society of Authors. International Copyright', *The Times*, p 14.
S92	30 Mar	'Afforestation and the State. Authors' Club Discussion', *Morning Post*.
S93	8 Apr	'Suffolk Territorials', *Eastern Daily Press*, p 8.
		Appeal.
S94	13 Aug	'Primrose League at Broome', *East Anglian Daily Times*, p 4.
S95	3 Sep	'Dr. Barnardo's Homes. Their Service to the Empire', *Eastern Daily Press*, p 6.
S96	17 Sep	'Scenes from *Montezuma's Daughter*', *East Anglian Daily Times* p 5.
S97	26 Nov	'Cheerful About Agriculture', *Eastern Daily Press*, p 3.

1910

S98	15 Feb	'Radium Wonders', *Daily Telegraph*, p 13.
S99	18 Feb	'Mr. H. Rider Haggard on Risk of Invasion', *Eastern Daily Press*, p 8.
S100	21 Feb	'Agriculture. Occupying Ownership', *Yorkshire Herald*.
S101	3 Mar	'The Protection of Children', *Eastern Daily Press*, p 8.
S102	11 Mar	'Booksellers' Provident Institution' (South Africa), *The Times*, p 12.
S103	18 Apr	'Royal Agricultural Benevolent Insitution', *Eastern Daily Press*, p 8.
S104	23 May	'Mr. Rider Haggard on Irish Agriculture', *The Times*, p 38.
S105	25 May	'The Progress of Smallholdings', *Morning Post*.
S106	11 Jun	'The Essex Show', *Essex County Standard*.
S107	18 Jul	'The Trend of Modern Education', *Eastern Daily Press*, p 9.
S108	23 Jul	'Smallholdings in Essex', *The Times*, p 8.
S109	16 Sep	'Mr. Rider Haggard on Agriculture', *The Times*, p 12.
S110	8 Nov	'Mr. Rider Haggard on Rat Destruction', *The Times*, p 14.
S111	21 Dec	'Mr. Rider Haggard Commends the Studious Danes', *The Times*, p 6.

1911

S112	16 Jan	'R.S.P.C.A. Annual Meeting', *Eastern Daily Press*, p 8.
S113	27 Jan	'Mr. Rider Haggard on Ownership', *Eastern Daily Press*, p 9. Agriculture.
S114	31 Jan	'Authors' Club. Mr. Rider Haggard on Smallholdings', *Standard*.
S115	6 Mar	'Sugar Beet Factories in Norfolk', *The Times*, p 13.
S116	6 May	'Land Problems', *The Field*.
S117	1 Jul	'Rural Education', *Eastern Daily Press*, p 5.
S118	15 Jul	'Mr. Rider Haggard on Poverty', *The Times*, p 11.
S119	28 Jul	'Mr. Rider Haggard and the Public Records', *The Times*, p 4.
S120	17 Aug	'Mr. Rider Haggard on the Strikers', *East Anglian Daily Times*.
S121	24 Nov	'Mr. Rider Haggard on a School for Smallholders', *Cambridge Independent Press*.
S122	9 Dec	'Rider Haggard the Prophet', *Eastern Daily Press*, p 8. The Insurance Bill

1912

S123	13 Jun	'Horror of Motors', *Daily Chronicle*.
S124	9 Nov	'Sir Rider Haggard Describes the Romance', *East Anglian Daily Times,* p 5. The plot of *Pearl Maiden*.

1913

S125	10 Mar	'People the Soil. Agriculture the Mainstay', *New Zealand Times*, p 8.
S126	21 Apr	'Ethics of Literature. Imagination and Imperialism', *Sydney Morning Herald*.
S127	25 Apr	'Yanco. Sir Rider Haggard's Visit', *Sydney Daily Telegraph*. On farming.
S128	26 Apr	'Australia's Need. Sir Rider Haggard on Immigration', *Sydney Morning Herald*.
S129	6 May	'Dominions Commission', *The Ballarat*.
S130	10 May	'Dominions Commission', *The Age* (Melbourne).
S131	5 Aug	'Sir Rider Haggard at Harleston', *Eastern Daily Press*, p 7. Dominions Commission visit to Australia and New Zealand.
S132	18 Nov	'Authors' Club', *Daily Telegraph*, p 7. On forestry.
S133	2 Dec	'Dr. Barnardo's Homes', *Daily Telegraph*, p 15.
S134	19 Dec	'Mr. Pretyman at Bungay', *Eastern Daily Press*, p 6. On farming.

1914

S135	28 Mar	'Echoes of the Past. Famous Novelist's Reminiscences', *Natal Witness*.
S136	1 Apr	'Co-operation Needed. Sir Rider Haggard on Agriculture', *Pretoria News*.

S137	3 Apr	'Wealthiest Land in the Empire', *Transvaal Leader*. pp 7 and 8.
S138	5 Sep	'The War Appeal', *Eastern Daily Press*, p 8.
		Printed as a pamphlet *A Call to Arms* — see PR12.

1915

S139	30 Jul	'War Savings Campaign', *East Anglian Daily Times*.
S140	5 Aug	'The War and After', *Eastern Daily Press*, p 4.
S141	17 Aug	'Sir Rider Haggard at Diss. Spirited Reply to Dr. Lyttleton',
		Eastern Daily Press, p 6.
		On Causes of the War.
S142	15 Nov	'Farmers Co-operative Association', *East Anglian Daily Times*, p 8.

1916

S143	2 Feb	'Colonial Institute Luncheon', *The Times*, p 6.
		Also printed in *United Empire*, Mar 1916 — the journal of the Royal Colonial Institute.
S144	4 Feb	'Authors' Club. The After-War Care of Sailors and Soldiers', *Daily Telegraph*, p 6.
S145	8 Apr	'Tasmania's Future. Land for British Soldiers', *Mecury* (Tasmania), pp 5 and 6.
S146	15 Apr	'Farmers and Co-operation. Aspects of the Wheat Scheme', *Argus* (Melbourne) p 22.
S147	18 Apr	'Colonial Institute Luncheon', *Argus* (Melbourne), p 6.
S148	19 Apr	'After the War', *Sydney Morning Herald*.
S149	27 Apr	'Visit to Trades Hall', *Brisbane Daily Standard*.
		After war settlement.
S150	29 Apr	'Empire's Need. Land Settlement', *Sydney Morning Herald*.
S151	10 May	'Civic Reception', *West Australian* (Perth).
S152	14 May	'Visit to Northam (Western Australia)', *Northam Advertiser*.
S153	6 Jun	'Imperial Lines in Overseas Policy', *New Zealand Times*, p 3.
S154	7 Jun	'Land and Safety. Population Problems', *New Zealand Times*, p 6.
S155	13 Jun	'Sir Rider Haggard's Mission', *New Zealand Herald*, p 9.
S156	13 Jun	'Building Up the Empire', *New Zealand Herald*, p 9.
S157	3 Jul	'Sir Rider Haggard Speaks on His Mission', *Victoria Daily Times* (Canada).
S158	5 Jul	'Sword of Damocles Hanging Over Empire', *Daily News Advertiser* (British Columbia).
S159	10 Jul	'Eloquent Appeals for Recruits', *Morning Bulletin* (Edmonton, Alberta).
S160	11 Jul	'Rider Haggard Thinks Present War Not the End', *Edmonton Journal*.
		On land settlement.
S161	12 Jul	'Let British People Go Where British Flag Flies', *Calgary Herald*. pp 1 and 11.
S162	13 Jul	'Large Turnout Greeted Sir Rider Haggard', *The Leader* (Regina).
		On the war and the future menace of Germany.
S163	14 Jul	'British Empire Must Be A Nation Armed Against The Inevitable Attack', *Saskatoon Phoenix*, p 4.

S164	15 Jul	'Sir Rider Haggard's Hopes Realised', *Manitoba Free Press*, pp 1 and 4.
S165	21 Jul	'Preparedness For The Next War', *Ottawa Free Press*.
S166	15 Nov	'Government and Land Settlement', *Daily Telegraph*, p 10. Also printed in United Empire, Dec 1916.
S167	17 Nov	'Sir H. Rider Haggard and the Liberal War Committee', *East Anglian Daily Times*.

1917

S168	27 Jun	'Women Supreme', *Newcastle Chronicle*.
S169	4 Jul	'Sir H. Rider Haggard at Southend', *Southend Observer*.
S170	6 Aug	'Norfolk Farmers and Meat Prices', *Eastern Daily Press*, p 5.
S171	25 Sep	'Sir Rider Haggard's Farewell to Farming. Why He Adopted Agriculture', *Eastern Daily Press*, p 5.

1918

| S172 | 13 Sep | 'Magical and Ceremonial Uses of Fire', *Norfolk Chronicle*. |

1919

| S173 | 17 Apr | 'Empire Birth-Rate. Sir Rider Haggard on Emigration', *The Times*, p 9. |
| S174 | 15 May | 'A Minister of Fine Arts. Mr. Bernard Shaw's View', *Daily Telegraph*, p 12. |

1920

S175	6 Apr	'King Solomon's Mines', *The Times*, p 8. South Africa exhibition.
S176	26 Jun	'Disease and the Birth-Rate', *The Times*, p 13.
S177	27 Oct	'Savages and Their Children. More Humane Than Some Civilised People', *Eastern Daily Press*, p 6.

1921

S178	28 Jun	'Plots For Novels. Sir Rider Haggard and the Real Umslopogaas', *Morning Post*.
S179	24 Sep	'Art the Consoler', *Liverpool Echo*.
S180	19 Nov	'The Delphian Coterie', *Daily Telegraph*, p 7. On the Empire of the Future.

1922

S181	18 Mar	'Woman and Life. Sir Rider Haggard's Views', *Daily Telegraph*, p 7.
S182	7 Apr	'Migration and Morals. Declining Birth-Rate', *The Times*, p 14.
S183	28 Apr	'London Society of East Anglians', *The Times*, p 11.
S184	15 Jun	'Agricultural Research. Importance of Seed Testing', *Eastern Daily Press*, p 8.

S185	6 Jul	'Peril of Pride. Sir Rider Haggard on Humility. What the War Revealed', *Eastern Daily Press*, p 4.
S186	8 Aug	'Harleston Show. Sir Rider Haggard Prophecies', *Eastern Daily Press*, p 6.
S187	24 Nov	'Sir Rider Haggard at Oxford. The Plough Club and British Agriculture', *Oxford Chronicle*.
S188	7 Dec	'Where Denmark Leads. A Successful Policy', *The Times*, p 9.

1923

| S189 | 24 Feb | 'Feeding the Children', *Hastings Observer*. |
| S190 | 26 Jul | 'Agricultural Parcel Post', *The Times*, p 9. |

1924

S191	24 Jul	'Plight of Agriculture. Sir Rider Haggard on Profits of Middlemen', *The Times*, p 11.
S192	6 Nov	'Two Centuries of Publishing', *The Times*, p 17.
S193	26 Nov	'Imagination and War', *The Times*, p 19.

8 Films, Plays and Radio Broadcasts Based on Haggard's Works (FPB)

Titles are listed in order of first book publication.

Films

DAWN

1917

FPB1 Made by The Lucoque Production Company, England. Black and white. Silent. 5500 feet.
Producer and Director: H. Lisle Lucoque.
Screenplay: Pauline Lewis.
Cast: Karina as Mildred Carr; Hubert Carter as 'Devil' Caresfoot; Madeleine Seymour as Angela; Edward Combermere as George Caresfoot; R. Heaton Grey as Philip Caresfoot; Annie Esmond as Lady Bellamy; Frank Harris as Sir John Bellamy; George Snazelle as Arthur Heigham.

Notices in *Bioscope* vol 35, no 553, 17 May 1917, Supplement p x; vol 38, 20 Dec 1917, p 79.

KING SOLOMON'S MINES

1919

FPB2 Made by The African Film Production Company at Killarney Studios, Johannesburg, South Africa. Black and white. Silent.
Director: H. Lisle Lucoque.
Cast: Albert Lawrence as Allan Quatermain; Holford J. Hamlin as Sir Henry Curtis; Ray Brown as Captain Good; Vivien Talleur as Gagool; Bebe Gordon as Foulata.

Notices in *Bioscope* 15 May 1919, p 73; *South African Pictorial Stage and Cinema*, vol VIII, no 205, 5 Jul 1919, p 5 (notice of London showing, repeating reviews from *Bioscope, Kine Weekly* and *The Cinema*). The same magazine (27 Sep 1919, p 19), reviews the first showing of the film at the Bijou Theatre, Johannesburg, on Monday 22 Sep 1919.

1937

FPB3   Made by Gaumont British Picture Corporation, England. Black and white. 8 reels. 80 minutes.
Producer: Geoffrey Barkas.
Director: Robert Stevenson.
Screenplay: Michael Hogan and Roland Pertwee.
Photography: Glen MacWilliam.
Cast: John Loder as Sir Henry Curtis; Anna Lee in an additional (totally unnecessary!) female part; Paul Robeson as Umbopa; Sir Cedric Hardwicke as Allan Quatermain; Roland Young as Captain Good; Sydney Fairbrother as Gagool.

Notices in *New Statesman*, 24 Jul 1937, p 148; *Spectator*, 30 Jul 1937; *The Listener*, 11 Aug 1937, p 297 ('Copybook Hollywood' by H.E. Turner).

Some of the location shots for this film were made in the Umgeni Valley, Natal. A local actress, Connie Barratt, doubled for Anna Lee in the female leading role.

1950

FPB4   Made by Metro Goldwyn Mayer, in America. Technicolour. 102 minutes.
Producer: Sam Zimbalist.
Directors: Comptom Bennett and Andrew Morton.
Screenplay: Helen Deutsch.
Photography: Robert Surtees.
Cast: Stewart Granger as Allan Quatermain; Deborah Kerr as Elizabeth Curtis; Richard Carlson as her son; Hugo Haas; Lowell Gilmore.

Notices in *Saturday Review*, 25 Nov 1950; *Public Opinion*, 22 Dec 1950, p 20 (under 'Jungle Jim's Adventure in Zooland').

1959

FPB5   Made by Metro Goldwyn Mayer, in America, under the title *Watusi*. Technicolour. 85 minutes.
Producer: Al Zimbalist.
Director: Kurt Neumann.
Screenplay: James Clavell.
Photography: Harold E. Wellman.

Cast: George Montgomery as Harry Quatermain; David Farrar as Rick Cobb; Tania Elg as Erica Neuler; Rex Ingram as Umbopa; Paul Thompson as Gagool; Dan Seymour; Robert Goodwin.

Harry Quatermain retraces his father's footsteps to King Solomoñ's Mines.

1963

FPB6

Made by the Panda Company, in Italy, under the title *Maciste Nelle Miniere di Re Salomoni* (Maciste in King Solomon's Mines, or, Samson in King Solomon's Mines). Technicolour. Techniscope. 8820 feet. 98 minutes.
Director: Piero Regnoli.
Cast: Reg Park; Wandisa Guida; Dan Harrison.

Maciste helps the inhabitants of an African kingdom against the army of a usurper and against a witch who is turning the people into slaves for the mines. This seems to be one of a series of 'Maciste' films.

Notices in *Kine Weekly*, 21 Jan 1965, p 9; *Daily Cinema*, 27 Jan 1965, p 6; *Bianco e Nero*, vol 26, no 1, Jan 1965; *Ciné Franc*, no 2123, 17 Jul 1965, p 14; Monthly Film Bulletin, vol 32, no 374, March 1965, p 41.

1985

FPB6A

Made by The Cannon Group Inc., in America. Technicolour.
Producer: Menahem Golan and Yoram Globus.
Director: J. Lee Thompson.
Screenplay: Gene Quintano and James R. Silke.
Director of Photography: Alex Phillips.
Cast: Richard Chamberlain; Sharon Stone; Herbert Lom; John Rhys-Davies.

This film might well appear under 'Parodies and Lampoons' in Section 10. Apart from its title, and the names of some of its characters, the film bears no relation to Haggard's book; it is merely a vehicle for gratuitous blood and violence. A special paperback version of Haggard's book was, however, produced (Beaver Books, published by Arrow Books, London, 1985), as a TV/film tie-in.

SHE

1899

FPB7

Made in France by George Méliès, with the title *La Danse du Feu*. Black and white. Silent. 65 feet. Listed in *Star Film Catalogue 1903–1908*, item 188.

1908

FPB8

Made by the Edison Production Company, in America. Black and white. Silent. 1000 feet. Released 13 Nov 1908.
Director and Screenplay: Edwin S. Porter.
Cast: Florence Auer as Ayesha.

Notices in *Moving Picture World*, vol 3, no 20, 14 Nov 1908, p 384; *Bioscope*, 10 Dec 1908, p 14.

1911

FPB9

Made by the Thanhauser Production Company, in America. Black and white. Silent. 2 reels.
Director: George O. Nichols.
Cast: Marguerite Snow as Ayesha; James Cruze as Leo Vincey; William C. Cowper; Viola Alberti.

Mentioned in *Classic Film Collector*, no 45 (Winter) 1974, pp 40–1. Reviewed in *Moving Picture World*, vol 10, no 12, 23 Dec 1911, pp 976 and 978 (W. Stephen Bush). This review was reprinted in *Selected Film Criticism 1896–1911*, ed. by Anthony Slide (New York and London, Scarecrow Press, 1982. 3 vols), in vol 1, pp 89–91.

1916

FPB10

Made by Barker Motion Photography, at Ealing in England, in association with C.B. Cochrane and H. Lisle Lucoque. Black and white. Silent. 5400 feet.
Director: Will Barker.
Screenplay: Nellie E. Lucoque.
Cast: Alice Delysia as Ayesha; Henry Victor as Leo Vincey; Sydney Bland as Holly; Blanche Forsythe as Ustane; Jack Denton as Job; J. Hastings Batson as Billali.
It appears that H. Lisle Lucoque had the sole distribution rights for this film in the United Kingdom. *Bioscope* (6 Jan 1916, p 79) forecasts the film's release in March. *Bioscope* (16 Mar 1916, p 1215) reports a private viewing at the Empire Theatre, London on 10 Mar. Another source gives a Trade Show date of 29 Feb 1916. The same source suggests that, at about this time in the history of films, the elaborate sets and costumes were sometimes adapted from stage shows; set designers began to be acknowledged in the credits. Lancelot Speed, the book illustrator, designed the set for this version of *She*.

This film was the subject of the National Film Archive Handout No. 337.

1917

FPB11

Made by Fox Films, in America. Black and white. Silent. Released 22 Apr 1917.
Director: Kenean Buel.
Screenplay: Mary Murillo.
Cast: Valeska Suratt as Ayesha; B.L. Taggart; Miriam Fouche.

1925

FPB12   Made by Reciprocity Films. An Anglo-German production, filmed at the E.F.A. Studios, Berlin, where the most modern equipment was available. Black and white. Silent. 8200 feet.
Director: Leander De Cordova.
Screenplay: Walter Summers.
Photography: Sydney Blyth (husband of Betty Blyth).
Cast: Betty Blyth as Ayesha; Carlyle Blackwell as Leo Vincey; Marjorie Statler; Mary Odette as Ustane; Tom Reynolds; Jerrold Robertshaw.

Notices in *Bioscope*, 28 May 1925, p 38; *Kine Weekly*, 16 Sep 1925, p 20; *Stoll Herald*, 18 Jan 1926, p 3; *Classic Film Collector*, no 32 (Autumn), 1971. pp 26–8; *Eyepiece — GBCT News*, vol 2, no 7, May/Jun 1980, pp 38–40.

Betty Blyth was chosen as Ayesha because she had already been successful as the star in the film production of *The Queen of Sheba*. This was not, however, based on Haggard's *Queen Sheba's Ring*.

1935

FPB13   Made by R.K.O. Productions Incorporated, in America. Black and white. 8800 feet. 95 minutes.
Producer: Merian C. Cooper.
Directors: Irving Pichel and Lansing G. Holden.
Screenplay: Ruth Rose and Dudley Nichols.
Photography: J. Ray Hunt.
Cast: Helen Gahagan as Ayesha; Randolph Scott as Leo Vincey; Helen Mack as Tania; Nigel Bruce as Holly; Samuel Hinds as John Vincey.

Notices in *Kine Weekly*, 29 Aug 1935; *Photoplay*, vol 48, no 4, Sep 1935, p 67; *Monthly Film Bulletin*, Aug 1935, p 129.

1953

FPB14   Made by Comedy Pictures, Bombay, in Hindi, under the title *Malika Salome*.
Director: Mohammed Hussein.
Cast: Krishna Rumari; Rupa Varman; Kamran (debut as a star and hero).
Music: Krishun Dayal and Iqbac.
An advance report appeared in *Film India* in December 1952.

1965

FPB15   Made by Hammer Film Productions — 7 Arts, in England.
Technicolour. Technicscope. 9475 feet. 105 minutes.
Producer: Michael Carreras.
Director: Robert Day.
Screenplay: David T. Chantler.
Photography: Harry Waxman.

Cast: Ursula Andress as Ayesha; Christopher Lee as Bill; Bernard Cribbins as Job; Rosenda Monteros as Ustane; John Richardson as Leo Vincey; Peter Cushing as Holly; Andre Morell.

Notices in *Daily Cinema*, 17 Mar 1965, p 4; *Kine Weekly*, 18 Mar 1965, p 8; *Variety*, 21 Apr 1965; *Monthly Film Bulletin*, vol 32, no 376, p 78.

1967

FPB16

Made by Hammer Film Productions, in England under the title *Vengeance of She*. It is based on characters created by Rider Haggard. Technicolour. 9088 feet. 101 minutes.
Producer: Aida Young.
Director: Cliff Owen.
Screenplay: Peter O'Donnell.
Photography: Wolfgang Suschitsky.
Cast: Olinka Berovo as Ayesha; John Richardson; Edward Judd; Derek Godfrey; Noel Willman; Andre Morell.

Notices in *Daily Cinema*, 25 Mar 1968, p 6; *Kine Weekly*, 30 Mar 1968, p 11; *Variety*, 10 Apr 1968, p 6; *Monthly Film Bulletin*, vol 35, 12 May 1968, p 80.

A girl, Carol, is possessed by the spirit of Ayesha.

JESS

1912

FPB17

Made by Thanhauser Production Company, in America. Black and white. Silent. 3000 feet.
Director: George O. Nichols.
Cast: Marquerite Snow as Jess; Florence La Badie as Bess; James Cruze; William Russell.

Notices in *Bioscope*, vol 17, no 318, 14 Nov 1912, Supplement p xx, and vol 17, no 320, 28 Nov 1912, p 673.

1914

FPB18

Made by Kennedy Features Inc. Production Company, in America. Black and white. Silent. Released 28 Feb 1914.
Screenplay: Arthur Maude.
Cast: Constance Crawley as Jess; Arthur Maude; Felix Modjeska

1917

FPB19

Made by the Fox Film Corporation, in America, under the title *Heart and Soul*. Black and white. Silent. 5 reels. Released 20 May 1917.
Director: J. Gordon Edwards.
Screenplay: Adrian Johnson.
Cast: Theda Bara as Jess; Claire Whitney as Bess; Harry Hilliard; Walter Law.

1919

FPB20   Made by African Film Productions, in South Africa. Black and white.
             Silent.
             Director: H. Lisle Lucoque.
             Cast: Albert Lawrence as Allan Quatermain; Halford J. Hamblin as
             Sir Henry Curtis; Ray Brown as Good; Mabel May as Queen
             Nyaleptha; Elise Hamilton as Queen Sorais.

             Notices in *Bioscope*, 6 Nov 1919, p 105; *Picture Plays*, 22 Nov 1919,
             p 8, and 24 Jan 1920, p 6; *South African Pictorial Stage and Cinema*,
             vol 8, 2 Aug 1919, p 5.

             Pyrotechnics by Brock. Chariot driving by George Taylor.

1979

FPB21   Made by the Barber Rose Production Company, England, under the
             title *King Solomon's Treasure*. Technicolour. 7901 feet. 86 minutes.
             Producers: Alvin Rakoff and Susan A. Lewis.
             Executive Producer: Harry Alan Towers.
             Director: Alvin Rakoff.
             Screenplay: Colin Turner and Allan Prior.
             Cast: David MacCullum as Henry Curtis; John Colicos as Allan
             Quatermain; Patrick Macnee as Good; Britt Ekland as Queen
             Nyaleptha; Ken Gampu as Umslopogaas.

MR. MEESON'S WILL

1916

FPB22   Made by Bluebird Photoplays Inc. Production Company, in America,
             under the title *The Grasp of Greed*. Black and white. Silent. 5 reels.
             Producer and Director: Joseph De Grasse.
             Screenplay: Ida May Park.
             Cast: Lon Chaney Snr.; Louise Lovely as Alice; C.N. Hammond; Jay
             Belasco; Gretchen Lederer.

             Notices in *Bioscope*, vol 35, no 553, 17 May 1917, Supplement p x;
             vol 33, no 526, 9 Nov 1916, p 16, and vol 36, 12 Jul 1917, Supplement
             p 33.

CLEOPATRA

1917

FPB23   Made by the Fox Film Corporation, in America. Black and white.
             Silent. 11 reels. Released 14 Oct 1917.
             Director: J. Gordon Edwards.
             Screenplay: Adrian Johnson.
             Cast: Theda Bara; Fritz Leiber; Thurston Hall; Albert Rosco.

Notices in *Bioscope*, vol 38, no 574, 11 Oct 1917, p 36, and 23 May 1918, p 23.

Pirated.

BEATRICE

1919

FPB24   Made in Italy. Black and white. Silent.
Director: Camillo de Risso.
Cast: Franchesca Bertini as Beatrice; Amleto Novelli; Livio Pavanelli.

1921

FPB25   Made by the Caesar-Film Roma Production Company, Italy/America, released under the title *Sister against Sister*. Black and white. Silent. 6500 feet.
Director: Herbert Brenon.
Cast: Alexander (Sandro) Salvini as Geoffrey Bingham; Marie Doro as Beatrice; Marcella Sabbatini; Mimi; Mina D'Orvella; Angelo Gallina.

Notices in *Bianco e nero*, no 1–3, Jan–June 1981, pp 366–8; *Kine Weekly*, 12 May 1921, p 61.

SWALLOW

1922

FPB26   Made by African Film Productions at Killarney Studios, South Africa. Black and white. Silent. 5 reels (4000 feet). Released 16 Dec 1922.
Director: Leander De Cordova.
Cast: Joan Morgan as Swallow; Hayford Hobbs; Dick Cruikshanks; Ena Soutar; M.A. Wetherell.

Listed in *Kine Year Book 1923*.

STELLA FREGELIUS

1921

FPB27   Made by Master Film Production Company, in England, under the title *Stella*. Black and white. Silent. 5500 feet.
Director: Edwin J. Collins.
Screenplay: Edwin J. Collins.
Cast: Molly Adair as Stella Fregelius; Manning Haynes as Morris Monk; Charles Vayne as Colonel Monk; Betty Farquhar as Mary Porson; Wilfred Fletcher as Stephen Lanyard; Mildred Evelyn as Eliza Lanyard.

Notices in *Kine Weekly*, 28 Apr 1921; *The Times*, 18 Apr 1921.

1924

FPB28   Made by Sascha Films, Austria, under the title *Die Sklavenköningin*.
Released in Britain as *Moon of Israel* by Stoll Pictures. Black and
white. Silent.
Director: Mihaly Kertesz (Michael Curtiz)
Screenplay: Ladislaus Vajda.
Cast: Maria Corda; Adelqui Millar; Arlette Marchal.

Notice in *Bioscope*, 6 Nov 1924, p 51.

Plays

DAWN

1887

FPB29   Under the title *Devil Caresfoot*.
'A new play, in four acts, adapted from Rider Haggard's novel *Dawn*,
by C. Haddon Chambers and J. Stanley Little. First produced at the
Vaudeville Theatre [London], Tuesday afternoon, July 12, 1887.'
Cast: Royce Carleton as Philip Caresfoot; Charles Charrington as
George Caresfoot (Devil); Fuller Mellish as Arthur Beaumont; Charles
Dodsworth as Sir John Bellamy; Eric Lewis as Lord Minster; M.J.
Hamilton-Knight as Rev. W. Fraser; Robb Harwood as Beckett; Janet
Achurch as Angela Caresfoot; Carlotta Addison as Lady Bellamy;
Fanny Brough as Mrs. Carr; Mrs. John Carter as Pigott.

Reviewed in *Theatre Magazine*, 1 Aug 1887, signed 'C.H.' (the same
issue carries photographs of Janet Achurch and Fuller Mellish, named
above); *Illustrated London News*, vol 91, 16 Jul 1887, p 71, and 13
Aug 1887, p 181.

The play moved to the Strand Theatre, London, from 6 Aug 1887.
Note: This adaptation differs considerably from the story in the book.
It appears completely to ignore the original character 'Devil'
Caresfoot, who, in the book, was Philip's father. In the play he
appears to be Philip's cousin.

SHE

1887

FPB30   A reference has been seen to 'She, an operatic spectacular drama, by
R.C. White, with new scenic effects, new music and new mechanical
workings.' Published in New York by C.R. Trumbull, printer, 1887.

FPB31   A William Gillette production in New York, USA, first performed in
November 1887. No other details found.

1888

FPB32

An adaptation of *She* was written by Edward Rose in collaboration with W. Sidney and C. Graves and first performed at the Novelty Theatre (sometimes known as the Toddrell Theatre, the New Queen's Theatre, the Eden Theatre and the Great Queen Street Theatre), Great Queen Street, London, on 10 May 1888.

On 6 September 1888, the play opened at the Gaiety Theatre, in the Strand. Miss Sophie Eyre was the producer and also played the title role.

Cast: Sophie Eyre as Ayesha; Mary Rorke as Ustane; Fanny Enson as Amenartas; Edmund Maurice as Leo and Kallikrates; Julian Cross as Holly; E. Cleary as Mahomed; H. Maxwell as Billali; Edmund Gurney as Chief Ugogo.

Some black African actors were introduced specially to play the parts of the Amhagger tribesmen, complete with native costumes and weapons. They were trained in their roles by John D' Auban.

Note: The play was well reviewed, with considerable praise voiced for the production and scenic illusion. Rider Haggard attended the first night and made a speech from his box. Harry Furniss apparently did not share the general view, for his satirical review of the play in *Punch* (see PL14), covering both the production and Haggard's speech, is less than flattering.

Reviewed in *Illustrated London News*, vol 93, 15 Sep 1888, p 306, with a full page of drawings by Dudley Hardy, of the play's leading characters on p 318.

JESS

1890

FPB33

Jess was adapted as a drama by Miss Eweretta Lawrence, in collaboration with J.J. Bisgood. It was first performed at a matinee at the Adelphi Theatre, London on 25 March 1890.

Cast: Eweretta Lawrence as Jess; J.J. Bisgood (?) as The Hero; J.D. Beveridge as A Farmer Settler; C. Dalton as A Boer Chief; Athol Ford as Hottentot Servant; Helen Forsyth as Bess; Julian Cross as Dutch Farmer.

Reviewed in *Illustrated London News*, vol XCVI, no 2659, 5 Apr 1890, p 427.

CLEOPATRA

1891

FPB34

Cleopatra was adapted for the stage by Arthur Shirley, as a farcical comedy, and was first performed at the Athen Hall Assembly Rooms, Shepherd's Bush, London on 14 Sep 1889. It was first performed in the West End, London, at a matinee performance on 25 Jun 1891, at the Shaftsbury Theatre. The review in the *Illustrated London News* (4 Jul 1891) by Clement Scott commented on the lavish production in 'a wild farce' and remarked that Maud Milton was very engaging in the title role.

1893

FPB35

The British Library catalogue records an opera, in three acts, based on Haggard's *Cleopatra*. Written by A.E. Christiansen (Sweden), it was performed in 1893. A version in German followed in 1897, and a French version (by G. Sandre, after Christiansen) in 1905 (date doubtful).

CHILD OF STORM

1914

FPB36

Under the title *Mameena*.
'Mr. Oscar Asche produced *Mameena*, a drama of Sir Rider Haggard's *Child of Storm*' at the Globe Theatre [London] last Wednesday [7 Oct 1914].
Cast: Lily Brayton as Mameena; Oscar Asche as Mameena's lover; Harcourt Beatty as Allan Quatermain; Herbert Grimwood as Zikali; Dora Barton as Princess Nandi.

Reviewed in *The Athenaeum*, 10 Oct 1914; *Illustrated London News*, 10 Oct 1914.

Radio Broadcasts

KING SOLOMON'S MINES

1946

FPB37

Broadcast as a serial play for several weeks on the BBC Light Programme from 16 Sep. Adapted by Alec Macdonald.

1956

FPB38

Broadcast as a serial play on the BBC Light Programme from 13 Jun. Produced by Archie Campbell, from Alec Macdonald's adaptation (FPB37).
In eight episodes: 1. The Legend of the Mines (13 Jun); 2. Solomon's Road (20 Jun); 3. The Witch Hunt (27 Jun); 4. The Eclipse (4 Jul); 5. The Battle (11 Jul); 6. Solomon's Treasure Chamber (18 Jul); 7. Buried Alive (25 Jul); 8. Found (1 Aug).
Cast: Derek Guyler as Allan Quatermain; Ralph Truman as Curtis; Raymond Williams as Good; Frank Singuinean as Umbopa; Roger Delgado as Jose; Lionel Ngakane as Jim; Charles Hodgson as African servant; Patience Collier as Gagool.

1966

FPB39   Broadcast as a drama on the BBC Home Service on 14 Apr. Adapted by H. Oldfield Box.

1970

FPB40   Broadcast on BBC Radio 4 'Story Time' on 14 Jul as *Allan Quatermain's Story*. Adapted by Barry Campbell as the second in 'The Treasure Hunters' series.

1981

FPB41   Broadcast on BBC Radio 4 'Story Time' on 13 Jul. Abridged by Ronald Russell.

SHE

1979

FPB41A   Broadcast on BBC Radio 4 on 14 Apr. Adapted by Victor Pemberton.

ALLAN QUATERMAIN

1948

FPB42   Broadcast on the BBC Light Programme, 23 May.

1956

FPB43   Broadcast on the BBC Light Programme 'A Book at Bedtime', in 20 instalments, 1 Jun–20 Jun. Read by Derek Birch. Abridged by Jocelyn Bradford.

1972

FPB44   Broadcast on BBC Radio 4 'Story Time', 9 Oct. Adapted by Ronald Russell.

BLACK HEART AND WHITE HEART

1981

FPB45   Broadcast on BBC Radio 4, 29 Sep.

Broadcasts about Rider Haggard

1961

FPB46   Broadcast on BBC Midlands Home Service, 28 May. Fifteen minute talk 'Rider Haggard', given by J.B. Priestley.

FPB47   Broadcast on BBC Midlands Home Service, Jun. Talk 'A Born
                 Storyteller' given by Lilias Rider Haggard.

                 1971

FPB48   Broadcast on BBC Radio 3, Jul 1971. Talk 'Can Haggard Ride Again'
                 given by Ian Fletcher.

9 Books and Articles About Haggard and His Works (BA)

1882

BA1   'The Modern Novel', *Saturday Review*, pp 633–4.

BA2   Reviews of *Cetywayo and His White Neighbours*.
         Vanity Fair, 29 Jul, p 73; *Saturday Review*, 12 Aug, pp 213–14;
         Spectator, 19 Aug, pp 1089–90; *British Quarterly Review*, Oct,
         pp 460–1; *The South African*, 5 Oct, p 5.

BA3   Macdonald, D. *Africana: or, The Heart of Heathen Africa*. London,
         Simpkin Marshall and Co.

1884

BA4   Reviews of *Dawn*.
         Academy, 22 Mar, p 200; Athenaeum, 22 Mar, p 372; Pall Mall
         Budget, 4 Apr; *Vanity Fair*, 12 Apr, p 206.

1885

BA5   Reviews of *The Witch's Head*.
         Athenaeum, 10 Jan, p 49; *Pall Mall Budget*, 16 Jan, p 29; *Academy*,
         17 Jan, p 41; *Saturday Review*, 17 Jan, p 84; *Literary World*, 6 Feb;
         Literary World (Boston), 2 May, p 158.

BA6   Reviews of *King Solomon's Mines*.
         Saturday Review, 10 Oct, pp 485–6; *Public Opinion*, 30 Oct, p 551;
         Athenaeum, 31 Oct, p 568; *Academy*, 7 Nov, p 304; *Queen*, 7 Nov,
         p 512; *Spectator*, 7 Nov, p 1473; *Independent*, 3 Dec.

1886

BA7   Notice of *King Solomon's Mines*. *Literary World* (Boston), 23 Jan,
         p 24.
         '. . . a bloody and ghastly tale.'

BA8   Shand, A.I. 'The Novelists and Their Patrons', *Fortnightly Review*,
           pp 23—35.
BA9   'London Letter', *Critic* (USA), 3 Apr.

           1887
BA10   Reviews of *She*.
               Pall Mall Gazette, 4 Jan, p 5; *Pall Mall Budget*, 6 Jan, pp 28—9;
           Literary World, 7 Jan; *Saturday Review*, 8 Jan, p 44; *Academy*, 15
           Jan (Andrew Lang); *Queen*, 15 Jan, pp 88—9; *Public Opinion*, 14 Jan,
           p 38; *Spectator*, 15 Jan, pp 78—9; *Athenaeum*, 15 Jan, pp 93—4;
           Vanity Fair, 22 Jan, p 66 (written in skittish blank verse!); *Pall Mall
           Gazette*, 22 Jan, p 13; *Critic*, Feb.
BA11   Reviews of *Jess*.
               Pall Mall Gazette, 15 Mar; *Athenaeum*, 19 Mar, p 375; *Murray's
           Magazine*, Apr, p 576; *Literary World* (Boston), 16 Apr, pp 116—17.
BA12   Reviews of *Allan Quatermain*.
               British Weekly, 5 Aug, p 218; *Pall Mall Gazette*, 18 Jul, p 3;
           Literary World (Boston), 23 Jul, p 236.
BA13   'A Letter From London', *Literary World* (Boston), 5 Mar, p 72.
BA14   'Who is She and Where Does She Come From?', *Pall Mall Gazette*, 11
           Mar, pp 1—2.
               Note: Thereafter, the question of plagiarism was a subject of
           continuous debate in the *Pall Mall Gazette* throughout March, April
           and May of 1887. It was revived in August, September and November
           of 1887, and was taken up by other periodicals. Items of particular
           interest are listed below.
BA15   'The Song of Jess and Who Wrote It', *Pall Mall Gazette*, 24 Mar.
BA16   'The Strange Case of She and Jess', *Pall Mall Gazette*, 26 Mar, p 3.
BA17   'Can Mr. Haggard Write?', *Court and Society*, 30 Mar, p 305.
BA18   'Mr. Rider Haggard and the Song of Jess', *Whitehall Review*, 31 Mar,
           p 7.
BA19   'The Ethics of Plagiarism', *Pall Mall Gazette*, 30 Mar, p 3 and 5 Apr,
           p 3.
BA20   'Literary and Art Notes', *Pall Mall Gazette*, 15 Apr, p 3.
BA21   'Mr. Rider Haggard and the Disputed Poem', *Public Opinion*, 15 Apr,
           p 456.
BA22   'The Song of Jess and How She Came By It. H. Rider Haggard's
           Explanation', *Pall Mall Gazette*, 19 Apr, p 5.
BA23   Mr. Rider Haggard and His Critics', *Public Opinion*, 29 Apr,
           pp 523—4.
               Quotes Haggard's letter to *The Times* of 27 Apr 1887.
BA24   'H. Rider Haggard', *Book Buyer* (New York), May, pp 156—7.
BA25   Moore, Augustus. 'Rider Haggard and The New School of Romance',
           Time, May, p 305.
BA26   Clark, S.M. 'Mr. Haggard's Romances', *Dial*, May, pp 5—7.
BA27   Lang, Andrew. 'Literary Plagiarism', *Contemporary Review*, Jun,
           pp 831—40.
BA28   Review of *Devil Caresfoot. Theatre*, 1 Aug, pp 100—1.
               Dramatization of *Dawn*.

BA29	Ogilvy, G. 'H. Rider Haggard', *British Weekly*, 5 Aug, p 218.
BA30	Saintsbury, George. 'The Present State of the Novel', *Fornightly Review*, 1 Sep, pp 410–16.
BA31	'H. Rider Haggard at Home', *Pall Mall Gazette*, 18 Sep, p 8.

1888

BA32	'The Culture of the Horrible: Mr. Rider Haggard's Stories', *Church Quarterly Review*, Jan, pp 389–411.
BA33	'Reality and Romance', *Spectator*, 28 Apr, pp 569–71.
BA34	Notice of *Mr. Meeson's Will. New York Times*, 3 Jun.
BA35	'London as a Literary Centre', *Harper's New Monthly Magazine*, Jun, pp 14–15.
BA36	Reviews of *Cetywayo and His White Neighbours*, 2nd edition. *Literary World*, 27 Jul; *Westminster Review*, Jul, pp 100–1.
BA37	Notice of *Maiwa's Revenge. Literary World* (Boston), 4 Aug, p 253.
BA38	'The Fall of Fiction', *Fortnightly Review*, 1 Sep, pp 324–6.
BA39	Review of *Mr. Meeson's Will. Literary World* (Boston), 1 Sep, p 275.
BA40	Review of *Maiwa's Revenge. Athenaeum*, 8 Sep, p 317.
BA41	'To the Author of "She" ', *The Month*, Sep, pp 60–3. A poem signed 'Theophilus'.
BA42	Reviews of a dramatization of *She*. (FPB29). *Illustrated London News*, 15 Sep, p 306; *Athenaeum*, 15 Sep, pp 361–2.
BA43	' "Squire" Haggard at Home', *Literary World* (Boston), 10 Nov, pp 393–4.
BA44	Review of *Mr. Meeson's Will . Athenaeum*, 17 Nov, p 659.
BA45	'Mr. Haggard and His Henchmen', *Fortnightly Review*, Nov, pp 684–88.
BA46	'The Profitable Reading of Fiction', *Forum*, p 65.
BA47	Notice of *Colonel Quaritch, VC. Literary World* (Boston), 8 Dec, p 453.
BA48	'Mr. Rider Haggard', *Illustrated London News*, 15 Dec, p 710.
BA49	Reviews of *Colonel Quaritch, VC*. *Illustrated London News*, 15 Dec, p 710; *Scots Observer*, 22 Dec, p 317.

1889

BA50	Lang, Andrew. 'The Dreadful Trade', *Scots Observer*, 16 Feb, pp 356–7.
BA51	Henley, W.E. 'Modern Men: H. Rider Haggard', *Scots Observer*, 27 Apr, pp 631–2.
BA52	Reviews of *Cleopatra*. *Scots Observer*, 27 Jul, pp 275–6; *Murray's Magazine*, Jul, p 287.
BA53	Haggard, David. *A History of the Haggard Family in England and America, 1433 to 1889*. Bloomington, Illinois.
BA54	Michael, L. *She: an Allegory of the Church*. New York, Frank F. Lovell & Co.

1890

BA55   Review of *Allan's Wife. New York Times*, 26 Jan.

BA56   'A Plea for Swaziland', *Review of Reviews*, Feb, vol 1, pp 41–2.

BA57   Runciman, James. 'King Plagiarism and His Court', *Fortnightly Review*, Mar, p 426.

BA58   'H. Rider Haggard', *Book News* (Philadelphia), Jun.

BA59   Review of *Beatrice. New York Times*, 6 Oct, p 3.

BA60   Reviews of *The World's Desire*.
   New York Times, 16 Nov, p 19; *British Weekly*, 20 Nov, p 54 (J.M. Barrie); *Literary World*, 28 Nov; *Athenaeum*, 6 Dec, p 773 ; *National Observer*, 13 Dec, pp 99–100 ('Culture and Anarchy').

1891

BA61   'Portraits of Celebrities — H. Rider Haggard', *Strand Magazine*, Jan, p 48.

BA62   'Rider Haggard Here', *New York Times*, 11 Jan, p 8.

BA63   Literary partnership with W.H. Ballou Fermet reported. *New York Times*, 28 Jan, p 4.

BA64   Review of *The World's Desire. Spectator*, 14 Feb, p 249.

BA65   Review of *Eric Brighteyes. New York Times*, 31 May, p 10.

1892

BA66   How, Harry. 'Illustrated Interviews No VII — Mr. H. Rider Haggard', *Strand Magazine*, Jan, pp 3–17.
   Later included in a book with the same title, of similar interviews with other celebrities, published by Newnes in 1893.

BA67   'Interesting People — H. Rider Haggard', *Winter's Weekly*, 19 Mar, pp 337–8.

BA68   Review of *Nada the Lily. New York Times*, 15 May, p 19.

BA69   'Rider the Ripper', *Critic*, 9 Jul, p 23.

BA70   Bremont, Anne. *Sonnets and Love Poems*. New York, J.J. Little.

1893

BA71   'The South African Difficulty. An Interview With H. Rider Haggard', *East Anglian Daily Times*, Oct.

BA72   *Collection of Letters Addressed to A.P. Watt by Various Writers*. London, Watt.

BA73   Review of *Montezuma's Daughter. New York Times*, 26 Nov.

1894

BA74   Thurston, Rev. Herbert. 'Mr. Rider Haggard and the Immuring of Nuns', *Month*, Jan, pp 14–29.

BA75   Dolman, F. 'How Mr. Haggard Works', *Review of Reviews*, Jan, p 31.

BA76   'How I Write My Books', *The Young Man*, Jan, pp 21–3.
   F. Dolman interview; with a photograph.

BA77   *Letters and Addresses to A.P. Watt.* London, A.P. Watt & Son.
BA78   Dolman, F. 'Mr. Rider Haggard at Home', *Black and White*, 11 Aug,
       pp 178–9.
       With a photograph.
BA79   Review of *The People of the Mist. New York Times*, 19 Nov.
BA80   Selous, F.C. *A Hunter's Wanderings in Africa.* London, Richard
       Bently & Son.
BA81   Jeaffreson, J.C. *A Book of Recollections.* 2 vols. London, Hurst &
       Blackett.

1895

BA82   'Mr. Rider Haggard as a Politician', *Saturday Review*, 24 Mar,
       pp 372–3.
BA83   'Rider Haggard in Parliament', *New York Times*, 24 Mar, p 23.
BA84   Wilcox, A. 'Agriculturists at Home — Mr. Rider Haggard at
       Ditchingham', *Cable*, 11 May, p 297.
       With three photographs.
BA85   Review of *Heart of the World. New York Times*, 25 May, p 3.
BA86   'Life Stories of Successful Men, No XXI — Mr. H. Rider Haggard',
       Answers, 15 Jun, p 67.
BA87   'Rescue of Rider Haggard', *Eastern Evening News*, 20 Jul, p 4; also
       22 Jul.
       From election riot.
BA88   'Rioting in East Norfolk. Interview with Rider Haggard', *Pall Mall
       Gazette*, 25 Jul, p 3.
BA89   'Election Ourtages', *Norfolk Chronicle*, 27 Jul, pp 4 and 7.
       Quotes Haggard's letter to *The Times* on 23 Jul, plus leading article.
BA90   'Tumble of Liberals', *New York Times*, 28 Jul, p 1.
BA91   Review of *Joan Haste. Saturday Review*, 21 Sep, p 386 (by H.G.
       Wells).
BA92   Review of *Joan Haste. New York Times*, 26 Oct.
BA93   Besant, Walter. 'Chronicle and Comment', *Bookman* (New York),
       Nov, pp 179–80.

1896

BA94   Review of *Heart of the World. Saturday Review*, 30 May, pp 562–3
       (by H.G. Wells).

1897

BA95   Graham , R.D. *The Masters of Victorian Literature.* London, Simpkin
       and Marshall, p 152.

1898

BA96   'A Novelist on "Land Suckers" ', *North British Agriculturist*, 7 Sep,
       p 567.
BA97   Review of an instalment of *A Farmer's Year* in *Longmans Magazine.
       North British Agriculturist*, 12 Oct, p 651.
BA98   Review of *Dr. Therne. Spectator*, 3 Dec, p 836.

1899

BA99　　　Review of *Swallow*. *New York Times*, 11 Mar.

BA100　　Woods, K.P. 'The Evolution of an Artist', *Bookman* (New York), Jun, pp 350–2.

BA101　　'Mr. Rider Haggard and His Orchids', *The Gardener*, 23 Sep, p 653.

BA102　　'Mr. Rider Haggard on the Crisis', *East Anglian Daily Times*, 9 Oct, p 5.

BA103　　Sanders, T.W. 'My Favourite Flowers. Mr. Rider Haggard as an Orchid Grower', *Amateur Gardening*, 16 Dec, p 384.

BA104　　Reviews of *A Farmer's Year*.
　　　　　Bookman, Dec; *Review of Reviews*, Dec, p 287 ('Rider Haggard as Prophet'); *Review of Reviews*, Dec, p 393 ('The End of the Farmer's Year').

1900

BA105　　Reviews of *A Farmer's Year*.
　　　　　Athenaeum, 6 Jan; *Agricultural Economist*, 1 Mar, p 78; *Literary World*, 23 Mar; *New York Times*, 19 Aug.

BA106　　'Notable Personalities: H. Rider Haggard, JP', *Agricultural Economist*, 1 Mar, pp 80 and 83.
　　　　　With photograph.

BA107　　Review of *Elissa*. *New York Times*, 23 Jun. .

1901

BA108　　Gregory, R.R.C. 'The Mission of Mr. Rider Haggard and Rural Education', *Longmans Magazine*, Jun.

BA109　　Reviews of *Lysbeth*.
　　　　　Review of Reviews, vol 23, May, p 504; *New York Times*, 4 May.

BA110　　Mackenzie, F.A. 'After the War — Mr. Rider Haggard's Prophecies', *Daily Mail*, 7 Dec.

BA111　　Review of *A Winter Pilgrimage*. *New York Times*, 7 Dec.

BA112　　'Literature Portraits — III: Henry Rider Haggard', *Literature*, 25 May, pp 430–1.

BA113　　'A Lobbyist'. 'Agricultural Politics', *Mark Lane Express*, 11 Nov, p 619.

1902

BA114　　Wilkinson, H.A. 'Living Talks With Men Who Are Alive — No III: H. Rider Haggard. The Rural Exodus', *Commonwealth*.

BA115　　'Mr. Rider Haggard's Reminiscences', *Great Thoughts*, Nov, p 81.

BA116　　Reviews of *Rural England*.
　　　　　Morning Post, 26 Dec, p 2; *Times Literary Supplement*, 26 Dec, p 387.

BA117　　'Mr. Rider Haggard on Agriculture', *East Anglian Daily Times*, 29 and 30 Dec.

1903

BA118   Reviews of *Rural England*.
Guardian, 14 Jan, p 63; *Contemporary Review*, Jan, pp 143–5; *New York Times*, 17 Jan; *Spectator*, 14 Feb, pp 540–68; *Quarterly Review* no 394, Apr, pp540–68 ('The Needs of Rural England'); *Edinburgh Review*, Apr, pp 475–500.

BA119   Reviews of *Pearl Maiden*.
Times Literary Supplement, 6 Mar, p 72; *New York Times*, 29 Aug.

BA120   'Real Places and Faces in Fiction — 1: Mr. Rider Haggard's Umslopogaas', *Black and White Illustrated Budget*, 19 Dec, pp 35–6.

1904

BA121   Review of *Stella Fregelius*. *Times Literary Supplement*, 5 Feb, p 36.

BA122   'Portraits of Great Writers', *Pearson's Magazine*, Jun, p[583].
Photograph and short article.

BA123   Reviews of *The Brethren*.
Times Literary Supplement, 7 Oct, p 304; *New York Times*, 31 Dec.

BA124   Review of *Ayesha*. *New York Times*, 17 Dec.

1905

BA125   Review of *A Gardener's Year*. *Times Literary Supplement*, 3 Mar, p 75.

BA126   'H. Rider Haggard Turned Coloniser', *New York Herald*, 19 Mar, p 3.

BA127   'Through America — Mr. Rider Haggard's Tour', *East Anglian Daily Times*, 29 Apr.

BA128   'A Man of the Moment — Mr. Rider Haggard', *Daily Mirror*, 21 Jun.

BA129   'Poverty and the Land. A Chat With Mr. Rider Haggard', *Daily News*, 23 Jun.

BA130   'Commissioner H. Rider Haggard', *Review of Reviews*, Jul, pp 20–7.
With two photographs.

BA131   'A Chat With Mr. Rider Haggard', *Graphic*, 29 Jul, pp 124–5.

BA132   Editorial on H. Rider Haggard's occupations. *New York Times*, 6 Aug, p 6.

BA133   Review of *Ayesha*. *Times Literary Supplement*, 6 Oct, p 329.

1906

BA134   'Where is Mr. Haggard?', *Review of Reviews*, Jan, pp 9–10.

BA135   Reviews of *The Way of the Spirit*.
Times Literary Supplement, 9 Mar, p 84; *Saturday Review*, 7 Apr, pp 432–3.

BA136   'Mr. H. Rider Haggard', *Literary World*, 15 Mar, pp 121–2.

BA137   Leyds, E.J. *The First Annexation of the Transvaal*. London, T. Fisher Unwin.

BA138   ' "Triangle Camp" Canard. Mr. Haggard Denies the Story of His "Promise" ', *Tribune*, 5 Sep.

BA139   Review of *Benita*. *Times Literary Supplement*, 28 Sep, p 329.

BA140	Review of *The Spirit of Bambatse*. *New York Times*, 29 Sep.
BA141	'An Interview With H. Rider Haggard', *Christian Commonwealth*, 1 Nov, pp 75–6.

1907

BA142	'Mr. Rider Haggard on Small Holdings', *Spectator*, 22 Jun, pp 968–9.
BA143	Review of *Fair Margaret*. *Times Literary Supplement*, 3 Oct, p 301.

1908

BA144	Northrop, W.B. 'H. Rider Haggard — Story Teller and Psychologist', *Cassell's Magazine*, pp 478–81.
BA145	Wheeler, H.F.B. 'Bookplates of Celebrities', *Bibliophile*, Sep, p 12.
BA146	Review of *The Ghost Kings*. *Times Literary Supplement*, 1 Oct, p 324.

1909

BA147	Review of *The Yellow God*. *Times Literary Supplement*, 11 Mar, p 96.
BA148	Review of *The Lady of the Heavens*. *New York Times*, 29 May.
BA149	'Mr. Rider Haggard', *Social Gazette* (A Salvation Army Organ), 15 Oct , p 2.
	An interview, signed 'D.C.'; with a photograph.
BA150	Review of The *Lady of Blossholme*. *Times Literary Supplement*, 11 Nov, p 427.

1910

BA151	Reviews of *Morning Star*.
	Times Literary Supplement, 31 Mar, p 113; *New York Times*, 2 Jul.
BA152	'Literary Men of the Month', *Captain*, Jun, pp 277–8.
BA153	Reviews of *Queen Sheba's Ring*.
	Times Literary Supplement, 8 Sep, p 317; *New York Times*, 15 Oct.

1911

BA154	Reviews of *Rural Denmark*.
	The Times, 18 Feb, p 13; *Times Literary Supplement*, 13 Apr, p 149; *New York Times*, 25 Jun.
BA155	Reviews of *Regeneration*.
	New York Times, 4 Jun; *Outlook* (New York), 1 Jul (by Theodore Roosevelt).
BA156	Review of *Red Eve*. *Times Literary Supplement*, 14 Sep, p 334.
BA157	'Writers of the Day — No 46: H. Rider Haggard', *New Zealand Times*, 5 Nov.

1912

BA158	Notice of *Marie*. *Times Literary Supplement*, 25 Jan, p 38.
BA159	Review of *Red Eve*. *New York Times*, 3 Mar.
BA160	'Our Portrait Gallery. Prominent Wardens — LXII: Sir Henry Rider Haggard', *Churchwarden*, 15 Jul, p 9.
	With a photograph.

BA161   Review of *Marie*. *New York Times*, 25 Aug.
BA162   'Sir Rider Haggard. A Short Sketch', *Amicus Illustrated Weekly*
            (Ceylon), 6 Dec, p 22.
                Signed 'F.H.G.'.

1913

BA163   'Sir Rider Haggard in Calcutta', *Stateman*, 18 Jan.
BA164   'Empire Trade Commission', *Commerce* (Ceylon), 22 Jan.
BA165   'The Visit of Sir H. Rider Haggard', *Evening Post and Advocate of
            Ceylon*, 1 Feb.
BA166   Review of *Child of Storm*. *Times Literary Supplement*, 6 Feb , p 53.
BA167   'Sir Rider Haggard — Fiction Writing and Agriculture', *The Age*
            (Melbourne), 18 Feb, p 1.
BA168   'Sir Rider Haggard. Empire Trade Commisson Arrival in
            Christchurch. Leading Article', *Lyttleton Times* (New Zealand),
            1 Mar, p 12; 'Not Interested in Romance', p 13.
BA169   'The Empire Trade Commission. Interesting Personalities', *The Press*
            (Christchurch, NZ), 1 Mar.
BA170   'Empire Trade Commission', *The Weekly Press* (Christchurch, NZ),
            12 Mar, p 32.
                With a group photograph, including Rider Haggard.
BA171   'Sir Rider Haggard — Story Writer and Farmer', *Sydney Evening
            News*, 30 Mar.
BA172   'Resources of the North. Sir H. Rider Haggard's Views', *Daily Mail*
            (Brisbane), 18 Apr, p 5.
BA173   'Sir Rider Haggard. His Opinion of Australia', *The Advertiser*
            (Adelaide), 12 May, p 9.

1914

BA174   Review of *The Wanderer's Necklace*. *Times Literary Supplement*,
            29 Jan, p 49.
BA175   'After 30 Years — Sir Rider Haggard Again in South Africa', *Cape
            Argus* (Cape Town), 2 Mar, p 7.
BA176   'Old Scenes — Sir Rider Haggard's Return to Natal', *Natal Witness*
            (Pietermaritzburg), 26 Mar, p 1.
BA177   'Saved His Master's Life. Novelist and His Faithful Servant', *Natal
            Witness* (Pietermaritzburg), 30 Mar, p 1.
                With photograph of servant Masuku.
BA178   'Sir Rider Haggard's Return. In Pretoria Then and Now', *Transvaal
            Leader*, 31 Mar, p 6.
BA179   'South Africa and the Empire — Sir Rider Haggard and Jess Cottage',
            Transvaal Leader, 31 Mar, p 7.
BA180   'Sir Rider Haggard and Masuku', *Pictorial* (Durban), 3 Apr.
BA181   'A Romantic Boarding House — Jess's Cottage', *Transvaal Leader*,
            3 Apr, p 9.
                Including photographs.
BA182   'Our Possibilities', *Transvaal Leader*, 4 Apr, p 6.
                Leading article.

BA183	'Sir Rider Haggard — Talks on Old Durban', *Natal Mercury*, 18 Apr.
BA184	Review of *Mameena. Athenaeum*, 10 Oct, p 364.
	A play based on *Child of Storm* (see FPB36).
BA185	'Boers Are Loyal, Says Rider Haggard', *New York Times*, 18 Oct, p 4.

1915

BA186	Review of *The Holy Flower. Times Literary Supplement*, 1 Apr, p 110.
BA187	Editorial on a forthcoming novel. *New York Times*, 18 Apr.
BA188	'Lord Selborne's Speech', *Eastern Daily Press*, 28 Aug.
	Interview.

1916

BA189	'Land Settlement After the War', *Morning Post*, 10 Jan.
BA190	Reviews of *The Ivory Child*.
	Morning Post, 10 Jan, p 2; *Times Literary Supplement*, 13 Jan, p 19.
BA191	Editorial (Haggard's World Tour), *New York Times*, 18 Feb.
BA192	'Land for Soldiers', *The Mercury* (Hobart, Tasmania), 4 Apr, p 3; 'Sir Rider Haggard's Mission', p 4.
BA193	'After the War. Peopling the Dominions', *Sydney Morning Herald*, 25 May.
BA194	'To Save the Race. Soldiers and Land', *The Dominion* (Wellington, NZ), 1 Jun, p 6.
BA195	'Seeking Avocations for Ex-servicemen', *Victoria Daily Times* (Vancouver), 30 Jun.
BA196	'British Empire Must Retain All Its Sons', *Evening Bulletin* (Edmonton, Alberta), 10 Jul.
BA196a	'Rocky Mountain Peak Named After Sir Rider Haggard', *Evening Bulletin* (Edmonton, Alberta), 11 Jul.
	'Mount Sir Rider': also a glacier named 'Haggard Glacier'.
BA197	Notice of Haggard visit. *Saskatoon Phoenix*, 12 Jul, p 1.
BA197a	Report of Haggard visit. *Saskatoon Phoenix*, 13 Jul, p 5.
	Note 'Rider' is spelt 'Sider'!
BA197b	Leading article. *Saskatoon Phoenix*, 15 Jul, p 4.
BA198	'Britain's Superfluous Women', *New York Tribune*, 22 Jul.
BA199	'Sir Rider Haggard's Colonial Tour', *East Anglian Daily Times*, 9 Aug.
BA200	'Sir Rider Haggard's Tour', *The Times*, 22 Jul, p 3; 31 Jul, p 5; 1 Aug, p 7.
BA201	'Land Settlement and the Empire', *Lloyd's Weekly News*, 26 Nov, p 5.

1917

BA202	'Sir Rider Haggard's Plea of "More From the Land" ', *Daily Chronicle* , 2 Jan, p 5.
	Plus leading article on p 4.
BA203	Report of Haggard's law suit over a film version of *She. The Times*, 13 Jan, p 4.

BA204   Blackman, A.M. 'The Nugent and Haggard Collections of Egyptian
         Antiquities', *Journal of Egyptian Archaeology*, pp 39–46.
BA205   Review of *Finished*. *Times Literary Supplement*, 6 Sep, p 428.

1918

BA206   Review of *Love Eternal*. *Times Literary Supplement*, 4 Apr, p 160.
BA207   Review of *Moon of Israel*. *Times Literary Supplement*, 7 Nov, p 538.

1919

BA208   Review of *Ivory Child*. *Times Literary Supplement*, 13 Jan, p 19.
BA209   Review of *When the World Shook*. *Times Literary Supplement*,
         27 Mar, p 164.

1920

BA210   'The Man of the Week — Sir H. Rider Haggard', *St. Leonard's
         Chronicle*, 9 Jan.
BA211   Review of *The Ancient Allan*. *Times Literary Supplement*, 12 Feb,
         p 104.
BA212   Review of The *Ancient Allan*. *Athenaeum*, 27 Feb.
         By Katherine Mansfield; also writes on Marge Askinforit, by Barry
         Pain.
BA213   Huddleston, S. 'A Rider Haggard Boom in France? — Has *She* Been
         Plagiarised?' *John O'London's Weekly*, 1 May, p 104.
BA214   'Parentage is Far Too Costly. Imperial Aspects', *Daily Sketch*, 28 Jun,
         p 2.
BA215   Review of *Smith and the Pharaohs*. *Times Literary Supplement*,
         11 Nov, p 737.

1921

BA216   Review of *She and Allan*. *Times Literary Supplement*, 3 Mar, p 143.
BA217   'She and Allan', *Bookman*, Mar, p 211.
         Biographical article with portrait.
BA218   Joseph, M. 'The Romance of Rider Haggard', *John O'London's
         Weekly*, 5 Mar, p 672.
BA219   Notice of *Moon of Israel*. *Times Literary Supplement*, 24 Mar, p 198.

1922

BA220   Review of *The Virgin of the Sun*. *Times Literary Supplement*, 26 Jan,
         p 59.
BA221   Randall, Wilfred L. 'Sir H. Rider Haggard and His Work', *Bookman*,
         Aug, pp 206–7.

1923

BA222   'Opening of the Inner Tomb on Sunday', *Westminster Gazette*,
         14 Feb, p 6.
         Interview re Tutankhamen.

BA223 'Desecrating the Dead. A Protest by Sir H. Rider Haggard', *Sunday Express*, 18 Feb, p 7.

BA224 Review of *The World's Desire*. *Times Literary Supplement*, 15 Mar, p 178.

BA225 Dark, Sidney. 'Ride On, Sir Knight, Ride On! Sir Rider Haggard and His Art', *John O'London's Weekly*, 17 Nov, p 242.

BA226 Brown, H.F. *Letters and Papers of John Addington Symonds*. London, John Murray.

1924

BA227 Review of *Heu-Heu*. *Times Literary Supplement*, 7 Feb, p 78.

BA228 Shanks, Edward. 'Sir Rider Haggard and the Novel of Adventure', *London Mercury*, Nov, pp 71–9.

BA229 Hamilton, C. *Unwritten History*. Boston, Little, Brown & Co.

1925

BA230 Review of *Queen of the Dawn*. *Times Literary Supplement*, 30 Apr, p 301.

BA231 Twenty lines of verse by J.E. Read, on the publication of *Queen of the Dawn*. *John O'London's Weekly*, 9 May, p 186.

BA232 Obituary notice. *The Times*, 15 May, pp 16 and 18.

BA233 Obituary notice and editorial. *New York Times*, 15 May.

BA234 Flower, Newman. 'Sir Rider Haggard. A Romantic Career. Some Personal Memories', *Sunday Times*, 17 May.

BA235 'Sir Rider Haggard. His Life and Career', *The Times*, 25 May, p 19.

BA236 'A Master of Romance. Sir Rider Haggard and His Many Novels', *John O'London's Weekly*, 30 May, p 276.
  With a photograph.

BA237 Twigg, J.B. 'A Memory of Sir Rider Haggard', *John O'London's Weekly*, 27 Jun, p 433. (Letter).

BA238 'Report of the Legacies in Haggard's Will', *The Times*, 1 Aug, p 15.

BA239 Cox, H. and J.E. Chandler. *The House of Longman*. London, Longmans, Green & Co.

1926

BA240 Reviews of *The Days of My Life*.
  Bookman, Nov, pp 108–10 (J.P. Collins; also a photograph on front cover); *Times Literary Supplement*, 7 Oct, p 665.

BA241 Hutchinson, H.G. 'Sir Rider Haggard's Autobiography', *Edinburgh Review*, Oct, pp 343–55.

1928

BA242 'The Sale of Kessingland Grange', *The Times*, 18 Nov.

BA243 Bensusan, S.L. *Latter Day Rural England*. London, Benn.

1929

BA244   Review of *Mary of Marion Isle*. *Times Literary Supplement*, 10 Jan, p 26.

BA245   Asche, Oscar. *Oscar Asche, His Life*. London, Hurst and Blackett.

BA246   Review of *Allan and the Ice Gods*. *Times Literary Supplement*, 30 June, p 454.

1930

BA247   McKay, George L. *Bibliography of the Writings of Sir Rider Haggard*. *The Bookman's Journal*, London
Limited edition of 475 copies. Originally appeared as supplements to *The Bookman's Journal*, vol 17, no 12 to vol 18, no 13.

BA248   Review of *Belshazzar*. *Times Literary Supplement*, 2 Oct, p 778.

1932

BA249   Conway, W.M. 'Episodes in a Varied Life', *Country Life*, 4, 18, and 25 Jun.

1933

BA250   Bergen, R.A. *Old Icelandic Sources in the English Novel. A Thesis*. Philadelphia, Pennsylvania Press, University of Philadelphia.

1935

BA251   Haggard, Lilias Rider. 'The Real Rider Haggard', *Pearson's Magazine*, pp 29–33.

1936

BA252   Partington, W. 'Champion of the British Farmer', *Farmer's Weekly*, 11 Sep, p 25.

BA253   Longman, C.J. *The House of Longmans (1724–1800)*. London, Longmans, Green & Co.

BA254   Pemberton, Max. *Sixty Years Ago and After*. London, Hutchinson & Co.

1937

BA255   Walpole, Hugh. 'Sir H. Rider Haggard' in *Dictionary of National Biography*, 4th Supplement. London, Oxford University Press.

BA256   Gissing, A. and E. Gissing. *Letters of George Gissing*. London, Constable.

1938

BA257   Witherby, H.F. and G. Witherby. *History of the English Novel*.

BA258   Kipling, Rudyard. *Something of Myself — For My Friends Known and Unknown*. London, Macmillan.

1939

BA259   McKay, G.L. and J.E. Scott. *Additions and Corrections to the Haggard Bibliography,* London, Mitre Press.

BA260   Elwin, Malcolm . *The Old Gods Falling*. London, Macmillan.

BA261   Lewis, C.S. *Rehabilitations and Other Essays*. London, Oxford University Press.

1941

BA262   Nash, Eveleigh. *I Like the Life I Lived*. London, John Murray.

1944

BA263   Scott, J.E. 'The New South Africa', *Papers of the Bibliographical Society of America*.
         An article indicating that, although a pamphlet of this title carried Haggard's name, it was not written by him.

BA264   Green, R.L. 'He, She and It', *Times Literary Supplement*, 27 May, p 264; and 17 Jun, p 300.

BA265   Green, R.L. 'King Solomon's Wives', *Times Literary Supplement*, 1 Jul, p 324.

1945

BA266   Colgan, N. 'Africa's Writer of Romance', *Everybody's Weekly*, 12 May.

BA267   Gamble, P. 'The Two Rider Haggards', *John O'London's Weekly*, 18 May, p 6.

BA268   Green, R.L. 'The Romances of Rider Haggard', *English*, summer.

BA269   Gibbons, S. 'Voyage of Discovery', *Fortnightly Review*, Dec, pp 401−6.

BA270   Buckley, J.H. *William Ernest Henley. A Study in Counter Decadence of the Nineties*. Princeton, Princeton University Press.

1946

BA271   *List of Books From the Library of Sir H. Rider Haggard*. London, Elkins Mathews.
         Catalogue.

BA272   Green, R.L. *Teller of Tales*. Leicester, Edmund Ward.

BA273   Green, R.L. *Andrew Lang. A Critical Biography*. Leicester, Edmund Ward.

1947

BA274   Scott, J.E. *A Bibliography of the Works of Sir Henry Rider Haggard 1856−1925*. London, Elkin Mathews.
         Only 500 copies printed.

1948

BA275 Bleiler, E.F. *Checklist of Fantastic Literature*. Chicago, Shasta.

BA276 Scott, J.E. 'Hatchers-Out of Tales', *New Colophon* 1, pp 348–56.

BA277 Elwin, Malcolm. 'Introduction' to new edition of *She*. London, Macdonald.

1949

BA278 Bryant, A.T. *The Zulu People*. Pietermaritzburg, Shuter and Shuter.

BA279 Connell, J. *W.E. Henley*. London, Constable.

1950

BA280 Webb, Jean Francis. *H. Rider Haggard's 'King Solomon's Mines': the tale of a fabulous treasure hunt*. New York, Dell Publishing Co.
       The story of the MGM motion picture.

BA281 Flower, N. *Just As It Happened*. London, Cassell.

BA282 Bentley, Nicolas, ed. *Fred Bason's Diary*. London, Wingate.

1951

BA283 O'Brien, E.D. 'The Adventurous Life of a Great Storyteller', *Illustrated London News*, 26 May, p 857.

BA284 Haggard, Lilias Rider. *The Cloak That I Left. A Biography of Rider Haggard*. London, Hodder & Stoughton.

BA285 Reviews of *The Cloak That I Left*.
       Spectator, 15 Jun (Arthur Ransome); *New Statesman*, 14 Jul, pp 45–6. (Graham Greene). Later published in Graham Greene's *Collected Essays*, Bodley Head, 1969.

1952

BA286 Miller, Henry. *The Books in My Life*. London, Peter Owen.

BA287 Article concerning 'The Ghost', at Brede Place (see M43). *Bulletin of the New York Public Library*, vol 56, no 12, pp 591–5.

1954

BA288 Greene, Graham. *The Lost Childhood and other Essays*. London, Eyre & Spottiswoode.

BA289 Muir, Percy. *English Children's Books*. London, Batsford.
       Second edition 1969.

BA290 Jung, C.J. *The Collected Works of C.J. Jung*. Edited by Sir Herbert Read, Michael Fordham and Gerhard Adler; translated by R.F.C. Hull. London, Routledge & Kegan Paul, 1954– . Vol 1– .
       Fascinating analysis of the psychology of Haggard's novels and romances. See volumes 10, 15, 16, 17 and 18.

1955

BA291 Carrington, C.E. *The Life of Rudyard Kipling*. London, Macmillan.

1956

BA292   Broughton, G. 'Rudyard Kipling and Rider Haggard', *Kipling Journal*, April, pp 8–10.

BA293   Trease, Geoffrey. 'The Spell of Rider Haggard', *Radio Times*, 1 Jun, p 6.

BA294   Campbell, Archie. 'In Search of Solomon's Treasure', *Radio Times*, 8 Jun, p 5.

BA295   Leading article on Rider Haggard. *Times Literary Supplement*, 22 Jun, p 377.

BA296   Green, R.L. 'H. Rider Haggard', *Eastern Daily Press*, 22 Jun.

BA297   Flower, Newman. 'The Most Amazing Book Ever Written', *Radio Times*, 29 Jun, p 6.

BA298   Baker, G. 'A Great Rider Haggard Accession', *Princeton University Library Chronicle* 17.

BA299   'H. Rider Haggard', *Literary World*, July.

1958

BA300   Nowell-Smith, S. *The House of Cassell 1848–1958*. London, Cassell.

1959

BA301   Ellis, H.F. 'The Niceties of Plagiarism', *Atlantic Monthly* , Jan, pp 76 and 78.

BA302   Green, R.L. 'Illicit Treasure Seekers: Another Literary Osmosis', *Sherlock Holmes Journal*, no 2 (Spring), pp 72–3.

1960

BA303   Cohen, Morton. *Rider Haggard — His Life and Works*. London, Hutchinson.
         Second edition 1968.

BA304   Pritchett, V.S. 'Haggard Still Riding', *New Statesman*, 27 Aug, pp 277–8.

BA305   Lewis, C.S. 'Haggard Rides Again', *Time and Tide*, 3 Sep, pp 1044–5.
         Review of BA303. Reprinted under the title 'The Mythopoeic Gift of Rider Haggard' in Lewis's collection of essays *Of This and Other Worlds* (Collins, 1982, ed. by W. Hooper). Another essay in the same collection, 'On Stories', also refers to Haggard.

1961

BA306   Brown, I. 'Teller of Tales', *New York Times Book Review*, 26 Mar, pp 5–18.

BA307   Review of *Rider Haggard — His Life and Works* (see BA303), *London Magazine*, Apr, pp 87–8.

BA308   DeMott, B. 'The Author of *She*', *Nation*, 20 May, pp 442–3.

BA309   Haggard, Lilias Rider. 'A Born Story Teller', *Listener*, 22 Jun, p 1078.

BA310   Lewis, C.S. *An Experiment in Criticism*. Cambridge, Cambridge University Press.

1962

BA311   Cohen, Morton. Introduction to a new edition of *She*. New York, Collier.

1964

BA312   Karrfalt, D.H. 'Anima in Hawthorne and Haggard', *American Notes and Queries*, pp 152–3.

1965

BA313   Cohen, Morton, ed. *Rudyard Kipling to Rider Haggard: The Record of a Friendship*. London, Hutchinson.

1966

BA314   Edwards, Oliver. 'Helen in Egypt', *The Times*, 12 May, p 16. *The World's Desire* (F13) discussed.

1967

BA315   Sandison, Alan. 'Rider Haggard: "Some Call it Evolution . . ." '. In *The Wheel of Empire*. London, Macmillan; New York, St. Martin's Press.

1968

BA316   Ascherson, Neal. 'He', *Spectator*, 26 Aug, p 314.
BA317   Doyle, B. *The Who's Who of Children's Literature*. London, Hugh Evelyn.
BA318   Hepburn, James. *The Author's Empty Purse and the Rise of the Literary Agent*. Oxford, Oxford University Press.
BA319   Reese, Trevor. *The History of the Royal Commonwealth Society 1868–1968*. Oxford, Oxford University Press.

1969

BA320.   Jackson, F. *Early Days in East Africa*. Folkestone, Kent, Dawsons.

1970

BA321   Harvey, F.J. *Children's Books in England*. Cambridge, Cambridge University Press.
BA322   Hutchinson, B., ed. 'Check List of Haggard's Works', *Book Collecting and Library Monthly* (Brighton), no 23, Mar.
BA323   Gardner, Brian. *The African Dream*. London, Cassell.
BA323a   Chapple, J.A.V. *Documentary and Imaginative Literature 1880–1920*. New York, Barnes and Noble.

1971

BA324	Fletcher, Ian. 'Can Haggard Ride Again?', *Listener*, 29 Jul, pp 136–8.
BA325	Harrison, Michael. *Fanfare of Strumpets*. London, W.H. Allen.
	Ayesha personifies Queen Victoria!
BA326	Carley, C.E. 'A Penetrating Look at a Famous Novel and Movie', *Classic Film Collector* (USA), Autumn.

1972

BA327	Atwood, Margaret. *Survival. A Thematic Guide to Canadian Literature*. Toronto, Anansi.
BA328	Gross, J., ed. *Rudyard Kipling — The Man, His Work and His World*. London, Weidenfeld and Nicolson.
BA329	Hinz, E.J. *Studies in the Novel*.
BA330	Greene, Graham. *The Pleasure Dome*. London, Secker and Warburg.
	Collected film criticisms.

1973

BA331	Moss, J.G. 'Three Motifs in Haggard's *She*', *English Literature in Transition*.
BA332	Aldiss, Brian W. *Billion Year Spree: The History of Science Fiction*. London, Weidenfeld and Nicolson.

1974

BA333	Carley, C.E. 'Haggard: A Biography and a Filmography', *Classic Film Collector* (USA), Winter.
BA334	Mullen, R.D. 'The Prudish Prudence of H. Rider Haggard and Edgar Rice Burroughs', *Riverside Quarterly* (Indiana State University), Vol 6, nos 1 and 2, Jan and Apr.
BA335	Townsend, J.R. *Written for Children*. London, Kestrel Books.
BA336	Zweig, P. *The Adventurer*. London, Dent.

1975

BA337	Street, B.V. *The Savage in Literature*. London, Routledge and Kegan Paul.

1976

BA338	Ellis, Peter Beresford. 'Rider Haggard as a Rural Reformer', *Country Life*, 9 Dec, pp 1796–7.
	Includes three photographs and a cartoon by 'Spy' reproduced from *Vanity Fair* (1887).

1977

BA339	Calder, J. *From Byron to Guevara*. London, Hamish Hamilton.
BA339a	Dixon, Bob. *Catching Them Young 2: Political Ideas in Children's Fiction*. London, Pluto Press.

BA340   Etherington, N. 'South African Origins of Rider Haggard's Early
        African Romances', *Notes and Queries*, Oct, pp 436–8.
BA341   Eagle, D. and H. Carnell, eds. *The Oxford Literary Guide to the
        British Isles*. Oxford, Oxford University Press.
BA342   Wilson, A. *The Strange Ride of Rudyard Kipling — His Life and
        Work*. London, Secker and Warburg.
BA343   Middlemas, Keith. *Pursuit of Pleasure: High Society in the 1900s*.
        London, Gordon Cremonesi.

1978

BA344   Ellis, Peter Berresford. *H. Rider Haggard: A Voice From the Infinite*.
        London, Routledge and Kegan Paul.
BA345   Barclay, Glen St John. *Anatomy of Horror: The Masters of Occult
        Fiction*. London, Weidenfeld and Nicolson.
        A chapter — 'Love and Death' — on Haggard.

1980

BA346   Green, Martin. *Dreams of Adventure, Deeds of Empire*. London,
        Routledge and Kegan Paul.
BA347   Higgins, D.S., ed. *The Private Diaries of Sir H. Rider Haggard
        1914–1925*. London, Cassell.
BA348   Ranger, Terence. 'The Rural African Voice in Zimbabwe Rhodesia:
        Archaism and Tradition', *Social Analysis*, Sep, pp 100–15.
BA349   Pritchett, V.S. *The Tale Bearers: Essays on English, American and
        Other Writers*. London, Chatto and Windus.
BA350   Parrinder, P. and R. Philmus, eds. *H.G. Wells's Literary Criticism*.
        Brighton, Harvester Press.

1981

BA351   Higgins, D.S. *Rider Haggard: The Great Storyteller*. London, Cassell.
BA351a Haining, Peter, ed. *The Best Short Stories of Rider Haggard*.
        Foreword by Hammond Innes. London, Michael Joseph.
        Two of the 'stories' published here are, in fact, chapters from
        Wisdom's Daughter (F52).
BA352   'Allan Quatermain to Rosa Burger: Violence in South African
        Fiction', *World Literature Written in English* (Univ. of Texas), vol 22,
        no 2, pp 171–82.

1984

BA353   Allen, R. 'Rider Haggard: The Author of King Solomon's Mines',
        Book and Magazine Collector, no 4, pp 16–23.
BA354   Etherington, N. *Rider Haggard*. Boston, G.K. Hall.
        'The first book-length study of Rider Haggard's fiction . . .' An
        interesting and provocative book.

1985

BA355   Simpson, Michael. *Thomas Adams and the Modern Planning Movement: Britain, Canada, and the United States 1900–1940.* London, Mansell.

BA356   Holloway, David. 'Haggard's Little Goldmine', *Daily Telegraph*, 7 Sep.

On the centenary of the first publication of *King Solomon's Mines* (F3).

BA357   Howkins, Alun. *Poor Labouring Men; Rural Radicalism in Norfolk 1870–1923.* London, Routledge and Kegan Paul.

References to *A Farmer's Year* (NF2) and *Rural England* (NF5).

BA358   Dalby, Richard. 'King Solomon's Mines. A Centenary remembered', *Antiquarian Book Monthly Review*, Oct.

1986

BA359   Fisher, Margery. *The Bright Face of Danger: An Exploration of the Adventure Story.* London, Hodder and Stoughton.

See in particular pp 65–71, and pp 198–211.

10 Parodies and Lampoons (PL)

1887

PL1   Barrie, J.M. 'An Interview with "She" ', by 'A Correspondent', *St. James's Gazette*, 16 Feb, p 6.

PL2   Lang, Andrew. A reply to Barrie's letter, by 'One Who Knows', *St. James's Gazette*, 18 Feb, p 13.

PL3   Walker Weird, *pseud.* 'Hee! Hee!', *Punch*, 26 Feb, pp 100–1.

PL4   Lang, Andrew and W.H. Pollock. *He.* By the Author of 'It', 'King Solomon's Wives', 'Bess', 'Much Darker Days', 'Mr. Morton's Subtler', and Other Romances. London, Longmans, Green.

This work was published by Longman on 23 Feb 1887 in Fcp, 8vo, 126 pp, price one shilling (sewed). Green paper wrappers with a design in red and black by W. Reader. A large paper edition (only 25 copies) was published on 2 Mar 1887. The book's dedication reads:

'Kor, Jan 30 1887.'

Dear Allan Quatermain — You, who with others have aided so manfully the Restoraton of King Romance, know that His Majesty is a Merry Monarch.

You will not think, therefore, that the respectful Liberty we have taken with your Wondrous Tale (as PAMELA did with the 137th Psalm) indicates any lack of loyalty to our lady AYESHA.

Her beauties are beyond the reach of danger from Burlesque, nor does *her* form flit across our humble pages.

May you restore to us yet the prize of her perfections, for we, at least, can never believe that she wholly perished in the place of the Pillar of Fire!

Yours Ever,
Two of the Ama Lo-grolla

He was reviewed in *The Athenaeum* on 12 Mar 1887.

PL5   'A Proposition and A Rider', *Punch*, 2 Apr, p 168.

Three mini-columns of doggerel, on plagiarism.

PL6   Biron, Henry Chartres. *King Solomon's Wives; or The Phantom Mines*. (Hyder Ragged). London, Vizetelly & Co.

An American edition was published by Munro, New York, in 1887. (No 736 in Munro's Library).

PL7   Walker Weird, *pseud*. Author of 'Hee-Hee', 'Solomon's Ewers', etc. 'Adam Slaughterman', *Punch*, 27 Aug, pp 88–9.

PL8   *He, A Companion to She. Being a history of adventure of J. Theodosius Aristophano on the island of Rapa Nui in search of his immortal ancestor.* New York, Munro. (No 721 in Munro's Library).

PL9   *It. A wild, weird history of marvellous, miraculous, phantasmagorical adventures in search of He, She and Jess and leading to finding 'It'. A Haggard conclusion.* New York, Munro. (No 726 in Munro's Library).

PL10   *King Solomon's Treasures.* By the author of 'He', 'It', 'Pa', 'Ma', etc. New York, Munro. (No 737 in Munro's Library).

PL11   *King Solomon's Wives.* By the author of 'He', 'It', 'Pa', 'Ma', etc. New York, Munro. (Pocket edition, Munro's Seaside Library, no 970).

PL12   *Bess. A Companion to Jess.* By the author of 'King Solomon's Wives', 'King Solomon's Treasures', 'He', 'It'. New York, Munro. (No 739 in Munro's Library).

There is debate about the authorship of items PL8–12. The *National Union Catalog, Pre-1956 Imprints* (London, Mansell), still links Andrew Lang's name with these parodies. The additional indication that W.H. Pollock was involved suggests that it has been assumed, because these two men did produce *He* (see PL4) that they were also responsible for the rest. I have not found the slightest evidence to support this idea and it seems most unlikely to be true. It seems more sound to believe the publisher's letter (also quoted in the *NUC, Pre-1956 Imprints*), naming J. De Morgan as the author.

1888

PL13   'The Doom of "She". Fragment of a Romance of Political Adventure', *Punch*, 31 Mar, pp 148–9.

With apologies to Mr. Rider Haggard.

PL14   Furniss, Harry. 'She-That-Ought-Not-To-Be-Played. A Story of Gloomy Gaiety', *Punch*, 22 Sep, p 132.

Author appeared as 'Lika-Joko'. A satirical review of the dramatization of *She* (see section 8).

PL15   Sims, G.R. 'The Lost Author'. *Hood's Comic Annual*, Christmas issue.

1889

PL16   Walker Weird, *pseud*. 'A Haggard Annual', *Punch's Almanac for 1890*, 5 Dec.

1890

PL17   Furniss, Harry. 'The Pick of the Pictures — Royal Academy, No 551.
        Two Tales of a Tiger — Advertisement for new Romance by Rider
        Laggard and Andrew Hang'. *Punch*, 24 May.

PL18   Lang, Andrew. *Old Friends. Essays in Epistolary Parody*. London,
        Longman.

1891

PL19   'Literary Stars', *Punch*, 3 Jan, p 2.
            A caricature by E.F. Wheeler — a trivial item, one of twelve small
        drawings of writers.

PL20   'Mr. Punch's Prize Novels. No XI. The Book of Kookarie. By Reader
        Faghard, Author of "Queen Bathsheba's Ewers", "Yawn", "Guess",
        "Me", "My Ma's at Penge", "Smallun Halfboy", "General
        Porridge, D.T.", "Me a Kiss", "The Hemisphere's Wish", etc. etc.',
        Punch, 17 Jan, pp 28–9.

1895

PL21   'An Election Address', *Punch*, 30 Mar, p 145.
            Seven verses, on Haggard becoming accepted as a Conservative
        candidate in Norfolk.

1899

PL22   'Allan Quatermain's Farm', *Punch*, 15 Nov, p 293.

1902

PL23   'The Song of a Fireside Ranger', *Punch*, 12 Mar, p 185.
            Seven verses on the works of Weyman, Hope, Barrie, Haggard,
        Kipling, Jacobs and Merriman.

PL24   'Authors at Bow Street. V', *Punch*, 19 Mar, p 204.
            Haggard in the dock — for abandoning the romantic novel?

1903

PL25   Marshall, S.J. *The King of Kor; or, She's Promise Kept*. Washington,
        Marshall.

1910

PL26   'A Poem on the Publication of "Queen Sheba's Ring" ', *Punch*,
        5 Oct, p 252.

11   Theses (T)

T1   Cohen, Morton. 'H. Rider Haggard. His Life and Work'. PhD thesis, Columbia University, 1958.

T2   Bear, N.H. 'The Presentation of War in English Prose Fiction'. MPhil thesis, London University (External), 1970.
        Includes special reference, *inter alia*, to Rider Haggard's works.

T3   Bursey, Wallace. 'Rider Haggard. A Study in Popular Fiction'. PhD thesis, Memorial University of Newfoundland, 1973.

T4   Gags, Beckett. 'Rider Haggard and the Male Novel. What is "Pericles"?' PhD thesis, Rutgers University, The State University of New Jersey (New Brunswick), 1974. (Lawrence Millman).

T5   Pierce, P.F. 'Rider Haggard'. BLitt, Oxford, 1975.

T6   Preedy, G. 'Fantasy as a Radical Form. A Study based on the work of Stevenson, Haggard, Wells, Peake and Burroughs'. MPhil thesis, Warwick University, 1975.

T7   Katz, Wendy R.H. 'Rider Haggard. A Study of Fiction in the Service of Empire'. PhD thesis, Dalhousie University, Canada, 1976.

Appendixes

Appendix 1: Some Popular Editions of Note

The following cheap, popular and uniform editions of Haggard's works are listed because they are early and scarce, or because they represent more recent and continuing interest in making a reasonably comprehensive range of works available in well produced editions. Many other editions exist but listing them all goes beyond the scope of this book.

EARLY AMERICAN EDITIONS

HARPER AND BROTHERS, NEW YORK.
  FRANKLIN SQUARE LIBRARY
King Solomon's Mines, no 552, Dec 1886.
She, no 558, Dec 1886
Jess, no 567, Feb 1887
Cleopatra, no 649 (New Series), 1889.
Beatrice, no 671 (New Series), 1890.
The World's Desire, no 684 (New Series), 1890.
Eric Brighteyes, no 698 (New Series), 1891.

M.J. IVERS AND CO, NEW YORK. AMERICAN
  SERIES
King Solomon's Mines, vol 1, no 4, 1885.
She
Allan Quatermain
A Tale of Three Lions, no 57.
Mr. Meeson's Will, no 81, May 1888.
Maiwa's Revenge
Colonel Quaritch, V.C.
Cleopatra, no 123, Feb 1889.
Allan's Wife
Beatrice

F.F. LOVELL CO, NEW YORK. HOUSEHOLD
  LIBRARY. ALL PUBLISHED IN THE 1880s.
She, no 12.
Jess, no 34.
Allan Quatermain, no 70.
A Tale of Three Lions, no 94.
Maiwa's Revenge, no 153.
Colonel Quaritch, V.C., no 185.
Cleopatra, no 236, 1889.
Allan's Wife, no 265.

J.W. LOVELL CO, NEW YORK. LOVELL'S
  LIBRARY
King Solomon's Mines, vol 18, no 813, 1886.
She, vol 17 (?), no 848, 1887.
Jess, vol 18, no 900, Mar 1887.
Dawn, vol 19, no 941, 1887.
Allan Quatermain, no 1020, Jul 1887.
A Tale of Three Lions, no 1100, Dec 1887.
  A later edition was entitled *Allan the Hunter*.
Mr. Meeson's Will, no 1183, 1888.
Maiwa's Revenge, no 1200, 1888. Includes stories by other authors.

Colonel Quaritch, V.C., no 1306, Nov 1888.
Cleopatra, no 1409, 1889.
Allan's Wife, no 1446, 1889.

GEORGE MUNRO, NEW YORK. SEASIDE LIBRARY POCKET EDITION. LATER GEORGE MUNRO'S SONS.
She, no 910, May 1886. (May 1886 is unlikely to be an accurate date because *She* did not start even its magazine appearance in *The Graphic* until October 1886).
Jess
Allan Quatermain, no 989, Jun 1887.
A Tale of Three Lions, no 1049, Nov 1887. Includes *On Going Back*.
Mr. Meeson's Will, no 1100, 1888.
Maiwa's Revenge, no 1105, 1888.
Colonel Quaritch, V.C., no 1140, Öct 1888.
My Fellow Laborer, no 1145, Nov 1888.
Cleopatra, no 1190.
Allan's Wife, no 1248.
Beatrice, no 1335.
The World's Desire, no 1635.
Eric Brighteyes, no 1849, 1891 (?).
The Witch's Head, no 1995.

N.L. MUNRO, NEW YORK. MUNRO'S LIBRARY
The Witch's Head, no 699, 1887.
She, no 700, 1887.
Jess, no 716, 1887.
Allan Quatermain, vol 50, no 738, 1887.
Mr. Meeson's Will, no 837, Jul 1888.

Also:
He, A Companion to She, vol 50, no 721, Apr 1887.
It, vol 50, no 726, Apr 1887.
King Solomon's Wives; or, The Phantom Mines, no 736, 1887.
King Solomon's Treasures, no 737, 1887.
Bess. A Companion to Jess, no 739, 1887.
King Solomon's Wives, no 970, 1887.

J.S. OGILVIE, NEW YORK. FIRESIDE SERIES
She, no 15, Jan 1887.
King Solomon's Mines, no 17, Jan 1887.
Jess, no 18, Jan 1887.

Allan Quatermain, no 27, 1887.
A Tale of Three Lions, no 35, Dec 1887. With stories by other authors.
Mr. Meeson's Will, no 53, 1888.
Maiwa's Revenge, no 59, 1888.
Colonel Quaritch, V.C., no 66, 1888.
Cleopatra, no 86.
Allan's Wife, no 100.

RAND, MCNALLY AND CO, NEW YORK. GLOBE LIBRARY
Jess, no 17, 1887.
She, no 18, 1887.
Allan Quatermain, no 26, 1887.
Mr. Meeson's Will, no 71, 1888.
Cleopatra, no 101, 1889.
Allan's Wife, no 113, 1889.
Beatrice, no 125, 1890.

STONE AND MACKENZIE, NEW YORK. THE WORKS OF H. RIDER HAGGARD. LATER MCKINLAY, STONE AND MACKENZIE.
She, 1886.
Jess, 1886.
King Solomon's Mines, 1886.
Allan Quatermain, 1887.
Eric Brighteyes, 1891.
Nada the Lily, 1892.
Cleopatra, 1894.
Swallow, 1898.
Pearl Maiden, 1902.
The Spirit of Bambatse, 1906.
Lysbeth, 1907.
Margaret, 1907.
Montezuma's Daughter, 1909.
Heart of the World, 1910.
Marie, 1912.
Child of Storm, 1913.
Allan and the Holy Flower, 1915.
People of the Mist, 1915.
Ivory Child, 1916.
Finished, 1917.
Ancient Allan, 1920.

POPULAR BRITISH EDITIONS

NEWNES SIXPENNY LIBRARY
Jess, no 17, 1899.
She, no 18, 1899.
Allan Quatermain, no 86, 1906.

Nada the Lily, no 91, 1906. Illus. by Cyrus Cuneo.

Montezuma's Daughter, no 96, 1906. Illus. by Maurice Greiffenhagen.

Pearl Maiden, no 102, 1906.

The People of the Mist, no 106, 1906. Illus. by Cyrus Cuneo.

Lysbeth, no 110.

The Witch's Head, no 114, 1907.

Dawn, no 117, 1907.

Colonel Quaritch, V.C., no 120, 1907.

The World's Desire, no 123, 1907.

Beatrice, no 126, 1907.

Joan Haste, no 128, 1907. Illus. by Cyrus Cuneo.

Stella Fregelius, no 132, 1907.

Swallow, no 136, 1907.

Black Heart and White Heart, 1908.

Eric Brighteyes, 1908. Illus. by Lancelot Speed.

Heart of the World, 1908.

Mr. Meeson's Will, 1908.

Maiwa's Revenge and *Elissa*, 1908.

Queen Sheba's Ring, 1913.

Allan's Wife, 1918.

Moon of Israel, 1918.

HODDER AND STOUGHTON SEVENPENNY LIBRARY

She, 1913. Another edition 1915.

Cleopatra, 1913.

Eric Brighteyes, 1913.

Allan's Wife, 1914.

Nada the Lily, 1914.

Montezuma's Daughter, 1914.

Heart of the World, 1914.

Beatrice, 1915.

Colonel Quaritch, V.C., 1915.

The World's Desire, 1916.

Pearl Maiden, 1916.

Elissa, or The Doom of Zimbabwe, 1917.

CASSELL'S SIXPENNY NOVELS

The Brethren, 1911.

King Solomon's Mines, 1911.

Benita, 1911.

The Ghost Kings, 1912.

The Yellow God, 1913.

MACDONALD ILLUSTRATED EDITION.

ALL ILLUSTRATED BY HOOKWAY COWLES, EXCEPT WHERE OTHERWISE STATED

Montezuma's Daughter, 10 Dec 1948.

She, 10 Dec 1948. With an introduction by Malcolm Elwin.

Allan Quatermain, 19 Mar 1949.

Eric Brighteyes, 19 Mar 1949. Illus. by Lancelot Speed.

Nada the Lily, 14 Jun 1949.

Allan's Wife, 17 Jan 1951.

People of the Mist, 14 Apr 1951. Illus. by Jack Matthew.

Child of Storm, 1 Dec 1952.

The Brethren, 10 Jul 1952.

The World's Desire, 10 Jul 1953. Illus. by Geoffrey Whittam.

Queen Sheba's Ring, 29 Oct 1953. Illus. by Geoffrey Whittam.

Heart of the World, 18 Jun 1954.

Allan and the Holy Flower, 12 Nov 1954.

King Solomon's Mines, 28 Sep 1956.

Ayesha, 26 Oct 1956.

Cleopatra, 4 Jul 1958.

The Ivory Child, 22 Oct 1958.

Marie, 25 Sep 1959.

She and Allan, 8 Apr 1960.

Finished, 23 Nov 1962.

Maiwa's Revenge, 3 Jun 1965.

Benita, 9 Sep 1965.

Appendix 2: Haggard Manuscripts in the Norfolk Record Office

1 *Dawn*, pp 1–493, folio. Dated 15th May–5th September 1883.
2 The original draft of *Dawn* under the title 'There Remaineth A Rest', pp 1–554, folio, and five pages of introduction.
3 *The Witch's Head*, pp 1–377, folio.
4 *King Solomon's Mines*, pp 1–216, folio.
5 *She. A Story of Adventure*, pp 1–231, folio, and four pages of introduction. Begun February 1886, finished 18 March 1886. The day of February on which the book was begun is obliterated, but the book was written in about six weeks.
6 *Jess*, pp 1–254, folio, and dedication 'To My Wife, 1886'; dated on the last page 31st December 1885.
7 *Maiwa's Revenge*, pp 1–91, folio. Dated on last page, 10 November 1887.
8 *Allan's Wife*, pp 1–125, folio, and dedication to Arthur H.D. Cochrane. Begun 25 February 1889, finished 16 April 1889.
9 *Colonel Quaritch, V.C.*, pp 1–336, folio. Commenced 29 July 1886, finished 26 December 1886.
10 *Cleopatra*, pp 1–267, folio, and ten pages of introduction. Begun 27 May 1887, finished 2 August 1887.
11 *Beatrice*, pp 1–281, folio. Begun 23 November 1887, finished 28 February 1888.
12 *Eric Brighteyes*, pp 1–266, folio. Begun 29 August 1888, finished Christmas Day 1888.
13 *Nada the Lily*, pp 1–275, folio. Finished 15 January 1890.
14 *Montezuma's Daughter*, pp 1–345, folio. Begun 15 June 1891, finished 3 September 1891.
15 *The World's Desire*, pp 1–53 by Andrew Lang; pp 54–145 by Haggard. Finished 9 January 1899.
16 One of the drafts of *The World's Desire* with the title 'The Song of the Bow'.
17 Copy of the Norfolk Roll of Honour with the manuscript of the introduction by Haggard.

It may also be of interest that the Norwich Reference Library holds the typed manuscript of an unpublished Haggard work entitled 'Diary of an African Journey 11 February 1914 to 3 June 1914', 265 pp.

Subject Index

Principal titles of works by Rider Haggard are printed in capital letters, and the main reference number is printed in bold. References are to item numbers.

171

Index to Newspapers and Periodicals

United Kingdom